305843

Contents

Introduction to the course

Components

FCE Expert consists of:

a Coursebook for classroom use

a Student's Resource Book for homework, private study or classroom use (with or without Answer key) with audio CD set

Teacher's audio cassette or CD pack

this Teacher's Resource Book

Five key features

1 *FCE Expert* is flexible. It is designed in a modular way so that teachers can either follow the order of the material in the book or choose their own route through the course to meet the needs of specific classes. Each page or double-page spread is freestanding, and almost always follows the same order in each module, making it easy to access and isolate separate elements of the course and integrate them in a different way.

So, a teacher might follow the linear route presented in the book:

(Units 1, 3, 5, etc.)
Reading ➜ Language development ➜ Writing

(Units 2, 4, 6, etc.)
Listening ➜ Speaking ➜ Use of English/Language development

Or a teacher might follow different, tailored routes, such as:
Language development ➜ Reading ➜ Writing

Writing ➜ Reading ➜ Speaking

Speaking ➜ Language development ➜ Use of English ➜ Listening

2 While each section can be taught independently, there are links between the sections to provide a coherent progression when the more linear route is chosen. For example, the Language development in the first unit of each module provides language which will be useful for students in the following Writing section; the Speaking has a topic which relates to the Listening in the same unit; in the second unit of each module, the grammar and vocabulary in the Language development sections are tested in the Use of English sections on the opposite page.

3 Most of the Use of English/Language development spreads follow a test–teach approach in which the language is first tested by means of a Use of English

task, then focused on in the Language development section using the examples from the Use of English task to clarify form and meaning.

4 The general skills required for Reading and Listening (e.g. for reading: skimming, scanning, predicting, etc.) are presented first in the early units, through tasks which simulate the exam but are graded in terms of their level of difficulty.

5 The Writing and Speaking sections focus more on approach than end-product. In other words, students are trained to build up good habits, develop the skill of self-monitoring and so become more independent learners.

Coursebook

The Coursebook consists of twelve modules, each divided into two units. Each module includes grammar consolidation and vocabulary development, and practises all the Papers of the exam.

Each module is designed around a theme. There is an Overview showing what is to be studied in the module, followed by a lead-in discussion. Then each of the two units is based around a topic linked to the overall theme of the module. For example, Module 5 (Units 9 and 10) has the theme Discovery. Under that general heading Unit 9 focuses on Human science whereas Unit 10 focuses on Invention.

After Modules 1, 3, 5, 7, 9 and 11 there is a Module review with revision and further practice of the language covered in the module.

After Modules 2, 4, 6, 8, 10 and 12 there is an Exam practice section, consisting of Paper 1 Reading tasks and Paper 3 Use of English tasks. At the same points in the course, this Teacher's Resource Book also contains photocopiable Exam practice for Paper 2 Writing and Paper 4 Listening.

Other elements of the Coursebook are:

- Top 20 Questions asked about FCE

- Exam overview, giving an at-a-glance outline of what is included in each paper

- Exam reference, giving more detailed information about what to expect in each part of each paper, and what skills or language are tested in each section

- Grammar reference, which gives detailed information about the main grammar points practised in the course

- Writing reference, which provides:
  - a checklist to help students monitor and edit their own writing

first certificate
expert

TEACHER'S RESOURCE BOOK

Longman

Pearson Education Limited
Edinburgh Gate
Harlow
Essex CM20 2JE
England
and Associated Companies throughout the world.

www.longman.com

© Pearson Education Limited 2003

First published 2003

Second impression 2003

ISBN 0 582 469295

Set in 10/12pt Times New Roman

Printed in Spain by Mateu Cromo, S.A. Pinto (Madrid)

Author's Acknowledgements

The author would like to thank Bernie Hayden, Fran Banks and Jacqui Robinson for their help and guidance, all his colleagues and students at Frances King School of English for their suggestions and Annie, Louis and Freya for their patience.

Publisher's Acknowledgements

We are grateful to the following for permission to reproduce copyright material:

Consignia plc for an extract adapted from their advertisement "Sorted … Royal Mail delivers a solution to the home delivery problem" published February 2000; Financial Times Limited for an extract adapted from "Jobs on the line" published in *FT Weekend: How to Spend It* February 2002; Focus Magazine for the article "A quick chat with Ellen MacArthur" by Sally Palmer published in *Focus Magazine* November 2002; Media Generation Limited for an extract adapted from "Best boot forward" by Kenric Hickson published in *Quicksilver Magazine* Autumn 2000; New Crane Publishing for an extract from "Roll up, roll up! Change your life" by Richard Barber published in *Sainsbury's Magazine* October 2002; Penguin Books Limited for an extract adapted from "The little girl and the wolf" by James Thurber published in *The Thurber Carnival* © James Thurber 1953; Peter Shepherd for a questionnaire adapted from www.trans4mind.com; Telegraph Group Limited for an extract adapted from "The man who was driven by jaguars" by Nigel Blundell published in *The Telegraph* 5th August 2000 © Telegraph Group Limited 2000; and Times Newspapers Limited for an extract from "Speechless? Now we're talking" by Elizabeth Judge published in *The Times* 10th August 2002 © Times Newspapers Limited, London 2002.

In some instances we have been unable to trace the owners of copyright material and we would appreciate any information that would enable us to do so.

Sample answer sheets are reproduced by kind permission of the University of Cambridge Local Examinations Syndicate.

Illustrated by Francis Blake, John Coburn, Fran Jordan, Sandy Nichols, Rachel Oxley, Chris Pavely, Nadine Wickenden and Russ Wilms

Cover photo © Raven Design

Designed by Jennifer Coles

Project Managed by Bernie Hayden

– a sample question for each type of writing task in the exam, with model answer, specific guidance, and another question for further student practice

– a spelling and punctuation section, giving useful support in these areas as practised in the Writing sections

- Speaking material, with photographs and tasks for Parts 2 and 3 of the Speaking paper

- Functions reference, which brings together all the language functions introduced in the Speaking sections, so that they can be easily accessed for reference and revision

Module and unit structure

Each module contains the following sections. For ease of use and flexibility, the sections are nearly always in the same order.

Units 1, 3, 5, 7, etc.

Reading

The texts have been chosen for their interest value and their potential to provide a 'window on the world' and generate discussion.

Stage 1 A *Before you read* section to establish the topic and a purpose for reading. It also aims to motivate students and generate vocabulary. For example, in Unit 7 (Personal challenges) students discuss a photo of the man featured in the article. Then they look at the title of the article and the introduction and write three questions they would like to find the answers to in the text.

Stage 2 An activity to encourage reading for gist, followed by a Paper 1 Reading exam task, with advice on the relevant task strategy. For example, in Unit 7 there are six Task strategy points to follow, including looking for grammatical links between the main text and the removed sentences in a gapped text. As the exam preparation is carefully graded and stepped throughout the course, these Task strategy sections are reduced as the course progresses.

Stage 3 A discussion and/or a vocabulary activity, both based on the text. In Unit 7 the vocabulary is phrasal verbs.

This Teacher's Resource Book contains photocopiable lead-in or follow-up activities.

In the Student's Resource Book, there is more extensive vocabulary work related to the reading texts, and further practice of each Paper 1 Reading exam task.

Language development 1

Language development 1 can be used independently of any exam training. However, the section revises and extends general grammar areas which students will need for the exam, not only because they are tested in the Use of English papers but because they will be needed for the Writing and Speaking papers.

This section follows a three-stage approach.

Stage 1 Students find examples of the grammar in context, and match them to form and meaning.

Stage 2 Controlled practice, linked to the context.

Stage 3 A practice activity which links the language to the exam task in the following Writing section. So, in Unit 7 the final Language development exercise involves students using narrative forms and time conjunctions to continue a story, then the Writing section consists of training in how to write a story for Paper 2.

At appropriate stages of the Language development sections, students are referred to the Grammar reference at the back of the book for a detailed grammatical summary of the language point being practised.

This Teacher's Resource Book contains photocopiable activities directly linked to these Language development sections, providing communicative language practice.

Writing

The Writing sections cover all the types of writing that students may be required to do in the exam, with particular emphasis on the compulsory transactional letter (Paper 2 Part 1). In terms of language, each Writing section has a link to the Language development section which precedes it, and a *Language spot* which practises an important area of language needed for writing.

The principle behind the Writing section is to establish 'good practice' through a clear set of procedures consistently applied and monitored, which can be used when completing any exam Writing task. Each spread is graded, and the aim is to give carefully guided preparation, so that students build up to complete the main task at the end of the section. In each section there is considerable language support; in particular a range of functional exponents is given and linked to the task.

In the units, the approach focuses on process more than end product. However, in the Writing reference there are exam tasks with model answers, notes for guidance, and more tasks for further practice.

The procedure in the Writing sections is as follows:

1 Lead-in → **2** Understanding the task → **3** Planning the task → **4** Thinking about the language and content needed → **5** Writing → **6** Checking and improving the writing

For example, in Unit 7 (Writing a story):

Stage 1 Discussion about stories

Stage 2 Analysing the exam task and discussing what will make a good story

Stage 3 Brainstorming ideas from pictures and making notes

Stage 4 Comparing opening/closing paragraphs and practising useful functional exponents and the use of adverbs

Stage 5 Writing the story

Stage 6 Editing the story using a checklist.

Students are then referred to the appropriate page in the Writing reference. The *Language spot* section gives practice in making language vivid. The *Language spot* sections are linked but not integrated with this procedure, and could be used at any point in the lesson, including the beginning.

Units 2, 4, 6, 8, etc.

Listening

This section can be covered before or after the Speaking section, which has a linked topic.

The sections are graded through the book to develop the skills needed to perform the tasks in the four parts of Paper 4 Listening. Early units have Task strategy sections in the margin to guide students.

Each Listening section has three stages:

Stage 1 *Before you listen*: This aims to establish the context, to build up motivation, to predict the content and to generate the vocabulary needed for the task. For example, in Unit 6 (*Our natural heritage*) the students are asked to talk about the photograph and guess the man's job and his likes/dislikes about being in the rainforest.

Stage 2 A task with relevant strategies. Unit 6 practises the general skill of listening for specific information and introduces the exam task of completing sentences.

Stage 3 Discussion and/or vocabulary related to the text. In Unit 6 there is a discussion about the way in which students completed the task.

Further practice of useful vocabulary linked to the topic can be found in the Student's Resource Book.

Speaking

This section follows similar principles to the Writing section, in that it aims to build up 'good practice' through a clear set of procedures consistently applied. The sections are graded throughout the book. They cover the strategies needed in the exam and provide useful functional exponents. These functions are all in the Functions reference at the back of the book.

In the earlier units, there are recorded sample answers on the cassette/CD for students to listen to critically from the point of view of appropriate language and effective strategies.

Each section has the following structure:

Stage 1 *Lead-in*. In this part, the students discuss the pictures and generate the vocabulary they will need to perform the task. For example, in Unit 6 students are asked to identify the jobs of two people who work with animals.

Stage 2 Guided exam preparation for the task. In Unit 6 the task is the 'individual long turn' (Paper 5 Part 2). First students compare and contrast the pictures, then they listen to a sample answer, identify the examiner's instructions, and analyse the student's answer for both content and language.

Stage 3 Students perform the exam task, following the guidelines provided in the Task strategy section, and afterwards reflect on how they performed.

Use of English 1

This section usually focuses on the more 'grammatical' Use of English tasks and so it is always either Paper 3 Part 2 (open cloze), Paper 3 Part 3 (key word transformation) or Paper 3 Part 4 (error correction). Its aim is to develop the exam strategies needed for each task and, in terms of language, follow a test–teach procedure, in that the Use of English task here tests the students' knowledge of the language, some of which is then practised in Language development 2.

Those sections which practise Paper 3 Part 2 or Part 4 include texts related to the topic of the unit and have the following structure:

Stage 1 *Lead-in*. This aims to build up motivation in relation to the topic of the text and generate some of the vocabulary needed. For example, in Unit 6 there is an 'animals quiz'.

Stage 2 Graded guidance for completing the exam task. In Unit 6 the students try and predict the content of the text from the title, read the text quickly and answer comprehension questions.

Stage 3 The students complete the exam task, supported by a Task strategy section and a Help section, which gives specific guidance for individual answers. This support is reduced throughout the book. This is followed either by discussion about the content of the text or analysis of the language tested in the task.

A similar procedure is followed for Paper 3 Part 3 (key word transformation) but since there is no specific text or topic, more attention is given to the exam strategies needed.

Language development 2

This section focuses on some of the language from the Use of English task on the opposite page. In Unit 6 the focus is on *-ing* forms and infinitives.

Some of the areas practised are 'large' grammar points, such as comparatives, quantity or articles; others are relatively small, such as *as/like*, but all are frequently tested in the Use of English paper.

Stage 1 Analysis of examples of the target language from the preceding Use of English task. Students are either guided to the grammar rules for themselves, or given input on the page. In some cases (e.g. comparatives) students are referred to the Grammar reference.

Stage 2 A range of controlled and semi-controlled practice activities.

Stage 3 A short personalised task.

Further communicative practice is provided in the photocopiable material in the Teacher's Resource Book.

Use of English 2

The task in this section focuses on vocabulary and is usually Paper 3 Part 1 (lexical cloze) or Paper 3 Part 5 (word formation). Since vocabulary is also tested in Paper 3 Part 3, one unit has a key word transformation task.

The texts are related to the topic of the unit and the page has a similar structure to Use of English 1 (see above).

Language development 3

This section practises and extends the vocabulary tested in the Use of English task on the opposite page.

The page has a similar structure to Language development 2 (see above).

Module reviews

These give revision of the grammar and vocabulary in the previous module in a non-exam format. They can be given as a test, set as homework or used as practice in the classroom.

Exam practice 1 – 6

These provide practice in Paper 1 Reading and Paper 3 Use of English. They can be used in conjunction with the Paper 2 Writing and Paper 4 Listening Exam practice in the Teacher's Resource Book.

You might wish to use these diagnostically, to determine whether extra practice of a particular area is needed.

Student's Resource Book

The Student's Resource Book is an integral part of the *FCE Expert* course. It contains 12 modules that mirror the themes and contents of the Coursebook units. It aims to consolidate areas of grammar practised in the Coursebook, extend vocabulary and give extra practice of Reading, Listening and Use of English.

There is an accompanying audio CD set. The Listening material is also available on the Teacher's cassette/CD pack.

Module and unit structure

Each module contains the following sections:

Units 1, 3, 5, 7, etc.

Vocabulary

Extension of topic vocabulary based on the Coursebook reading text; other vocabulary areas such as phrasal verbs; exam practice exercises for the vocabulary-based tasks in Paper 3 Use of English.

Language development 1

Consolidation and practice of language covered in Language development 1 in the Coursebook; extension of certain language areas; graded exam practice exercises.

Writing

Further practice of the exam task type covered in the Coursebook, focusing on structure and organisation based on analysis of a sample answer.

Listening

Paper 4 Listening text and task, practising strategies and task types that have already been covered in the Coursebook.

Units 2, 4, 6, 8, etc.

Vocabulary

Extension of topic and other vocabulary or functions based on the Coursebook listening and/or speaking tasks.

Language development 2

Consolidation and practice of language covered in Language development 2 in the Coursebook; extension of certain language areas; graded exam practice exercises.

Reading

Paper 2 Reading text and task, practising strategies and task types that have already been covered in the Coursebook.

Complete practice exam

A complete exam which you can use when you think your students are ready for it, or in separate parts at any stage in the course.

Teacher's Resource Book

As well as this Introduction, the Teacher's Resource Book contains:

Unit-by-unit teacher's notes

Guidance on how to use the Coursebook material, with further suggestions; 'books closed' activities to set the ball rolling at the beginning of modules and units; annotated answers for exercises and exam tasks.

OMR Answer sheets (photocopiable)

Replicas of the Answer sheets students have to use in the exam. They can be photocopied and given to students when they do the Exam practice sections in the Coursebook, and the complete Practice exams in the Student's Resource Book.

Photocopiable activities

A pre-course exam quiz; three photocopiable activities to supplement each coursebook module, providing further lead-in and follow-up material and communicative language practice; full teacher's notes and answer keys for each activity.

Module tests: How much do you remember? (photocopiable)

One photocopiable page per module, testing the grammar and vocabulary covered in the module. There are five exercises on each page. The items reflect the five Paper 3 tasks, but for ease of administration and checking, they use discrete sentences rather than full-length texts. Answer keys are at the appropriate points in the unit-by-unit teacher's notes.

Exam practice (photocopiable)

Six exam practice sections for use after Modules 2, 4, 6, 8, 10 and 12, i.e. the same points as the Coursebook Exam practice. This material provides practice in Paper 2 Writing and Paper 4 Listening, and so complements the Coursebook Exam practice (Papers 1 and 3). The recordings for the Paper 4 Listening tests can be found on the Coursebook cassettes/CDs after Modules 2, 4, 6, 8, 10 and 12. Answer keys are at the appropriate points in the unit-by-unit teacher's notes.

Tapescripts

These are all at the back of the book for ease of reference.

Teacher's cassette/CD pack

The Teacher's cassette pack (four cassettes) contains all the listening material from the Coursebook, Teacher's Resource Book and Student's Resource Book. There are two cassettes for the Coursebook, (which include the listening tests in the Teacher's Resource Book) and two cassettes for the Student's Resource Book. The material is also available in a pack of four audio CDs.

Abbreviations used in the Teacher's Resource Book
CB = Coursebook
TRB = Teacher's Resource Book
l./ll = line/lines
p./pp = page/pages
para. = paragraph

Module 1 Lifestyles

Units 1 and 2 are linked by the theme of 'Lifestyles' and include topics such as family, homes, routines, festivals and celebrations.

••
Photocopiable activity

Photocopiable activity (pre-course) on page 125 provides an introduction to the FCE exam. After the quiz, it would be useful to show students other features of the book, by asking questions such as *Where can you find the Grammar reference?* (pp. 192–205) *What can you find on pages 206–217?* (Writing reference).
••

To set the ball rolling ...

Lead-in p.7

Get students to discuss the dictionary extract together, then ask them for the key points: *way someone lives; place they live; things they own; job they do; activities they enjoy.* Then they should discuss the other questions in pairs or small groups before feedback to the class to compare ideas.

Unit 1 Ways of living

To set the ball rolling ...

With books closed get students to tell a partner about their home and family. If necessary provide prompts such as *Who do you live with? What do other members of your family do? Describe your house/home.*

Reading p.8

1 Get students to look at the first strategy box before they do this. Ask them to give reasons and so encourage them to give fuller answers.

2 Use the strategy box to clarify what the term *skimming* means and why it is important. As well as giving a general understanding, skimming helps to establish the type and style of the text, the writer's intention (to inform, amuse, entertain) and the general organisation and layout of the text. Suggest a suitable time to skim this article. Suggestion: 1–2 minutes.

2c This question would best be discussed as a whole class.

3 Before students scan the article, use the strategy box to clarify what scanning is and why it is useful. In the exam it is important to use time well and scanning will help students do this.

3c Students should do this in pairs or small groups.

4 This discussion would be best in small groups.

••
Photocopiable activity

Photocopiable activity 1A on p.126 could be done at this point. It is a board game about students' lifestyles, containing questions typical of those asked in Paper 5 Parts 1 and 4.
••

Language development 1 p.10

1a First get students to describe the picture. What is the relationship of the people and what are they doing? Check/Clarify the difference between *grow* – to become physically bigger, used for people, plants, animals, towns, etc. – and *grow up* – to develop from a child to an adult, used only for people.

1b Check that students are familiar with the basic names of the verb forms before they do the exercise. When they have completed the exercise, you may want to show them the Grammar reference on page 197.

2a Students should work on their own to complete the dialogues before checking their answers with the Grammar reference and each other.

2b Before students practise the questions together point out how the answers in the book are more than simple responses; the answers are expanded to give further information. E.g. in question 2 the answer *My father* is expanded to say why. Encourage students to do the same.

3a You may need to clarify the difference between a state and an action, e.g. by saying: *I live in Madrid. It's not an action, I don't actually do anything, I just live. Every day I ride a bike to work. It's a physical action, something that I do.*

3b After students have completed the box give them time to read the Grammar reference on page 197.

4 Students can either refer to the Grammar reference as they do the exercise or try on their own before checking. Ask them to justify their answers and say whether each one is a state or an action.

5a First check that students know who Alan Shearer is.

Background

Alan Shearer was captain of the England national football team. He scored 30 goals in over 60 matches for England between 1992 and 2000.

5c After completing the box, students should read the Grammar reference on page 199.

7a Students should write their answers, to give them time to think about the structures, before comparing their experiences with other students. If necessary, give them one or two examples about you.

7b This would work well in small groups.

Photocopiable activity

Photocopiable activity 1B (p. 127) would work well after any of Exercises 6, 7 or 8. It is an information exchange activity giving further practice of language used to describe past and present habits.

▶ **Student's Resource Book page 7**

Writing p.12

1 Get students started by describing who you might write a formal letter to, such as a bank, and eliciting one example of who you would write an informal letter to, such as friends or family. Paper 2 part 2 often includes an informal letter to a friend. Ask if anyone has ever had a pen friend, and if so how long they kept up correspondence.

2 Point out that students should establish the style of any writing task by considering who the reader is, and they should establish the purpose in order to use suitable language and complete the task.

3a Tell students that, in the exam, marks are given for task completion, so they should think about what the task requires. In this case they will need to cover three points: themselves, their family and suggesting a meeting.

3b When students are completing the paragraph plan, remind them that it is only an exam and not a real life situation. Although it is better to write true things about themselves – e.g. they will know more vocabulary about their own real hobbies – it is not necessary. In this case they should, e.g., invent a hobby rather than say they don't have one. Remind them that the aim is to demonstrate what they can do in English, not to write a true description of themselves.

4a Check that students understand why the sentences are inappropriate (they are too formal) before they attempt the task. Remind them that contractions such as *I'm* are acceptable in informal letters.

4b If students are unsure of any of the *True/False* statements get them to look again at the examples in Exercise 4a.

4d Get students to read the question again before they do the task.

5 The letter should now take students only about 20 minutes to write and could be done in class or for homework.

6 Point out that there is a more complete list of points to check when editing in the Writing reference on page 206.

LANGUAGE SPOT: sentence word order

The aim of this exercise is to revise basic English sentence structure and word order, in particular with adverbs of frequency and other adverbials. The sentences are typical of what students might want to write in the writing task for this unit, so it could be done at any time during the writing lesson, or at the end of it, or at another appropriate moment during Module 1.

▶ **Student's Resource Book page 9**

Unit 1 Key

Reading p.8

3b 1 A; **2, 3** B,C; **4, 5** A,B; **6** C; **7** B; **8** C; **9** A

3c **2, 3** B (*their greatest wish is for a permanent home*)
C (*to have a larger house*)
4, 5 A (*Jose Maria is comfortable cooking for the family*)
B (*Dividing household chores is a necessity*)
6 C (*a turn at the microphone (in a karaoke bar)*)
7 B (*Batsuury and Oyuntsetseg commute each day to city jobs*)
8 C (*the family dog*)
9 A (*their daughter … they do not want any more children*)

Language development 1 p.10

1a 1 wife; 2 husband; 3 grandfather; 4 schoolgirl; 5 grandfather; 6 older girl

1b **A** 1 a temporary situation: He*'s staying* with the family at the moment.
2 a changing situation: His children *are growing up fast!*
B an annoying or surprising habit: She*'s always* making long calls on the phone.
C a habit: 1 She *usually goes out* in the evening.
2 a long-term situation: She *lives* in a small house … .
D typical behaviour: He*'ll sit and doze* in an armchair all evening.

2a 1 Do you live; 're living; 're looking for
2 do you get on; 'll tell/tells
3 Does anyone annoy; 's always taking (always takes)
4 do you go out; go out; 'm studying; 'm only going out
5 Do you like; 's getting

3a 1 S; 2 S; 3 S; 4 A

3b **A** understand, know; **B** have

4 1 I'm having *have* two brothers. S
2 Jan*'s having* has a shower A
3 What is it meaning *does it mean*? S
4 Marina thinks *'s thinking* about A
5 We are not owning *don't own* our house S
6 The house look*s* old S
7 What do *are* you look*ing* at? A
8 Phil*'s seeing* sees a client A

5a Past habits: *used to put*; *would play*
Past state: *used to like*

5b 1 Many times
2 Many times
3 *used to, would*
4 *used to*

5c **A** *used to, used to, would, would*
B *used to, used to*; **C** *liked, played*

6 1 forgot
2 lived/used to live; had/used to have
3 always went/always used to go/would always go; had/used to have/would have
4 was/used to be; worked/used to work/would work; retired

7 Answers will vary.

8 1 c; 2 e; 3 f; 4 a; 5 d; 6 b

Writing p.12

1 A letter to a new pen friend would usually contain personal information about family, lifestyle, interests, routines, aspirations, etc.

2 b

4a 1 It would be great to meet you sometime.
2 I live in a small town …
3 We get on (well) …
4 Next time I write, I'll send a photo.
5 … we would always go on holiday …
6 She looks like me, but she can be a bit talkative.
7 I hear you're looking for a pen friend.
8 Do you ever get the chance to visit my country?
9 I'm writing because …
10 Let me tell you about my family.

4b 1 T; 2 F; 3 F; 4 F; 5 T; 6 T

4c 1 Any of the expressions in 'Giving a reason for writing' or 'Talking about the future'.
2 It would be great to meet you sometime.
3 We get on (well) …
4 Do you ever get the chance to …?
5 Let me tell you about my family.
6 I hear you're looking for a pen friend.

4d *Dear pen friend* would not be appropriate – students should never begin a letter with *Dear friend* or *Dear pen friend*.
Dear Mrs Watson is too formal.
Dear Sue, i.e. using the other person's first name, is an appropriate opening for an informal letter.
I hope to hear from you at your earliest convenience. is too formal.
Looking forward to hearing from you. is fairly 'neutral' and would be appropriate.
Well, that's all for now. Do write back soon. is possibly too informal for a first letter to someone you don't yet know, but could be used in subsequent letters to a pen friend.
Lots of love would be too informal/personal in this letter.
Best wishes is fairly 'neutral' and would be appropriate.
Yours sincerely is too formal.

5 Sample answer:

Dear Ana

I hear you're looking for a pen friend and so am I! Let me tell you a little bit about myself and my family.

My name's Ivan and I live in Prague. I used to work for a chemical company but now I'm learning to be a salesman. In the future I want a job where I can travel for my work. I've already been to a few places in Europe, but I've never been to your country.

I live at home with my parents, which is comfortable as I don't have to do much housework. My younger brother is studying at university. Although he is four years younger than me we get on quite well. We both enjoy snow-boarding and music.

What about you? Do you ever get the chance to travel? It would be great to meet you one day. Why don't you come to Prague next summer? Next time I write I'll send a photo.

Best wishes
Ivan

(172 words)

LANGUAGE SPOT: sentence word order

1 I don't always speak English very well.
2 My mother and father always eat fish on Fridays.
3 My sister's having a great time in Paris right now.
4 Usually her friends all gave her a lot of help.
5 My grandmother would always listen to music in bed.
6 Everyone enjoyed themselves very much at the party.
7 I'll send you an email on Tuesday next week.
8 Please write back as soon as you can.

Unit 2 Festivals and traditions

The topic of festivals and traditions continues the lifestyles theme.

To set the ball rolling ...

With books closed, ask students what kinds of festivals they celebrate. Give birthdays and national holidays as examples of a range of possible festivals.

Ask them to discuss what makes festivals special (traditional clothes, food, processions, etc.).

Listening p.14

1 It doesn't matter if students can't identify the festivals at this stage but they may be asked to guess which country they are in (A shows the Songkran festival held in Thailand to celebrate the solar New Year; B shows a public parade organised to celebrate Thanksgiving in the USA; C shows Hindus celebrating Diwali in India. For further details, see the tapescript on page 197.) Before they move on to Exercise 1b, use the strategy box to point out how prediction is a useful tool to help understanding.

2 Point out the listening strategy before students listen. When students have matched speakers to the pictures ask them what words/phrases they remember from each and, by combining them with the pictures, work out the gist of each speaker.

3 Before students listen again, ask them to read the strategy box and remind them that they are listening for specific information, not specific words or phrases. Give them time to mark the important words in each statement before listening.

4 At this stage of the course it is useful to give students time to prepare what they are going to say and to have time to look up key vocabulary. However, remind them that it is a speaking activity and check that they are just making notes rather than writing out sentences in full. The discussion itself would work best in small groups. If all your students are from the same place, you could ask them within each group to think of different festivals to talk about. As each student describes their festival, encourage the others to ask questions.

Speaking p.15

1 Discuss ideas as a class and then elicit other types of family celebrations not shown, e.g. engagement, new baby, house warming, christening/naming ceremony, retirement. Clarify any new vocabulary, and in particular get students to think about word-

building, e.g. *to get engaged, to be engaged, engagement,* etc.

2a Point out the speaking strategy. Remind students that in Paper 5 part 2 they will be asked to speak for a minute and compare and contrast two pictures, but not to describe them in detail. They will also be asked to respond to them personally in some way, e.g. here they have to say which celebration they would prefer to be at and why.

2b When students have decided which pictures the woman is describing, ask them what words or phrases they heard to help them.

2c Give students enough time to read the expressions before they listen for them. You could model them for the students, either before or after listening, so that they can recognise the stress patterns. Show the class the complete list of useful expressions in the Functions reference on page 224.

2d Before students do the speaking task, remind them of the strategy box and get them to think about how long they will speak on each section (similarities, differences and preference). As they speak, encourage partners to listen attentively but not to interrupt. They could also time the speaker and give feedback on his/her fluency.

3 This could be done in pairs, groups or as a whole class, and could produce some interesting stories. If any students seem to have little to say, you could prompt them to talk about any planned future celebrations, or other family celebrations that are not shown in the photos.

▶ **Student's Resource Book page 10**

Language development 2 p.16

The language in Exercise 1 should largely be revision for students at this level, but it is important to check that they have a good grasp of these basics. Ask students to look at the photo and ask if anyone knows anything about the carnival.

Background

The Notting Hill Carnival takes place on the last Sunday and Monday of August, in and around the streets of Notting Hill in West London. The Carnival was started in the 1960s by Caribbean immigrants, to promote their culture. It features a procession, food and music, both traditional and modern. Up to two million people crowd into the narrow streets, making it the most popular street festival in Europe.

1a/b Students should do this in pairs, or at least discuss their answers in pairs, before checking in the

Grammar reference. Discuss and clarify any points students are not sure about.

1c Students may need access to dictionaries for this task. If so, encourage them to work out the correct form of the words before they look up the meanings. Again, get them to compare answers before checking them as a whole class.

2 Give students plenty of time to study the information in the box before attempting the exercise. Point out to students that to do well at FCE level it is not enough just to use basic comparative and superlative structures, and they should be able to demonstrate use of these modifiers when using adjectives and adverbs.

3a Remind students to modify their comparisons as they write them.

3b Discussion could be in pairs or small groups, with brief class feedback.

▶ **Student's Resource Book page 11**

Use of English 1 p.17

1a As this is the first time students encounter Key word transformations, and they are an area of the exam that students often find problematic, it is important to go through the example carefully with the class. Demonstrate how the example sentence expresses the same idea in two different ways and take time to work through the strategy box and example before starting the exercise.

1b Ask concept questions to check students' understanding of the rubric, such as *Can you change the word given? Which words do you write?* Students can use the Help clues if needed. Explain that some of the language has not been covered in the book yet and refer them to the contents map to show them when it will be covered.

3 When students have discussed the questions you could discuss strategies for further practice in areas they found difficult, such as using the Students' Resource Book, referring to grammar practice materials, the school study centre, etc.

Use of English 2 p.18

1 Check that students understand *hospitality* (friendly behaviour towards visitors) before they discuss the question.

2a With all text-based questions, students should understand the gist before attempting to complete the task. Give students a minute to first skim the text then scan it to find the answers to the three questions.

2b It would be useful to stop after students have

answered the first one or two questions and go through them with the whole class before students go on and complete the exercise. Remind them to use the Help clues where they have difficulty.

2c This exercise points out some of the areas that are frequently tested in Paper 3 Part 1.

2d Remind students that they will need to learn a lot of vocabulary during the course and discuss with them ways to use a vocabulary book to help them.

Language development 3 p.19

This section is designed to familiarise students with the concept of collocation. They will need encouragement throughout the course to notice collocations as they occur and to record them.

LOOK When students have found the five collocations it might be useful to elicit the opposites for some of them, e.g. *heavy meal – light meal,* to further demonstrate how collocation works.

1 Students may be unfamiliar with this type of diagram, which is sometimes known as a spidergram. If so, spend a little time explaining how they can be a useful memory aid, as they help learners with strong visual memories and may help to categorise vocabulary in a similar way to the brain.

2a Although some other adjective + noun combinations might be possible, e.g. *strong clothes, wide heels,* they are not common and therefore cannot really be regarded as 'strong' collocations.

....
:   **Photocopiable activity**   :
: Photocopiable activity 2 (pp. 129–130) gives   :
: practice of these, and more adjective + noun   :
: collocations.   :
....

3 This might be a good point in the course to show students how phrasal verbs are listed in dictionaries.

4a Emphasise that students should learn the phrasal verbs with the nouns they collocate with, e.g. *turn the heat up, keep costs down.*

5 It would be useful to revise some of the phrasal verbs in a future lesson. One good way of doing so is to play 'Noughts and crosses'. Divide the class into teams. The object of the game is for one team to complete a row of three squares (vertical, horizontal or diagonal) in a grid with their symbol, either 'noughts' (0) or crosses (X). Draw a square on the board and divide it into nine smaller squares by drawing two horizontal lines and two vertical lines inside it. Write one phrasal verb into each square. Teams take it in turns to choose a verb and put it into a sentence which shows the meaning. If it is correct, they can put their symbol in the square. The first team with three squares in a row wins.

▶ **Module 1 Review CB page 20**

▶ **Module 1 Test: How much do you remember? TRB page 174**

Unit 2 Key

Listening p.14

1b A: river, statue, religious procession
B: parade, flag, traditional costumes
C: lamps

2a 1 C; 2 A; 3 B

3a Important words in each statement:
A Live animals
B dresses
C tales, acted out
D food
Speaker 1 C (*we watch plays based on ancient Diwali stories*)
Speaker 2 A (*People buy birds and fish … and set them free*)
Speaker 3 D (*The food that people always eat*)

Speaking p.15

2b 1 C then B in that order
2 She prefers the birthday party ('I think I'd prefer the birthday party … as it's more relaxed and probably more fun than …')

2c **Similarities:**
Both of … are
They both seem to be …
In this one … and this one …
Differences:
The main difference between … and … is
… whereas … This one is … .
Likes, dislikes, preferences:
I would like … but …
Although … I'd like … because …
I think I'd prefer … as …

Language development 2 p.16

1a 1 Notting Hill Carnival in London is ~~more~~ *the most* popular one I know.
2 It is ~~most large~~ *the largest* street carnival ~~of~~ *in* Europe.
3 But ~~more big~~ *the bigger* it gets, ~~more friendly~~ *the friendlier* it becomes.
4 The costumes are ~~prettyest~~ *the prettiest* I have seen.
5 But the ~~goodest~~ *best* thing is the music.
6 Each year it seems ~~more loud that~~ *louder than* the last time!
7 Luckily, the weather is usually as good ~~than~~ *as* the music.
8 Next year I will go ~~more early~~ *earlier*, to see everything.

1c 1 more enthusiastically; 2 the most popular;
3 more widely; 4 better-known; 5 bigger;
6 wider; 7 as enthusiastic; 8 liveliest; 9 most sensational; 10 more commercialised

2 1 by far the largest; 2 much more crowded;
3 not quite as long; 4 a lot more colourful;
5 far spicier; 6 easily the mildest; 7 just about the worst

Use of English 1 p.17

1a isn't nearly as old as
1b 1 aren't as/so widely read
2 apart from
3 a much better swimmer than
4 turned it down
5 much less popular than

HELP **Question 1** passive
Question 2 *from*
Question 3 you need the article *a*
Question 4 *turn s.th. down*

2 6 is more difficult to study
7 always borrowing my things without
8 been good at
9 hasn't/has not seen Jane for
10 only a little more slowly

3 vocabulary: 2, 4, 8
comparative or superlative structures: 1, 3, 5, 6, 10 tense forms: 7, 9

Use of English 2 p.18

2a 1 They washed their feet.
2 An object in the house that the guest has admired.
3 Because they might be too embarrassed to refuse food when it is offered.

2b 1 C world – collocates with *ancient* and concerns people
2 A look – phrasal verb *look after*
3 D journey – must be countable – c.f. *travel* (uncountable) and collocate with *long*
4 B survived – continued to this day
5 D particular – specified one of a number
6 A typical – normal/common
7 C required – passive, the tradition calls for it
8 B off – *breaks off*, removes
9 B foreign – from abroad
10 D heavy – collocates with *meal*
11 A keeps on – continues
12 B turn – phrasal verb *turn s.th. down*, to refuse s.th.

HELP **Question 1** *world*
Question 2 *look after*
Question 6 *typical*
Question 10 *heavy*
Question 12 *turn down*

2c 2 • the correct word from a set with similar meanings: 4, 6, 7
• phrasal verbs: 2, 8, 11, 12
• adjective + noun combinations: 1, 3, 9, 10

Language development 3 p.19

LOOK ancient world (opposite: modern)
long journey (opposite: short)
old customs (opposite: new)
special cloth (opposite: ordinary)
foreign guests

1 apples; milk; look; grapes

2a strong: <u>influence</u>, possibility, feelings, argument
wide: variety, grin, choice, gap
plain: English, clothes
high: heels, number, speed

2b 1 strong feelings; 2 plain English; 3 wide grin;
4 high speed; 5 wide choice/wide variety;
6 strong influence; 7 High heels;
8 strong possibility

3 1 literal/obvious meaning
2 idiomatic

4a 1 up; 2 down; 3 down; 4 up; 5 down; 6 up

4b 1 d; 2 f; 3 e; 4 g; 5 c; 6 h; 7 b; 8 a

4c a – 8; b – 5; c – 7; d – 6; e – 2; f – 3; g – 4;
h – 1

Coursebook
Module 1 Review p.20

1a 1 on; 2 in; 3 for; 4 at; 5 after; 6 to; 7 on;
8 to; 9 on; 10 for

2a 1 ~~are~~ *do* many people speak~~ing~~ more than one
language?
2 ✓
3 ~~would~~ *were* people ~~be~~ happier 20 years ago?
or: *did* people *use to be* happier 20 years ago?
4 ~~would~~ *do* people work harder nowadays?
5 ✓
6 do women do less housework than they ~~would~~
used to?
7 what sort of things ~~are~~ *do* people ~~doing~~ *do* on
national holidays?
8 how did people ~~use to~~ celebrate on 31
December 1999?

3a Possible answers:
1 Going out is not as exciting as staying at
home.
2 Living in a village is nowhere near as
dangerous as living in a city.
3 Working in an office is not quite as relaxing as
working from home.
4 Keeping pets is much easier than looking after
children.
5 Giving presents is far more satisfying than
receiving presents.
6 Men's cooking is slightly better than women's
cooking.

3b 1 What's *the most comfortable/the prettiest/the
quietest* room in your house or flat?

2 What's the *most enjoyable/the biggest/the
liveliest* party you've been to?
3 What's *the healthiest/the quickest/the easiest*
way of travelling to college or work?

4 1 wide; 2 wide; 3 strong; 4 plain; 5 strong;
6 wide; 7 strong; 8 high

5 1 take it down
2 look her up
3 do up my room/do my room up
4 settle down
5 tidy up
6 let my friends down/let down my friends

Teacher's Resource Book
Module 1 Test: How much do
you remember? p.174

1 1 C; 2 B; 3 B; 4 A; 5 C

2 1 use; 2 like; 3 would (could); 4 between; 5 Is

3 1 He *always forgot/was always forgetting* to lock
the back door.
2 Jane's cooking *is not nearly as good* as John's.
3 Shall *I pick you up* at 8.00 p.m.?
4 I don't have *(quite) as many books as* he does.
5 My boss *is always interrupting me* when
I speak.

4 1 were; 2 to; 3 more; 4 ✓; 5 to

5 1 inhabitants; 2 personality; 3 international;
4 outskirts; 5 talkative

Module 2 Careers

Units 3 and 4 are linked by the theme of careers and include topics such as growing up, schools/education and work.

To set the ball rolling ...

Elicit the difference between the words *job* and *work* (*job* – countable – the specific thing that you do for a living; *work* – uncountable – the general concept) and between *job* and *career* (*career* – a job or profession that you plan to do for several years).

Lead-in p.21

Elicit the names of the jobs shown in the photos. Ask students if they would like to do any of the jobs shown, and to give reasons why/why not.

Then get them to discuss the lead-in questions.

Unit 3 Work

Reading p.22

1 To extend the discussion you could ask *What other films has Sean Connery been in?* and *Who plays James Bond now?*

2 Students should first read the strategy box giving more advice on skimming. Choosing a suitable title is a good way of demonstrating a general understanding. From skimming, students should learn that the article is about his tough childhood, his first jobs and his determination.

3a The skimming should also have given students some idea of the structure of the text, making it easier to decide which paragraph to look in for each question.

Spend some time on the technique, as it is important that students develop strong strategies from the start. Summarise as: Read for gist – read questions only – scan text for answers – read in detail – answer in own words – select answer that expresses same idea. If students have time they should also think about why the other answers are wrong.

Remind students that in the exam there will be four possible answers for each question.

Note pronunciation of Edinburgh: ˈed-ᵊn-ˌbr-ə

4 This could be done as a race (First to find eight jobs, or How many can you find in 30 seconds?) to further encourage scanning.

As they discuss the jobs, encourage them to expand their answers with reasons.

5 Students are likely to encounter words with which they are unfamiliar. If the words are in an important part of the text, students should use the reading strategy to deduce the meanings. The definitions in this exercise help students to check their guesses.

d Students often need lots of encouragement initially to keep vocabulary books.

> **Photocopiable activity**
>
> Photocopiable activity 3A (p. 131) could be done at this point. It is a group discussion on various aspects of a variety of jobs.

▶ **Student's Resource Book page 14**

Language development 1 p.24

With books closed ask students for ways of finding jobs (asking around, job centres, advertisements, relatives) and the process of getting them (see an advertisement, write a letter of application, attend an interview).

Discuss students' experiences of applying for jobs and attending interviews.

1a Get students to discuss the question in pairs.

1b If students are not familiar with the names of the tenses, give them some examples before they do the exercise.

1c This is to draw students' attention to the different use of the tenses and is preparation for completing the grammar summary. You may want to let students discuss the questions in pairs before class feedback.

2a Students should do the exercise on their own and check in pairs before referring to the Grammar summary to check their answers.

3e *for* and *since* are frequently tested in the FCE exam. One way to give further practice is to give each student two pieces of paper, one with the word *for* and the other with the word *since*. Then call out a list of time expressions, e.g. *six months, last month, October, Friday, five days, five o'clock, Christmas,* and as you say each one students hold up the correct piece of paper. To make it a game you could award points for correct answers.

4 Remind students that this type of checking and correcting is important with their own written work. Get them to justify their answers.

5b This is an opportunity for less controlled personalised practice of the structures. Encourage students to try and write interesting true sentences, but to use their imagination if they can't think of anything true to write.

6 This could be done with a competitive element. E.g. students could work in pairs and see which pair is the quickest to find and correct the eight mistakes.

· ·
Photocopiable activity

Photocopiable activity 3B (p. 132) would work well here. It is a roleplay with candidates being interviewed and selected for a job.
· ·

▶ **Student's Resource Book page 15**

Writing p.26

1 Point out to students that in Paper 2 Part 2, they may be asked to write either an informal letter (as in Unit 1) or a formal letter.

2 In the exam, as with all writing, the writer needs a clear focus on the reason for writing. Students should consider these four questions for every piece of writing they do now.

3a Again emphasise that the planning stage is vital if students are to include all the important information within the word count and use a range of structures/vocabulary.

3b Encourage students just to make notes at this stage, not to start writing the actual paragraphs.

4a Point out that the only problem here is the level of formality. All the sentences contain good English and interesting phrases.

4c Although addresses should not be added, there should be a suitable opening and closing.

5 Now that students have done detailed work on the planning of the letter, the writing should not take more than 20 minutes.

6 Checking should take another ten minutes. Remind students that contractions and direct questions are not used in formal letters.

When they check the number of words, teach them at this stage to calculate the average number of words per line and then just count the lines. By the time of the exam they should have a good feel for the right number of words in their handwriting, and therefore won't need to waste time counting every word.

▶ **Student's Resource Book page 17**

Unit 3 Key

Reading p.22

1a 1 a Sean Connery
  b *Indiana Jones and the Last Crusade; Dr. No*
  c Indiana Jones's father; James Bond

2 **B** is the best title as the text mainly concerns the various jobs he had before playing the role of James Bond. **A** only summarises the first paragraph and **C** only refers to the last paragraph concerning his looks. He didn't actually win Mr Universe.

3b 1 C
  2 A line 20 (*keen to extend his experience …*) Not B as *despite his parents' objections*
  3 B lines 31–32 (*he had to leave for medical reasons*)
  4 B he had boasted about joining, but he had made a mistake – lines 28–29 (*doubting whether the Navy was really the right thing for him*)
  5 A line 41 (*as long as the job paid him enough …*) Not B as he *didn't mind what he did* or C as he played football but *turned down a job with Man Utd.*
  6 C lines 53–54 (*on the strength of his looks alone*) Not A as he didn't win.

4 milk delivery boy, Royal Navy, coal delivery, labourer, French polisher, lifeguard, actor, fashion model

5b 1D; 2E; 3F; 4B; 5G; 6C; 7A

Language development 1 p.24

1a Yes. Good English and some experience of computers.

1b past simple: helped; attended
present perfect simple: have often been; have learned; haven't had

1c 1; No; No; Yes, a year ago; Yes, last year
  2 Present perfect simple
   Present perfect simple
   Past simple
   Past simple
  3 a year ago; last year
   often; over the years

1d A 1 I have often been to the United States
  2 I have learned quite a lot of English
  3 I haven't had much experience
  B 1 I helped to organise a children's holiday club
  2 I attended a short training course

2a 1
A: Have you ever lived abroad?
B: Yes, I have.
A: Where did you live?
B: In Dublin.
A: When did you go there?
B: In 2002.
2
A: Have you ever worked in an office?
B: No, I haven't.
3
A: Have you ever been to the USA?
B: Yes, I have.
A: When did you go there?
B: Last year.
A: Why did you go there?
B: To study English.
4
A: Have you used English in your work before?
B: No, I haven't.

3b present perfect simple: have lived; have just taken; haven't had
present perfect continuous: have been studying; have been reading

3c 1 Yes; 2 Yes; 3 1; 4 Yes; 5 Maybe. We don't know.

3d A I have lived in Krakow since 1990.
B I have been studying French at university for two years.
C I have just taken my exams.
D Recently I have been reading more about Krakow.

3e 1 for; 2 since; 3 for; 4 since; 5 for; 6 since

4 1 ✓ Recent activity.
2 Incorrect. Recent finished action. Should be *I've had some good news.*
3 ✓ Recent activity.
4 ✓ Recent finished action.
5 Incorrect. Recent finished action. Single action, not a repeated action. Should be *Emma's fallen over.*
6 Incorrect. Recent repeated activity. Should be *We've been using the stairs all day.*

5a 1 've/have been
2 haven't written
3 haven't been waiting
4 've/have been working
5 haven't had
6 felt
7 've/have made (viewed as a recent finished action)
OR 've/have been making (viewed as a recent activity, maybe unfinished)
8 've/have been trying
9 've/have found
10 've/have been staying

6 I ~~have been~~ *was* born in Poland 26 years ago and I've lived here all my life. I ~~am~~ *have been* married for two years but we don't have any children yet. I've been studying at teacher training college ~~since~~ *for* four years and I enjoy it a lot. In my spare time I'm learning the clarinet – I've played it ~~since~~ *for* five years. I also love reading. Last year I ~~have~~ read a lot of novels in English. I ~~go~~ *have been going* to the country for my holidays ~~during~~ *for* six years because I love the mountains. ~~I've also gone~~ *I also went* to the USA two years ago to work.

Writing p.26
1 formal: c, d, e; informal: a, b, f

2 1 The Manager of the hotel
2 to apply for a job
3 personal information, ability to speak English, suitability, availability
4 positive, enthusiastic

3a **Paragraph 1** – Where you heard about the job (your name comes at the end)
Paragraph 2 – knowledge of the area, training/qualifications, previous experience, languages, other skills and personality.
Paragraph 3 – suitability
Paragraph 4 – availability (referees would normally be given in the accompanying CV)

4a appropriately formal: 2, 6, 10
too informal: 1, 3, 4, 5, 7, 8, 9

4b 1 I would like to apply for the position of hotel receptionist which I saw advertised in the student magazine.
3 At present I am studying at university and I have a reasonable command of English.
4 – I regret I have had no experience of this kind of work but I have a good knowledge of computers.
5 – I very much enjoy working with people.
7 – I think I would be a suitable candidate for this job because …
8 – I would be happy to provide references and attend an interview.
9 – I hope you will consider my application.

4c Opening: *Dear Sir or Madam* As the name of the manager is unknown, this is the only suitable opening.
Closing: *Yours faithfully* This is the best ending when no name has been used at the beginning. In British English, if there is a name at the beginning, e.g. *Dear Ms Smith, Yours sincerely* is usually used at the end.

5   Sample answer:

Dear Sir or Madam

I would like to apply for the position of hotel receptionist which I saw advertised in my university's student newspaper. I am hoping to find hotel work during the summer holiday.

I am 20 years old and at present I am studying Marketing. I have a reasonable command of English and I also speak a little German. I very much enjoy working with people and for the last two summers I have been working in a restaurant, where I had to serve customers from different countries. Now I am looking for something better. I have a good knowledge of computers and database systems.

I think I would be a suitable candidate for the position because I have been described as calm and organised. I am keen to learn more about the travel industry.

I am available from June 10 and would be happy to attend an interview at any time. I look forward to hearing from you in the near future.

Yours faithfully

Eduardo Palazzo

Eduardo Palazzo

(169 words)

Unit 4 Education

This unit continues the theme of careers, focusing on the topic of education.

To set the ball rolling ...

With books closed, put students in pairs or groups to talk briefly about the school(s) they went to. Give suitable prompts if necessary, e.g. *State or private? Single sex or mixed? Strict or relaxed?*

Listening p.28

1 Students look at the photos and read the strategy box before discussing the two questions.

2 In this radio discussion two speakers give their opinions on the differences between boys and girls at school. Students can refer back to the strategy on page 14 (Unit 2) before listening for the first time. Give them plenty of time to read the notes before they listen.

3 Students should first read the listening strategy. Before they listen, remind them that opinions might be expressed in different words and that they need to recognise who expresses the opinions.

4 Students could also discuss their opinions on separating girls and boys at school and how they think it would have affected their own education.

5 A list of school subjects is a useful lexical set under the topic of education. A spidergram in a vocabulary book would be a good way to record them.

Speaking p.29

1 Give students a few minutes to think of points before they speak.

2a At this stage students should not discuss the list. They will do this later.

2d Students should read the speaking strategy first. Give them time to look at the list again and to prepare before the discussion. Monitor and check that they are using the language for giving opinions, agreeing and disagreeing, and give feedback on this afterwards.

3 Give students time to look at the statements and think about them first. Remind them to use the functional language as they discuss the points, and again provide feedback on this afterwards.

▶ **Student's Resource Book page 18**

Use of English 1 p.30

1 This is just intended as a quick introduction to the topic of the text. Don't spend long on it, and don't expect students to come up with too much detail!

Background

Albert Einstein (1879–1955) was born German but became a Swiss citizen in 1901. He emigrated to the USA in 1933. His theory of relativity was just one of many great theories. When the first atom bomb was used, he said that if he had known what his discoveries would be used for, he would have been a watchmaker. After the Second World War he campaigned against nuclear weapons.

2a Remind students that the purpose of the three questions is to get a general understanding of the text, and that they should only spend a minute or so looking at the article to find the answers.

2b First go through the task strategy with the class. Elicit ways of identifying whether the missing word is a noun, article, verb, pronoun, etc., e.g. *What word follows the gap? What type of words are followed by –ing forms?*, etc. When students first work through the text, point out that they don't have to work through in order; harder ones can be left until others have been filled in, by which time they might seem easier.

2c It might be useful for students to discuss these questions before giving them the answers and explanations.

3 Another question to discuss could be:
Do you think that, generally speaking, school/university exams are a good indication of how successful someone will be?

Language development 2 p.31

LOOK It might be useful to elicit some uses of articles with books closed before students read the grammar box.

1a Do the first question as an example with the whole class, asking suitable concept questions for each part. For example, sentence 1:

- How many *best courses* can you have? *The* is often used with superlatives.
- *… the one* – do we know which one?
- *the economics* – what type of word is *economics*? (a subject of study)
- *The teacher* – do we know which teacher?
- *a good progress* – Is *progress* countable or uncountable?

Encourage students to work through the other sentences in the same way.

1b Students should work through the gapped text with the same systematic approach. Note how *college* is used in different ways in the text, illustrating different uses of articles; students wanted *a* college (indefinite), the attitude of *the* college (definite), to go to Ø college (fixed expression).

2 Give students time to read through the grammar box before doing the exercise.

• •
Photocopiable activity
Photocopiable activity 4 (pp. 133–134) would work well here. Students complete the missing articles in a story and retell it to a partner.
• •

▶ **Student's Resource Book page 19**

Use of English 2 p.32

1 First get students to compare and contrast the two pictures as in Paper 5 Part 2. This should help lead in to the discussion on what children learn at school (social skills/interaction, relationships, respect, etc.).

2a As with other Use of English tasks, it is important for students to have a general understanding of the text before attempting the task.

2b Students should read the task strategy and the rubric carefully before starting the task. Look at the example and do question 1 together to help students with the strategy. In 0, the word must be a noun as it is between an adjective and *for. Oblige* is a verb. We form the noun by dropping *e* and adding *-ation*. In 1, after an article and two adjectives it must be a noun. *Educate* is a verb. We form the noun by removing *e* and adding *-ation*.

2c These questions focus students on the strategy and introduce expressions such as suffix and prefix, which students may not be familiar with.

3 You could also ask students whether they would think of educating their own children at home.

Language development 3 p.33

LOOK This is the first time suffixes are dealt with in the book. Emphasise that many types of words are formed by adding suffixes and that this section only looks at adjectives. Give students advice on recording suffixes in a vocabulary book. Suggest that each time they learn a new word they also record the related words formed with suffixes. (e.g. suit; suitable, unsuitable, suitability, suitably)

3a Students could either do this with a partner or by using dictionaries. If they use dictionaries, demonstrate how phrasal verbs are listed in the dictionary.

3b Do the first question with the class to ensure they are thinking about both the correct verb and the correct tense.

▶ **Module 2 Test: How much do you remember? TRB page 175**

▶ **Exam Practice 1. Papers 1 and 3 CB pages 34–35; Papers 2 and 4 TRB page 176**

Unit 4 Key

Listening p.28

1 2 Girls are doing better than boys in public exams.

2 1 Girls are more intelligent than boys.
2 Girls are more intelligent than boys.
Most boys think that studying hard is not masculine.
Very few primary school teachers are men.
Girls and boys have different learning styles.
Girls are studying harder than in the past.
3 separating boys and girls

3b/c 1 F The reporter thinks that a report published today will not shock people who work in education (*I don't think it comes as a surprise to educationalists*).
2 F Caroline does not believe that girls are more intelligent than boys of the same age (*There's no evidence at all to show that girls are brighter than boys*).
3 T
4 T
5 T
6 F Tim and Caroline don't agree that there are advantages if boys and girls study in separate classes. (*... just separating groups of boys within the class and having a boy–girl seating plan works just as well ...*).
7 T

Speaking p.29

2b Most important factors:
• small classes – individual attention
• being near home – more free time and friends
• live nearby
• uniform – important that they all wear the
• same clothes
• least important factor:
• lots of equipment – doesn't matter at this age

2c Giving opinions:
<u>For</u> me, one of the most important <u>things</u> is ...
I just <u>don't think</u> it matters ... .
The <u>least</u> important factor for me is ... .
Strong agreement:
That's <u>true</u>.
I agree <u>absolutely</u>.
I couldn't <u>agree</u> more.
Disagreement:
I agree <u>up</u> to a <u>point</u>, but I
Do you <u>think</u> <u>so</u>?
But don't <u>you</u> <u>agree</u> that ... ?
Actually, I think it's <u>more</u> <u>important</u> ... .

Use of English 1 p.30

2a 1 Science.
2 He didn't like exams or going to classes.
3 He worked in the Swiss patent office.

2b 1 a – student = singular countable noun
2 all – *nearly + all*
3 what/as
4 neither/nor – linking two negative ideas
5 few – determiner with plural noun (months)
6 Despite/After – before *-ing*
7 the – name of a unique institution
8 Although/Though – contrast
9 because – expresses reason
10 a – school = singular countable noun, one of many
11 both – good at two things
12 All/Throughout
13 lot – *a lot of*
14 was – before past participle in passive structure
15 the – a particular, defined history

2c 1
articles – 1, 7, 10, 15
determiners – 2, 5, 11, 12, 13
connecting expressions – 4, 6, 8, 9
2 passives

Language development 2 p.31

1a 1 The best course was the one I did on ~~the~~ economics. The teacher was very good and I made ~~a~~ good progress.
2 Nina's studying ~~the~~ German at evening classes in ~~the~~ London.
3 My brother is 19. He's at ~~the~~ university in ~~the~~ Africa and wants to become **an** English teacher because it would give him **a** good opportunity to travel.
4 When we were in Japan we noticed that most Japanese students work harder than the American students I met in **the** USA.
5 I go to college by ~~the~~ train. Unfortunately, the train is often late.

1b 1 Ø – students in general
2 a – one of many
3 Ø
4 the – superlative
5 the – defined noun
6 the – referring to something known
7 the – still connected to the superlative in 4
8 the – defined
9 the – known buildings
10 The – only one
11 a – college = singular countable noun
12 Ø – in general
13 a – as 11
14 a – timetable = singular countable noun
15 Ø – fixed expression

16 Ø – in general
17 Ø – fixed expression

2 1 some – a large amount of
2 any – negative, before uncountable noun
3 anything – negative
4 some – positive, before uncountable noun
5 anything – negative
6 some – positive, before uncountable noun
7 hardly any – almost no
8 some – in a question, hoping for a positive answer
9 some – positive, before uncountable noun
10 anything – it doesn't matter what

Use of English 2 p.32

2a 1 No. *In the UK there is no legal obligation for children to go to school.*
2 Other adults think children don't have the opportunity to socialise. *... the attitude of other adults, who say children don't socialise.*

2b 1 education; 2 responsibility; 3 academically;
4 necessary; 5 suitable; 6 impressive;
7 inattentive; 8 biggest; 9 unsympathetic;
10 perfectly

2c 2 nouns – 1, 2
adjectives – 4, 5, 6, 7, 8, 9
adverbs – 3, 10
3: 1, 2, 3, 5, 6, 9, 10
4: 7, 9

Language development 3 p.33

LOOK Add a suffix: suitable, impressive
Change the stem: *unsympathetic*
Make internal changes: *necessary*
Add a prefix: *inattentive, unsympathetic*

1 1 harmless; 2 natural; 3 courageous;
4 childish; 5 helpful; 6 passionate; 7 dirty;
8 horrible; 9 dramatic; 10 lively

2 take on (responsibility)

3a 1 g; 2 a; 3 h; 4 c; 5 j; 6 i; 7 b; 8 d; 9 e; 10 f

3b 1 turned up (to suddenly appear); 2 staying on;
3 carry out; 4 got down to; 5 Go over;
6 handed in; 7 keep up with; 8 pick up;
9 get (his meaning) across; 10 work out

Teacher's Resource Book
Module 2 Test: How much do
you remember? p. 175

1   1 C; 2 B; 3 C; 4 A; 5 D

2   1 hearing; 2 does; 3 has; 4 the; 5 some/many

3   1 Paul *has been playing tennis for* three years.
2 Susan *has liked jazz since* she was a teenager.
3 There *is hardly anything to do* at the weekends.
4 Nina's looking for a *more suitable* job.
5 I *am available to attend/am available for* an interview at any time.

4   1 been; 2 am; 3 ✓; 4 the; 5 have

5   1 irresponsible; 2 disability; 3 dirtiest;
4 flexible; 5 strength

Coursebook
Exam practice 1 p.34

Paper 1 Reading
Part 4   1 A; 2 C; 3 B; 4 D; 5 B; 6 C; 7 B; 8 D;
9 C; 10 A; 11 B; 12 A; 13 D

Paper 3 Use of English
Part 1   1 D; 2 B; 3 A; 4 C; 5 D; 6 B; 7 A; 8 D;
9 B; 10 D; 11 A; 12 D; 13 C; 14 C; 15 B

Part 2   1 for; 2 would; 3 At; 4 one/a; 5 the;
6 were; 7 any; 8 as; 9 to; 10 although; 11 up;
12 all; 13 kept; 14 than; 15 most

Part 3
1   I have *not seen Jane for a / not seen Jane since last* week.
2   Nobody in our club is *as good as Ann (is)* at chess.
3   He *will usually fall asleep* in the armchair in the evenings.
4   John asked Caroline to marry him but she *turned him down/turned down his/the offer / turned his/the offer down* because he was too old.
5   Mark is *one of the tallest people* I know.
6   I don't *want you to say anything* to Tom about last night.
7   This car *was far less expensive than* my last one.
8   Nick *has been (doing) boxing for/has been a boxer for* three years.
9   I *used to ride my bike* to college every day when I was seventeen.
10 The louder the music got, the *more difficult it was* to hear anyone speak.

Part 5   1 traditional; 2 successful; 3 suitable;
4 original; 5 enthusiastic; 6 unable;
7 farther/further; 8 failure; 9 shortage; 10 likely

Teacher's Resourse Book
Exam practice 1 p.176

Paper 2 Writing
1   Style: Informal letter – avoid formal expressions.
Content:
Tell your friend where you went, who you went with, what you ate and how enjoyable the picnic was. Include one or two interesting things that happened and say how your friends reacted.

2   Style:
Formal letter of application.
Content:
Say why you are interested in the job. Explain in detail the things you could write about, mentioning any experience you have of this sort of work and saying why you are a good candidate for the job.

Paper 4 Listening
Part 4   1 F; 2 T; 3 T; 4 F; 5 F; 6 T; 7 F

Module 3 The world around us

Units 5 and 6 are linked by the theme of 'the world around us' including topics such as cultural heritage, the environment, weather and animals.

Lead-in p.37

With books closed, get students to think of three man-made and three natural things which they see around them on a normal day. Compare ideas as a class. Then ask them to look at the two photos, and say which place they would prefer to visit and why. Explain *World Heritage sites* briefly (see 'Background' below). Get students to discuss the questions together, followed by class feedback.

Background

World Heritage sites are a list maintained by UNESCO (the United Nations Educational, Scientific and Cultural Organization) of over 730 'natural and cultural properties of outstanding universal value, protected against the threat of damage in a rapidly developing world.'
The Kremlin and Red Square, Moscow, were chosen as World Heritage sites because the Kremlin is 'inseparably linked to all of the most important historical and political events in Russia since the 13th century' and 'on Red Square, the Saint Basil Basilica is one of the most beautiful monuments of Russian Orthodox art.'
The Galapagos Islands, in the Pacific Ocean 1,000 km off the coast of Ecuador, were chosen because they are 'a unique living museum and showcase of evolution … unusual animal life – such as the land iguana, the giant tortoise and the many types of finch – inspired Charles Darwin's theory of evolution following his visit in 1835.'

Unit 5 Our cultural heritage

To set the ball rolling ...

With books closed, brainstorm what students know about Italy, such as where it is, what Italians typically eat and drink, famous places. Students may mention Venice as a famous place.

Reading p.38

1a Let students discuss the questions in pairs, then elicit ideas from the class.

Background

Venice is a port on the north east coast of Italy, and a regional capital, with a population of about 300,000. It is famous for its canals – about 150 divide the city – and the bridges which cross them, the most famous of which is the Rialto. There are no cars in the city; transport is by boat or on foot. Popular tourist sites are St. Mark's Square and Cathedral and The Doge's Palace. Apart from tourism it has a famous glass industry. Its famous opera house burned down in 1996. Research has been going on for a number of years to find ways to stop the city 'sinking' into the advancing sea.

2 If necessary, set a time limit of about $1^{1}/_{2} - 2$ minutes.

3a Draw students' attention to the strategy box, emphasising how the summary sentences express the same ideas in other ways. E.g. in paragraph 0 Venice is *unique* and in summary sentence G it is *different from other cities*. Give students a maximum of 15 minutes to match the summary sentences.

4 Give students time to think about the questions before they discuss them in small groups, then as a whole class.

Photocopiable activity

Photocopiable activity 5A (pp. 135–136) fits well here. It is a structured debate on the pros and cons of tourism.

5 Multiple matching often requires the recognition of near synonyms. Encourage students to build their vocabulary by recording near synonyms.

▶ **Student's Resource Book page 22**

Language development 1 p.40

1a Ask students if they know what the three sites are and where they are.

Background

The Taj Mahal, near Agra in India, was built by the Mughal emperor Shah Jahan in memory of his wife, Mumtaz Mahal ('Chosen One of the Palace'), of which the name Taj Mahal is a corruption. She died in 1631, and the building was commenced around 1632. It took 22 years to complete and cost 40 million rupees (830,000 US dollars).

The Statue of Liberty stands in New York Harbor. It is 92 metres high and made of copper sheets over a steel frame. Begun by the French sculptor Frédéric-Auguste Bartholdi in 1875, it was dismantled in 1885, shipped to New York and reassembled.

Marrakesh was founded in 1071–1072. The lively medina contains an impressive number of architectural masterpieces, including the walls and the monumental gates, the Kutubiya Mosque with its 77-metre-high minaret, the Saadian tombs and characteristic old houses.

1b After they have read the text, ask students if they know any other World Heritage sites, perhaps in their own country. A complete list by country can be found on the UNESCO website: http://whc.unesco.org/heritage.htm .

2b You might want to go through these questions one by one with students. If necessary, use further examples to highlight the difference between the adverbs *hard* and *hardly: He works hard* = He works a lot. *He hardly works* = He doesn't work very much at all, he does almost no work.

3a Students could work on their own or in pairs, then check by looking in the Grammar reference on pages 193–194.

3b Remind students that World Heritage sites can be cultural and/or natural and should be of 'outstanding universal value'. It would be interesting for students to check whether their chosen place is already a World Heritage site – they may not even know that it is!

4 Tell students that this language is frequently tested in Paper 3, and that it can make their writing and speaking more interesting in Papers 2 and 5.

5 This is an opportunity for less controlled, personalised practice of the language, probably best in small groups followed by class discussion.

6 Correcting is a vital element of writing and students should be encouraged to check their own writing, looking for typical mistakes such as these.

Photocopiable activity

Photocopiable activity 5B (pp. 137–138) gives further practice of adjectives and adverbs.

▶ Student's Resource Book page 23

Writing p.42

1 If necessary, for question 1 you could suggest two or three cities locally for students to choose from, outlining briefly what attractions each one has.

2 Emphasise that it is very important for students to think about these four questions in all their FCE writing, and the transactional letter in particular.

3a Remind students that their writing needs to be well organised. A good plan should include both the organisation of key points into paragraphs, and language (vocabulary and structure) to include at each stage. A good composition should contain a range of structures and vocabulary relevant to the topic.

4a Explain that a good opening is important. It makes the reader want to read on, and in the exam it will make a good first impression on the examiner.

4b Elicit what kind of language makes a letter informal. E.g. contractions, informal vocabulary such as *great, thrilled, loads,* and phrasal verbs such as *put you up.*

4c Explain that the expressions match the points in the paragraph plan and are informal. Students could compare in groups or as a whole class to establish the range and use of the structures.

4d Get students to discuss these in pairs and encourage them to give reasons for their choices – again, it is a question of the level of formality in the sentences.

5 As students now have a detailed paragraph plan and expressions to use, the writing should take only about 20 minutes. In the exam, if students aim to spend 15 minutes planning and 20 minutes writing, they will have ten minutes to check their work.

6 Encourage students to get into the habit of systematic checking. They should use the checklist in the Writing reference on page 206. In addition, they should check for errors with particular language areas that they have problems with.

LANGUAGE SPOT: punctuation

Although poor punctuation is not specifically penalised in the exam, the overall impression mark may be adjusted if communication is impeded. Students could use the Punctuation section of the Writing reference on page 217 to help them with any they are not sure about, and/or to help check when they have finished.

▶ Student's Resource Book page 25

Unit 5 Key

Reading p.38

1a **1** In the north east of Italy, on the Adriatic coast.
2 It is built around a network of canals – there are no roads or cars in the city.
3 Students may know or be able to guess that tourism has become more important and industry has declined.

1b Venice is changing and not necessarily for the better.

2 **a** 0; **b** 5; **c** 3; **d** 2; **e** 6; **f** 1; **g** 4

3a **1** B (*… on the frontiers of east and west … control important trade routes. As a result, Venice became a strong commercial and naval force …*)
2 C (*… one of the great qualities of the Venetians is their inner strength and ability to fight back.*)
3 E (*… water buses and tourist gondolas have now replaced trading vessels … churches and palaces … have become shops, hotels and flats … warehouses have been turned into art museums.*)
4 A (*National and international efforts are now being made to protect Venice and its art treasures …*)
5 D (*The resident population has shrunk … great concern that Venice is turning into a museum city for tourists … an effort to attract residents back …*)
6 F (*… should Venice's heritage be preserved at all costs … or should it move with the rhythm of modern life …?*)

5 **1** remarkable (line 2); **2** influence (l. 13); **3** impressive (l. 34); **4** fragile (l. 42); **5** shrunk (l. 54)

Language development 1 p.40

1a The Taj Mahal, the Statue of Liberty and the Islamic centre of Marrakesh

1b They are all UNESCO World Heritage sites.

2a Adjectives: natural, cultural, best-known, lively, fascinating, bleak, worrying, political, full, extremely, impressive
Adverbs: fast, hard, actively, hardly, well

2b **1** fast, hard, well; **2** lively; **3** hard, hardly.

3a **1** easy – *be* + adjective
2 incredibly – adverb before an adjective (*well-preserved*)
3 fast – adverb after *spoke. too quickly* would be possible.
4 classic – adjective describing the noun *site*
5 late – adjective; hard – adverb = a lot

6 surprising – adjective describing *sites*; imaginatively – adverb before an adjective (*created*)

4 **1** D – a remarkably + adjective + noun (*quite a simple idea*)
2 C – quite + a + adjective + countable noun (*a pretty/very fast car*)
3 A – a little + adjective (*a little/bit of* + noun)
4 C – very + gradable adjective
5 B – rather + a/an + adjective + noun (*a/an + fairly/rather/extremely/pretty* + adjective + noun)
6 D – very + gradable adjective (*gorgeous/wonderful/marvellous* = ungradable adjective)
7 B – absolutely + ungradable adjective (*very/extremely/remarkably* + gradable adjective)

6 **1** … a ~~very~~ huge statue …
2 … the new theatre is ~~very~~ fantastic.
3 … to be ~~smart~~ *smartly* dressed.
4 … are working very ~~hardly~~ *hard* to restore …
5 … the streets are sometimes *a* bit noisy …

Writing p.42

2 **1** An old friend.
2 To give information and suggestions.
3 Four – trains, accommodation, what to see, clothes.
4 Informal – she is an old friend and the style of her letter is informal.

3a Five paragraphs.
3b **Paragraph 2:** Travel instructions: Hourly train connections.
Paragraph 3: Places to go: 1 Lovely park.
2 Medieval castle.
Paragraph 4: Clothes: Shorts. T-shirts.

4a B. It is less formal.
4b Formal language in A:
Thank you very much …
… your letter of 10 July …
… your visit to my home town …
… I am writing to invite you to stay with me at my house.
Informal language in B:
It was great to hear from you …
I'm thrilled you're coming …
I hope you'll stay with me …
I've got loads of room to put you up now I've unpacked!

4d **1** A – All the language in A is informal, whereas all of B is extremely formal.
2 B – This is less formal (contraction, use of continuous not simple) and makes it clear they have met before, whereas in A *meeting you* makes it sound as if they are going to meet for the first time.

3 B – Again, this is less formal, with contractions and *Let me know*.

4e *Love* if they are very good friends, or *Best wishes*

5 Sample answer:

> Dear Sue,
>
> It was great to hear from you and I'm really excited that you're coming to visit me. You and Tom don't need to stay in a hotel – you can both stay at my house.
>
> It's quite easy to get here from the conference centre as there's a fast train every hour and it's only about 20 minutes away. If you call me I'll pick you up at the station.
>
> My town's fairly small so there isn't much to do but you really must visit the castle, which is incredibly old. There's quite a large park, which is a lovely place for a picnic in the summer.
>
> It tends to be very hot here in July, so just bring a few casual clothes such as shorts and T-shirts.
>
> Let me know if there's anything else you'd like to know – just call or email. I can't wait to see you again.
>
> Love
>
> Daisy

(154 words)

LANGUAGE SPOT: punctuation

Chester itself is a very pretty town. It dates back to Roman times, so there are a lot of fascinating ruins and lovely architecture which I'm sure will interest you. The Roman amphitheatre is well worth a visit with its guides dressed up as Roman soldiers. There is also a cathedral and a church, and there are red sandstone walls all round the town. It takes about an hour and a half to walk around them but it's a lovely walk. Henry James, the American writer, wrote about how much he loved the walls. You'll also find a river in Chester where you can go for a boat trip or have a picnic. If you have time to go shopping, there are lots of wonderful shops.

Unit 6 Our natural heritage

The 'world around us' theme continues in this unit with the topics of animals, natural phenomena and weather.

Listening p.44

1a First ask students to describe the photo. Elicit/Check the words *jaguar* and *rainforest*. Let students discuss the questions in pairs, then explain that they will hear the actual answers on the recording.

2a Get students to do this in pairs. It is important that students think about what kind of word could go into each space. Look at the example with them, and perhaps do number 2 together, to make sure they know what to do.

2c Point out that Exercise 2b is similar to Paper 4 Part 2, in which three words is normally the maximum necessary. Numbers can be written as numbers or words; e.g. question 1 could be *5.30* or *half past five*. In question 4, *a hundred and seventy kilometres* would obviously be more than three words, and this would not usually occur in the exam. Note also that in question 4, an abbreviation such as *km* would be acceptable. The most important thing is to show the examiner that you have understood the material on the recording.

After checking all the answers, ask students if they would like to do the job that Nick Gordon does, and why.

Speaking p.45

1 There may be some discussion about exactly what each person's job is, which gives you the opportunity to teach some useful vocabulary. The man in the photo on the left could be a farmer or a shepherd. The woman in the photo on the right could be a vet, a veterinary nurse or a veterinary assistant. In British English, *vet* is the most common word; *veterinary surgeon* is more formal. In American English, *veterinarian* is more common.

2 This activity aims to train students to compare and contrast the pictures, rather than simply describe each one separately, a common mistake in Paper 5 Part 2.

3a Point out that the instructions usually have two parts: First 'compare and contrast' and then 'say ...' (i.e. give a personal reaction of some kind).

3b As students listen, they should think about what the student says compared with what they said in Exercise 2.

3d Get students to discuss the questions in pairs. Play the recording again if they can't answer the questions. Point out that in Paper 5, if students don't know a word, they should explain it in another way, just as the student does on the recording. They will be given credit for this by the examiner. If they make no attempt to explain a word they don't know, they could lose marks.

4 Students should read the task strategy first.

5 Encourage students to discuss their own and each other's performance in the task.

▶ **Student's Resource Book page 27**

Use of English 1 p.46

1 This is to generate interest in the topic of animals' unusual abilities – you might want to reassure students that they don't need to know facts like these for the exam! Use the photo to teach *cricket*. Students should discuss the questions in pairs before turning to page 218 to check their answers.

2a Students should always look at the title of a Use of English text, as it will give them a clear indication of the content.

2b Again, students should always read any text for a general understanding before they start the exam task.

2c If you think it necessary, do the first one or two gaps with the whole class so that they can see the process of deciding what the missing words are.

2d This focuses students on choices they made and highlights typical areas tested in this part of the exam.

Language development 2 p.47

Look Point out the section in the Grammar reference on verbs of the senses, which can be followed by an infinitive without *to* or an *-ing* form.

1a This is a brief lead-in to the grammar exercise.

2a These three verbs are commonly tested at FCE.

2b Get students to check in pairs then perhaps look at the Grammar reference to check their answers.

3a Ask students what they know about the phenomenon.

Background

The Northern Lights is the popular name for the *aurora borealis*, which occurs when solar particles enter the earth's atmosphere over the north pole and react with gases, causing them to emit light. In the southern hemisphere, the corresponding phenomenon is known as the Southern Lights or *aurora australis*.

3b If students find any of the verb + preposition combinations hard, encourage them to note them down to learn.

4a Encourage students to write true sentences.

Photocopiable activity

Photocopiable activity 6 (pp. 139–140) would work well here. It is a card game in which students have to connect two verbs together correctly.

▶ **Student's Resource Book page 28**

Use of English 2 p.48

1 Any students who have seen the film will be familiar with Groundhog Day. Get them to explain it briefly to the others.

Background

In the fantasy comedy film *Groundhog Day* (1993) a weatherman, fed up with reporting on the Punxsutawney story every year, suddenly wakes up and finds himself in a world where every day is 2 February, and all the events of that day are repeated daily.

2a Give students a limit of one minute to read the text, ignoring the spaces.

2b Remind students to use the strategy on page 18 and the help questions if they need to.

2d Weather collocations are practised further in Exercise 3a on page 49. Knowledge of collocation is tested in various parts of the exam. Encourage students to note down collocations as they hear them rather than only writing down individual words.

Language development 3 p.49

1 This could be in pairs or small groups, followed by class discussion. Get students to expand their answers and to support them with reasons.

2a Make it clear that some words may go into more than one category. E.g. *hurricane* could go with wind or storm; *snow* and *hail* could go with rain or storm. Encourage students to discuss them together; if they give reasons for their answers, it will help them to understand the meanings of the words. Use the short definitions in the Key on TRB page 31 to help clarify meaning.

2b If there is time, students can make sentences of their own using the other items from the exercise.

3a If students have already done Exercise 2d on page 48, remind them of the collocations they found then.

3b Get students to think of the context of each sentence before completing it.

4a There may be more than one possibility, but students should look for the strongest collocations.

5 Check that students understand all the vocabulary in the questions. Obviously there are no 'right' answers here, but encourage students to give reasons for their choices.

▶ **Module 3 Review CB page 50**

▶ **Module 3 Test: How much do you remember? TRB page 177**

Unit 6 Key

Listening p.44

1b Nick is a wildlife photographer/film-maker. (*I was sent out to the Amazon … to make a TV documentary about monkeys and birds.*)
He liked: the heat, the humidity, the snakes, the insects, the animals, the people.
He didn't like: the loneliness, sweating so much, getting bitten by the insects, the feeling of claustrophobia caused by lack of daylight. (*You pour sweat … . The insects … you're bitten all the time. … claustrophobic … no real daylight … It's lonely.*)

2a 1 a time
2 two colours
3 a countable noun – get a … of sth.
4 measure of area
5 adverb – describing how jaguars move
6 noun – something edible but unusual
7 noun – describing a feeling
8 noun – something researchers fix to an animal
9 noun – something or someone that kill jaguars
10 two animals

2b 1 half past five/five thirty/05.30; 2 (deep) yellow; black; 3 photograph;
4 170/kilometres/kilometres/km; 5 quietly;
6 spider; 7 (great) respect; 8 radio collars;
9 (cattle/sheep/livestock) farmers; 10 domestic cats; dogs

2c 1 No more than three words.
2 Yes. All the words needed are used by the speakers.

Speaking p.45

3a … is difficult about these jobs.

3c Personally, I …
… if I had to choose …

3d vet – a kind of doctor who looks after animals
… a doctor for sick animals.
pets – small animals who live in the home

Use of English 1 p.46

1a See Coursebook page 218

2a **Possible answer:** animals can help us to predict when an earthquake is coming.

2b 1 Fish jump onto land; mice seem dazed and are easy to catch.
2 They evacuated a city and saved many lives, after the strange behaviour of some animals alerted the authorities to a major earthquake.
3 Some animals' senses are very sensitive, so perhaps they can detect seismic activity before an earthquake.

2c 1 have – present perfect with plural subject (people)
2 them/themselves – plural object or reflexive pronoun (fish/mice)
3 to – *begin* + to – infinitive
4 by – past passive + *by* + agent
5 more – compares with previous sentence
6 of – after *many*
7 had – past perfect
8 too – *too* + adjective + to do sth.
9 the – city (Haicheng) referred to earlier
10 in – *succeed* + in + -ing
11 Since –present perfect and a point in time, *then*
12 for – *prepare* + for sth.
13 It – subject
14 which/that – relative clause
15 be – infinitive after *would*
HELP **Question 1** present perfect
Question 7 before
Question 9 the
Question 13 It
2d articles – 9
auxiliary verbs – 1, 7
verb + verb patterns – 3, 10
verb + preposition – 4, 12

Language development 2 p.47

LOOK main verb + infinitive with *to*: ... *scientists* **began to receive** *reports* ...
main verb + infinitive without *to*: People **have seen** fish **jump** out ...
preposition + -ing form: ... *leaders had* **succeeded** *in saving* ...
adjective + infinitive: ... *too* **frightened to enter** *buildings/... may be* **able to detect** *the seismic activity* ...
noun + infinitive: ... **a pity to ignore** *the signs* ...

1a 1 The moon passes exactly in front of the sun and blocks out its light.

1b 1 to settle; 2 sleeping; 3 fly; 4 noticing; 5 solving; 6 go; 7 not bringing; 8 feel; 9 to talk; 10 not to drive

2a 1 a He remembered that he needed to wear them, and then put them on.
b He remembered that he had worn them at some point before then.
2 a She experimented with using one to see if it would work or was a good idea.
b She physically attempted to do it. Maybe she didn't succeed.
3 a He stopped doing something (e.g. driving) in order to look at the lights.
b He was looking at the lights and then he didn't look at them.
2b 1 to buy; 2 to get; 3 drinking; 4 to post; 5 calling; 6 adding

3b 1 of seeing; 2 to going; 3 in getting; 4 on putting up; 5 for not helping; 6 to go; 7 to her going; 8 on walking; 9 her from doing; 10 of getting lost

Use of English 2 p.48

2a 1 The groundhog 'Punxsutawney Phil' comes out of his hole and people make weather predictions based on his behaviour.
2 The 1993 film *Groundhog Day* has made the event better-known in recent years.
2b 1 B – *come out of a sleep* (*get up* is intransitive)
2 C – *clear* collocates with *sky*
3 B – *severe* is the only adjective here that collocates with *weather*
4 C – collocates with *spring* and contrasts with *six more weeks of winter*.
5 A – *gather in* a place (*combine with, crowd into*)
6 B – *a large number of* + plural noun
7 D – *just around the corner* – idiom = soon
8 B – *hard* collocates with *winter* to mean *severe/cold*
9 C – *heavy* collocates with *snow*
10 A – *of the same name* is a fixed expression
11 D – *turn s.b. into s.th.* = to make somebody become something different.
12 A – *turned up* = arrived
13 B – *although* followed by a clause
14 A – *hope for* + noun (hope to + infinitive)
15 C – *last for* + a period of time
2c words that go together – 2, 3, 4, 8, 9
the correct word from a set of similar meanings – 4, 5, 6, 10, 15
fixed expressions – 7, 10, 14
phrasal verbs – 1, 11, 12
linking words – 13
2d clear sky; severe weather; cloudy day; early spring; long, hard winter; heavy snow; good weather

Language development 3 p.49

2a rain:
drizzle (light rain)
hail (frozen rain)
shower (a short period of rain)
snow (soft flakes of frozen rain)
downpour (a lot of rain in a short time)
wind:
breeze (a light wind)
gust (a sudden, short, strong wind)
hurricane (a violent storm, especially in the Western Atlantic; we often associate hurricanes with strong wind)
gale (a very strong wind)

storm:
hurricane (a violent storm, especially in the Western Atlantic; we often associate hurricanes with strong wind)
thunder (a loud noise in the sky)
lightning (light in the sky caused by electricity)

2b 1 lightning; 2 gusts; 3 hail; 4 Hurricanes; 5 snow

3a 1 c, e, g; 2 b, c, e, g; 3 a, f; 4 b, c, e, g; 5 f; 6 a, b, e, f; 7 d; 8 f; 9 e; 10 e; 11 a, f

3b 1 high/strong; 2 heavy; 3 gentle/light; 4 loud; 5 heavy; 6 chilly; 7 torrential/tropical

4a 1 d; 2 c; 3 e; 4 a; 5 b

Coursebook
Module 3 Review p. 50

1 1 commercial; 2 shrink; 3 fragile; 4 affordable; 5 growth; 6 cope; 7 remarkable; 8 achievement

2a 1 surprisingly; 2 Interestingly; 3 hard; 4 late; 5 fast

2b 1 There is *a* quite *a* large number of foxes in Britain's cities.
2 Camels can lose *a* fairly *a* large amount of water without harming their bodies.
3 Dogs are extreme*ly* faithful pets.
4 The life of a performing animal in the circus can be *a* pretty miserable.
5 When it's ~~very~~ freezing most animals try to find shelter.

3 1 I'm watching a programme called 'Our Disappearing World'. Have you seen it?
2 According to the presenter, many people's lives have changed dramatically.
3 'I think it's a tragedy,' he said, 'that so many languages are disappearing.'
4 Ongota, an Ethiopian language, is only spoken by 78 people.
5 However, some regional languages like Catalan, Welsh and Trentine are surviving.

5 1 in; 2 of; 3 to; 4 of; 5 from; 6 on

6 1 clear; 2 gentle; 3 heated; 4 high; 5 heavy; 6 torrential; 7 loud

Teacher's Resource Book
Module 3 Test: How much do you remember? p.177

1 1 D; 2 C; 3 A; 4 C; 5 B

2 1 away; 2 fancy; 3 where; 4 in; 5 to

3 1 I *stopped smoking when I was/reached* 26.
2 Do *you remember paying/if/whether you paid* that bill?
3 Dan's office *is fairly close to/near (to)* his house.
4 There *were hardly any tourists in* the city five years ago.
5 The children had been *looking forward to going to* the zoo for ages.

4 1 ✓; 2 at; 3 for; 4 to; 5 ✓

5 1 threatened; 2 similarities; 3 scientifically; 4 friendliest; 5 Tourism

Module 4 Challenges

Units 7 and 8 are linked by the theme of 'Challenges' and include topics such as fund raising, an adventure race and various aspects of sport.

Lead-in p.51

A challenge is something that tests skill, ability or strength. Get students to look at the photos and talk about what challenge the people in each picture are facing. They should then discuss the lead-in questions. For the second question, you may want to start students off by giving one or two examples of your own.

Unit 7 Personal challenges

Reading p.52

1a This is a quick introduction and students only need to identify what they can from the pictures, e.g. he's running in a desert, he's famous.

Background

Ray Mouncey successfully completed the run described here (his fourth desert run) in 2000. The following year he returned and ran 1,001 miles, the equivalent of 38 marathons, in 42 days in the harshest conditions. Temperatures reached 55°C and dropped to only 40°C at night.

1b Students could write the questions individually or in pairs. Write some of their questions on the board.

2 Before students skim and scan the article they could refer to the strategies on pages 8 and 22. They should first skim for general understanding (60–90 seconds) then scan to find answers to their questions. Explain that they may not find all the answers. Check which questions remain unanswered, and help students find those answers which you know to be in the text.

3 As this is the first time students have encountered gapped texts, spend some time going through the rubric and strategy box with them. Point out that the missing sentences must fit logically and also grammatically.

Go through the example with them showing how this is so, and do number one together as a whole class. Set a time limit of 15 minutes for the exercise.

4 Students discuss the questions in groups. The second one links to the photocopiable activity.

5 The article uses a number of phrasal verbs which students need to identify. Point out that they are not used only in informal writing.

Photocopiable activity

Photocopiable activity 7A (p. 141) would work well here. It is a discussion similar in format to Paper 5 Part 3, with students deciding on the best way to raise money.

▶ **Student's Resource Book page 32**

Language development 1 p.54

With books closed, write the three words *unlock*, *door*, *noise* on the board and ask students to try and combine them in a sentence.

1a Ask students to cover the second part before they read the opening sentence and compare it with their own.

1b Students uncover the next part to check their predictions.

1c Establish that the story takes place in the past. It is not important if students don't know the names of the past verb forms at this stage.

1d When students have completed the table, they should look at the Grammar reference on pages 198–199.

2 Get students to skim the text first and find out what the noise was. They could then do the exercise individually and compare answers at the end, or work in pairs to discuss their answers.

3 As students read the information in the box, check understanding of the vocabulary and concepts, such as *cross the finish line*, *fill up*. It would also be useful to compare and contrast some of them by rephrasing examples with other conjunctions and asking students if there is any change in meaning, e.g.:
By the time the police arrived, the robbers had run away.
When the police arrived, the robbers had run away.
When the police arrived, the robbers ran away.
The police arrived after the robbers had run away.

Get students to compare answers in pairs. As you go through the answers with them, ask concept questions to check understanding, such as:

1 How late was he? (Very!)
2 Did they catch the plane? (No)
3 Did she say it during the call or before? (During)
4 Did she finish the book? (No)
5 Did he see the end of the programme? (Yes)
6 Did they check during the race? (No, before)
7 Was the search before or after we arrived? (Just after)
8 Why was I relieved? (I found the purse.)

4a Students should try to make true statements about themselves, as they are more likely to be remembered. But they could make up sentences if they can't think of any true ones.

5 Point out that there may be more than one answer and try to elicit all possible answers when checking with the class.

6 This could be set as a writing task for homework. Encourage students to use a range of tenses.

Photocopiable activity

Photocopiable activity 7B (p. 142) would work well here. It is a group work activity in which students devise a scenario and write a story from picture clues.

▶ **Student's Resource Book pages 33**

Writing p.56

1 With books closed, brainstorm the different types of stories before the Lead-in.

2 There are no 'right' answers here.

Question 1: The opening words given allow for the students to write any kind of story.

Question 2: Obviously, all these things will make for a good story, and students' opinions may differ as to which are more important.

Question 3: Again, this will be up to the students.

Point out how the exam rubric clearly establishes the writing task. Who is it for? The readers of a student magazine. What is it? A short story that must follow on from the opening words. The purpose? To engage/interest the readers.

3a Students should do this in pairs or small groups. Help with vocabulary where necessary.

3b Make sure students only write notes at this stage, and don't start writing the actual story yet. As they make notes, encourage them to start thinking of vocabulary and verb tenses they might use in each part. Emphasise that in such a composition they need to use a range of narrative tenses.

4a/b Point out that the level of the language is not higher in the 'better' paragraphs, just slightly fuller and more complex, making it more engaging and interesting for the reader.

4c The phrases in the box will add depth to students' narrative writing. Encourage them to use as many as possible.

4d Ask students if the gapped sentence makes sense as it is, before eliciting possible adverbs. Then compare the sentences with and without the adverbs and ask students to comment on the difference. The sentences with the adverb are more vivid.

5 Give students just 20 minutes to write the composition.

6 Allow ten minutes for this checking stage. Go through the four points here in detail.

- Have they stuck to the plan? Does the story have a strong beginning, middle and end?
- Have they used a range of different narrative tenses? And some linking words?
- Have they used a range of adjectives and adverbs to make the story more vivid?
- Is it within the acceptable range? Too long and the story could be marked without an ending.

▶ **Student's Resource Book page 35**

Unit 7 Key

Reading p.52

3b 1 G; 2 A; 3 D; 4 E; 5 F; 6 B; 7 C

5 1 to set out; 2 to set up; 3 to look forward to;
4 to give up; 5 to look after; 6 to point out;
7 to set off; 8 to get through

Language development 1 p.54

1c was unlocking, heard, closed, ran out, tried,
wasn't working, I'd been talking, had run down

1d **A** an action or event at a point in the past:
heard; closed; ran out; tried
B an activity in progress at a point in the past:
was unlocking; wasn't working
C a single action which happened before a point
in the past: *had run down*
D an activity which happened before a point in
the past: *I'd been talking*

2 1 ran (action at a point in the past)
2 was talking (activity in progress)
3 was arguing (activity in progress)
4 had been waiting (viewed as an activity before
a point in the past)/had waited (viewed as an
action before a point in the past)
5 came (action at a point in the past)
6 had been crying (activity before a point in the
past – when I saw her she was no longer
crying)/was crying (activity in progress)
7 told (action at a point in the past)
8 had happened (action before a point in
the past)
9 was talking (activity in progress)
10 came (action at a point in the past)
11 was carrying (activity in progress)
12 was going (activity in progress)
13 was (event at a point in the past)
14 had been waiting (viewed as an activity
before a point in the past/were waiting (viewed
as an activity in progress)
15 explained (action at a point in the past)
16 went (action at a point in the past)
17 was laughing (viewed as an activity in
progress – they were already laughing)/laughed
(viewed as an action at a point in the past –
they started laughing at that point)
18 started (action at a point in the past)
19 felt (action at a point in the past)
20 had reacted (action before a point in
the past)

3 1 C; 2 B; 3 C; 4 D; 5 B; 6 A; 7 A; 8 D

5 1 As soon as I heard the news I phoned my
sister./I phoned my sister as soon as …
2 After I'd been to see a friend, I went home./I
went home after I'd been to see a friend.
3 By the time he arrived, I had waited for
around an hour./I had waited for around an
hour by the time he arrived.
4 When the boss resigned, the business
collapsed./The business collapsed when the boss
resigned.
5 I had been gardening for hours when she
phoned me./When she phoned me, I had been
gardening for hours.
6 While his owner was talking, the dog ran into
the road./The dog ran into the road while his
owner was talking.
7 By the time we got to the airport, the plane
had left./The plane had left by the time we got
to the airport.
8 Before I went to Russia I had never eaten
caviar./I had never eaten caviar before I went to
Russia.

Writing p.56

4a A
4b B
4d Example answers:
1 absolutely, totally
2 immediately, at once
3 well, brilliantly, expertly
4 exactly, precisely
5 excitedly, interestedly
6 definitely, probably

5 Sample answer:

That day, my life changed forever. I had just arrived on the beautiful island of Cyprus for a two-week holiday with three friends. We had been planning to spend the time relaxing on the beach and visiting the ancient monuments.

In the afternoon, while we were exploring a small village, I saw a sign advertising a diving school. I had never been scuba diving before and decided to try it. I signed up for a beginner's course and started the next day. My friends weren't interested and went to the beach. First I learnt some basic skills and what the equipment was for. While my friends were sunbathing I was sitting in a classroom. However, that afternoon I went for my first dive. As soon as I went underwater, I was hooked.

I went diving every day after that and hardly saw my friends for the rest of the holiday. By the time the holiday had finished, I had decided to give up my job and work in a diving school so I could continue my new passion.

(179 words)

LANGUAGE SPOT

1 beautiful, wonderful, warm
2 heavy, considerable
3 set off
4 exhausted, worn out
5 seldom, hardly ever, rarely
6 Eventually

Unit 8 Sport

The 'challenges' theme continues with the topic of sport, including a listening on the challenge of taking up a new sport.

To set the ball rolling ...

With books closed, ask students in pairs to write a definition of *sport*. Compare definitions and ask, e.g., if all sports use a ball/are competitive/are physical. Longman *Dictionary of Contemporary English* defines sport as: *a physical activity in which people compete against each other.*

Listening p.58

1a Check that students understand *take up* (start doing an activity). If not many students have tried the sports, ask which they would most like to try and why.

1b As this is the first time students encounter multiple matching in Paper 4 give them plenty of time to read the rubric and answer the questions.

2a As you go through the task strategy, point out the highlighted points in the first two options.

3 For question 2 it might help to elicit other risk sports with the whole class, such as *climbing, caving, hang gliding*. Question 3 is a matter of opinion, but statistically horse riding and winter sports are among the most dangerous.

4 If students find any of the words in italics difficult, e.g. *keen on, enrol,* remind them of strategies for guessing unknown words.

Speaking p.59

In Paper 5 Part 3, the candidates speak together in a collaborative task based on a visual stimulus (usually several pictures). It is not important to come to an agreement; it is interactive communication that matters.

1 Getting students to look at both sides at this stage will help to develop the discussion later.

2a After checking students' answers, point out that this task usually has two parts: first 'talk about' and secondly 'choose/select/decide', etc.

2c Give students enough time to read the expressions in the table before they listen again.

3 Refer students to the task strategy and remind them of the importance of turn-taking. If the class is not divisible by three, it would be better to have extra examiners with some pairs than a pair without an examiner, so everyone can have some feedback. Remind the 'examiners' that as well as giving the instructions (on CB page 218) and keeping time, they will need to be noting the two candidates' performances.

4   Try to encourage the students to be constructive rather than just polite.

▶ **Student's Resource Book page 37**

Use of English 1 p.60

1   Even if students don't recognise or know Tiger Woods, encourage them to say what they can see from the photo, e.g. *He's a golfer,* and to try and make some guesses about him, e.g. *Maybe he's from the US.* When students speak about the sportspeople they admire, remind them to back up their choices with reasons.

Background

Tiger Woods was born in December 1975. He turned professional at 20 and became world number one in less than a year. In 2001, he became the first ever golfer to hold all four major championship titles at the same time. In his first five years as a professional, he earned $32 million in prize money.

2a   Give students 45–60 seconds to scan the text and answer the questions.

2b   Here, the second sentence of the text is used to teach the grammatical terminology. Note that although articles and determiners are listed as two items, articles are in fact a type of determiner, i.e. a word that is used before a noun, limiting its meaning in some way. Other types of determiner are: demonstratives (*this, these*), quantifiers (*some, much*), possessives (*his, their*) and numerals (*two, second*). There is more work on determiners in Language development 2 on page 61.

2c   Get students to explain why the extra word should not be there.

2d   Students should first read the task strategy. Remind them that they should check sentence by sentence, but mark the text line by line, and that they have to find words which need to be removed because they are wrong, not just words which could be removed.

Language development 2 p.61

The concept of countable and uncountable nouns is not usually a problem for students, but it can be difficult for them to know which nouns are which.

1a   It might be useful to show students how countable and uncountable nouns are marked in a dictionary ([C] and [U]) before they do this exercise, so they can check any that they are unsure of.

2   These are typical FCE level mistakes; remind students to check their own work for similar mistakes.

3   Get students to skim the text first and answer the question *Who was most seriously injured?* As a follow-up, you could put students in groups to discuss which sports are popular in their country, which are more popular with men and with women, and whether any dangerous sports are popular. Give an example first, such as: *In the UK a lot of people play football, but not so many play basketball and very few play baseball.*

▶ **Student's Resource Book page 38–39**

Use of English 2 p.62

With books closed, get students to 'guess the sport' (tennis) by giving clues, e.g. *it's a sport, it's got six letters, it's played with two or four players,* etc.

1   Students don't need to come up with much here. You could limit question 1 to two similarities and two differences, and encourage them to make guesses for question 2.

2a   Ask the students to guess the answers to the questions before reading.

2b   Refer students back to the task strategy on page 18 before they begin the task.

Language development 3 p.63

You could introduce the language point with books closed by putting the pairs of words *actual/current*, *old/ancient* and *great/big* on the board. Ask students if the words in each pair are the same or different and if they are different, what that difference is. They then look at the examples and explanations.

1   Check students understand that the words and definitions are in pairs. They may need to use a dictionary to check some of the words.

2a

Background

Larry 'Buster' Crabbe (1907–1983) started his film career as a stunt double, performing dangerous swimming scenes. He went on to play various action heroes, including Tarzan, Flash Gordon and Buck Rogers. He also starred in a number of Westerns, playing Billy the Kid on many occasions. He is often compared to Johnny Weissmuller, another Olympic swimmer who famously played Tarzan. A popular performer, he made over 100 films.

2b   Students could discuss the questions in small groups

··

Photocopiable activity

Photocopiable activity 8 (pp. 143–144) would work well here. It is a board game with students answering questions using adjectives that are often confused.

··

3 Adjectives ending in *–ing* and *–ed* are often confused. Further help could be given with a drawing on the board of a person reading. Label the person 'interested' and the book 'interesting'. Elicit the difference before looking at the examples from the text.

4a When students have completed the exercise, ask them if they agree with sentences 1, 3, 5, 7.

7 Whichever way students record phrasal verbs, encourage them to record examples or notes on usage as well as the meaning of the phrasal verbs. It would be a good opportunity to revise the grammar of phrasal verbs:

1 Tennis *took off* in the 16th century. [I]
2 He *took off* his tracksuit/*took* his tracksuit *off* before the race. [T]
3 He *took after* + parent
4 *take to* + *someone/thing*: He took to it, not ~~He took it to.~~

▶ **Module 4 Test: How much do you remember? TRB page 178**

▶ **Exam Practice 2: Papers 1 and 3 CB pages 64–66; Papers 2 and 4 TRB pages 179–180**

Unit 8 Key

Listening p.58

1a 1 skiing; football; swimming; cycling; golf; running; tennis

1b 1 five speakers; they will talk about their reasons for taking up a sport.

2a/b 1 C (*get people to give donations*)
2 D (*the expressions of amazement on my kids' faces*)
3 A (*I had to be talked into it by friends*)
4 F (*determined to show Tony that he was wrong*)
5 E (*the only way I can really unwind*)

4 1 from the word go; 2 into; 3 sign up; 4 fancy; 5 give it a go

Speaking p.59

2a First, talk to each other about the advantages and disadvantages of doing each of these sports. Then decide which one would be best for someone who doesn't have much spare time.

2b Running, because it's easier and quicker than the others.

2c **Starting a discussion:**
Let's begin with …
Interrupting/Showing you want a turn:
Yes, and as well as that,
Sorry to interrupt, but …
Involving the other person:
What would you say?
What do you think?
Bringing the discussion to an end:
Anyway, we have to decide …
So let's decide which …

Use of English 1 p.60

2a 1 He has shown that anyone can succeed, even in a seemingly exclusive sport like golf.
2 An introvert.

2b pronoun: us, everyone, one
preposition: from, for, to, of, in
article: a, the
determiner: that, every
auxiliary verb: has, can
linking word: and

2c *the*: can be successful in ~~the~~ life. (life in general)

2d 1 ✓
2 the – see 2b
3 some – *a number of* or *some*, but not both
4 she – *his mother* is the subject so we don't need *she*
5 any – no determiner needed, but if one were used here it would be *some* as it is a positive statement.
6 a

7 which – *like something about someone*
8 much – *a great deal of = much*
9 ✓
10 many – *cash* uncountable (*much* possible but neither necessary)
11 ✓
12 to – *enjoy + -ing* without *to*
13 lots – *movies* countable
14 ✓
15 not – *cannot + not* is repetition of negative
2e • articles – 2, 6
• determiners with countable/uncountable nouns – 3, 5, 8, 10, 13
• subject + verb – 4
• verb + verb –12

Language development 2 p.61

LOOK Countable: years, father, army, number, mother, balls, champion, thing, opponents, people, hotels, bed, shirts, megastar, man, movies, fishing, scuba diving, video games, problems, languages
Uncountable: golf, confidence, cash, scuba diving
Both: sport, life

1a 1 spectator (C) fan (C) excitement (U) (*excitement* different because (U))
2 advice (U) fact (C) information (U) (*fact* different because (C))
3 skiing (U) athletics (U) football (Both) (*football* different because both)
4 money (U) salary (C) coin (C) (*money* different because (U))
5 racket (C) equipment (U) glove (C) (*equipment* different because (U))
6 temperature (C) weather (U) sunshine (U) (*temperature* different because (C))
7 exercise (Both) tracksuit (C) trainer (C) (*exercise* different because both)

1b football:
The physical object is countable: *We gave him a football for his birthday …*
The sport is uncountable: *… because he likes playing football so much.*
exercise:
Particular examples of exercise are countable: *I know three different exercises for leg muscles.*
The general idea is uncountable: *It's important to do some exercise every day.*

2 1 Our trainer gives us good advices.
2 I've heard the results. The news ~~are~~ *is* very bad.
3 People likes Tiger Woods.
4 Some footballers have long hairs.
5 It was ~~a~~ terrible weather so the match was cancelled.

6 Beckham has very expensive furnitures in his house.
7 My shorts ~~was~~ *were* very dirty after the match.
8 I had to do some hard works to beat the champion.
9 The national team stayed in ~~a~~ luxury accommodation.
10 I need informations about tickets.

3 1 Many – *sports* [C]
2 a number of – *hours* [C]
3 much – *time* [U]
4 several – *friends* [C]
5 any – *didn't see* (negative) + *any*
6 lots – followed by verb *to eat*
7 much – followed by adjective *better + luck* [U]
8 a lot of – positive
9 few – *hours* [C]
10 a few – significant number
11 a few – *sounds* [C]

Use of English 2 p.62

2a 1 The palm of the hand, and a wall or a rope.
2 Each point scored was marked by a 15-minute section on a clockface – when it reached 60 minutes the game was over.

2b 1 B – state that something unproven is true
2 A – collocates with *ancient*
3 D – phrase *to lead a* + adjective + *life*
4 A – *a + similar* (*the + same*, verb + *like/alike*)
5 B – *hit* could be with the hand open or closed, but *punch* is always with a closed fist, and *kick* with a foot.
6 C – *took up* = started (an activity)
7 B – *Later* + clause; *Following* + noun; *Soon, Shortly* = a short time after, not four centuries!
8 A – *use a piece of equipment; wear clothes/jewellery/glasses*
9 D – *early days* = collocation
10 C – *made of* = fixed phrase
11 B – *took off* = became popular/a success
12 A – *keen* + noun (= enthusiastic)
13 D – *caused* = made s.th. happen
14 A – *win a point* (*beat an opponent* = win the match)
15 C – *abbreviate* + *to*

Language development 3 p.63

1 1 b; **2** a; **3** c; **4** d; **5** f; **6** e; **7** h; **8** g

2a 1 current; **2** pleasant; **3** great; **4** excited; **5** sensitive; **6** old; **7** usual; **8** typical

3 -ed adjectives describe a reaction to something. -ing adjectives describe the person/thing that causes the reaction.

4a 1 boring; 2 disappointed; 3 tiring; 4 annoyed;
5 terrifying; 6 depressed; 7 interested;
8 amusing

5 The French upper classes became interested,
and they *took up* the sport.
The game soon spread to England and *took off*
in a big way.

6 1 took up; 2 took off; 3 took over; 4 took
after; 5 took to

Teacher's Resource Book
Module 4 Test: How much do
you remember? p.178

1 1 C; 2 B; 3 A; 4 B; 5 D

2 1 by; 2 in; 3 had; 4 much; 5 to

3 1 The course was cancelled because *of a/the lack
of* people.
2 Nick *had been working since/had been at work
since* 6.00 a.m. that day.
3 Ann *was watching TV at* 9.00 p.m.
4 He *had left by the time* I arrived at his house.
5 She got married *as soon as she (had)* left
university.

4 1 he; 2 ✓; 3 two; 4 to; 5 us

5 1 untreatable; 2 sensible; 3 boring;
4 informative; 5 invaluable

Coursebook
Exam practice 2 p. 64

Paper 1 Reading
Part 1 1 E; 2 C; 3 G; 4 D; 5 A; 6 F

Paper 3 Use of English
Part 1 1 A; 2 D; 3 C; 4 B; 5 B; 6 A; 7 D;
8 A; 9 B; 10 D; 11 A; 12 B; 13 C; 14 B; 15 C

Part 2 1 where; 2 little; 3 after; 4 to; 5 on/about;
6 than; 7 took; 8 however; 9 into; 10 were;
11 of; 12 by; 13 in; 14 a; 15 gone

Part 4 1 did; 2 ✓; 3 by; 4 for; 5 many; 6 any;
7 ✓; 8 been; 9 to; 10 of; 11 ✓; 12 so;
13 more; 14 plenty; 15 whole

Part 5 1 fairly; 2 easily; 3 terrified; 4 unfortunate;
5 remarkably; 6 actively; 7 exciting;
8 nervously; 9 arrival; 10 impressive

Teacher's Resource Book
Exam practice 2 pp.179–180

Paper 2 Writing
1
Style:
Formal letter.
Content:
1 Say that you want a course.
2 Ask about the level of the classes and whether you
need your own instrument.
3 Find out about the timing and length of lessons,
and how to pay.
4 Ask about the price of practice rooms.

Paper 4 Listening
Part 3 1 D; 2 E; 3 A; 4 F; 5 B

Module 5 Discovery

Units 9 and 10 are linked by the theme of 'discovery' and include texts on human science, talking about the future, museums, inventions, discoveries, computers, robots and explorers.

Lead-in p.67

Start off by eliciting what scientific advances the photos show (computing, vaccinations, genetics), before students discuss the questions in pairs or small groups.

Unit 9 Human science

Photocopiable activity

Photocopiable activity 9A (p. 145) is designed to be an introduction to the unit and will help to pre-teach some of the vocabulary. It is a quiz about the human body.

Reading p.68

1a It would be a good idea to check the pronunciation of the fields of science before students do the exercise.

1b The title of the article makes it quite clear what students are going to read. The sub-headings A–D are harder and might throw up a number of possibilities, which would generate interest in the text.

2 Set a suitable time limit, e.g. two minutes, so that the skimming doesn't become detailed reading.

3a The reading task in Unit 1 gave students an introduction to multiple matching tasks. This activity is much more like the exam in terms of text length, options and number of questions. Refer students to the task strategy. Point out that only when they have skimmed the article will they be able to predict which part to look in for each question. It would be useful to set the students a suitable time limit (e.g. 15 minutes) to do the task, so that they become aware of the time available in the exam, although you could give them a few minutes more at this stage if necessary.

4 Additional questions could include:

Have you ever studied any of these subjects? Would you like to?

▶ **Student's Resource Book page 42**

Language development 1 p.70

1a Look at the first sentence and elicit that *I don't feel well* is in the present and *I'm going to be sick* is the consequence in the future. See if students can think of any other possible situations, e.g. someone on a roller coaster or someone who has seen/eaten something disgusting.

1b Encourage students to look at the sentences in their contexts and not just identify future forms that they may already be familiar with.

1c When students have completed the table, give examples of how a decision might become an arrangement. E.g., you read a restaurant review and think it sounds good, so you decide: 'I think I'll take X there'. Later, when someone asks what your plans are for the weekend: 'I'm going to take X to …'. Then after you ring and book the table you could say 'I'm taking X to …'

Time clauses

Refer students to sentence 4 in Exercise 1a: *If you tell her, she'll tell everyone.* Remind students that although the first part uses the present tense, the sentence refers to the future. The time clauses here work in the same way.

2 Get students to compare and explain their answers.

3b When students have matched the forms to their uses it might be useful to compare the structures with those practised in earlier units:

The present continuous refers to an action in progress now. The past continuous refers to an action in progress at a point in the past. Hence the future continuous refers to an action in progress at a point in the future.

The present perfect refers to an action before now. The past perfect refers to an action before a point in the past. Hence the future perfect refers to an action before a point in the future.

4 Students should complete the predictions with positive verb forms. They have a chance to agree or disagree in 5b.

5a When students have completed the exercise, show how the 'certainty' language is often stressed, e.g. *We **may** have … but I **doubt** it.*

5b As students give their opinions on the predictions for 2100, encourage some discussion leading in to the questions in 5c.

6 Give students time to think about the statements and make a few notes before they discuss them in groups.

7 The text contains mistakes typically produced by FCE students. Point out that all the errors are with verb tenses. Checking through a piece of writing systematically, in this case just checking the tenses, is an important strategy in the exam.

··
Photocopiable activity

Photocopiable activity 9B (p. 146) would work well here. It is designed to get students using all the tenses covered here while talking about their futures.
··

Writing p.72

1 Check that students know the difference between a museum and a gallery. A museum contains objects that are scientifically or culturally important, possibly including art objects. A gallery specifically contains works of art. Suggested answers for question 2 would be the points in handwriting in the exam task below on page 72.

2 This is the second time that students practise a transactional letter, Paper 2 Part 1 (see Unit 5). Elicit some of the key points:

• The transactional letter might be formal or informal.

• The overall aim is to achieve a positive effect on the reader. This is done through organisation, layout, and cohesion as well as accuracy of language.

• Candidates must include the key points from the input if they are to achieve good marks.

3a Remind students that a logical strategy is to think first about what to include, then in what order, and finally how to divide it into paragraphs.

4a The expressions can be used in any formal letter of this type. Look at the grammar of each expression by eliciting the next word in each case, e.g. *grateful if*, *possible to*, *arriving at/on*.

┌──┐
LANGUAGE SPOT: polite questions

Polite or indirect questions are a feature of more formal writing. Compare the efficiency and directness of the form *Where's the café?* with the more polite forms.
└──┘

▶ **Student's Resource Book page 45**

Unit 9 Key

Reading p.68
1a 1 astronomy; 2 archaeology; 3 psychology;
4 linguistics; 5 genetics; 6 forensic science

3a 1 D (*amusing anecdotes …*)
2 A (*even if you don't have a scientific background*)
3 B (*an ideal birthday present*)
4 D (*examples of language taken from various sources*) (ll.82–83)
5 A (*… people believed that family traits were carried in the blood. Today we know that they were wrong*) (ll.16–18)
6 D (*his personal belief*) (l.78)
7 C (*… gets better and better with age …*) (ll.61–62)
8 B (*… scientific studies … thirty minutes after birth …*) (ll.25–29)
9 C (*… main objective is to encourage the greater public understanding of scientific ideas.*) (ll.48–51)
10 A (*… up-to-date with the latest influential theories.*) (ll.2–4)
11 C (*… television audiences in mind (a tie-in series has just begun on BBC1) …*) (ll.64–65)
12 B (*… packed with eye-catching photos … *) (l.43)

3b 1 In A his earlier books were on other subjects and therefore this book doesn't follow on.

Language development 1 p.70
1a **Suggested answers:**
2 Two colleagues or friends are trying to arrange to meet tomorrow, but the speaker can't because he/she has a driving test.
3 One friend to another. The speaker has bought something, such as a radio, and has found that it doesn't work.
4 One friend to another. They have a secret, and the speaker doesn't trust the third person not to reveal the secret if she is told about it.
5 Friends, or husband and wife. They are going to the cinema or theatre, and the speaker is waiting for the other person who is still getting ready.
6 Two strangers at a supermarket or station. One is offering to carry the other's heavy bag.

1b 1 'm going to be; 2 'm taking; 3 'm going to take it back; 4 'll tell; 5 starts; 6 'll carry

1c **A** Planned, a definite arrangement (e.g. in a diary): *I'm taking my driving test.*
B Planned, fixed event (e.g. a public timetable): *It starts at eight.*
C Planned, decided earlier (intention): *I'm going to take it back.*
Prediction: we notice something in the present that will make something happen: *I'm going to be sick.*
D Unplanned, decided now (e.g. an offer, a promise): *I'll carry it.*
Prediction: we expect something to happen (it is our opinion or we have experience of it): *She'll tell everyone.*
Time clauses
3 Are you going to have a drink before the show ~~will~~ starts?

2 1 will be; 2 'm going to visit; 3 get; 4 starts; 5 'll cook; 6 'm having lunch; 7 's going to have; 8 go

3a Future continuous: *will be having*
Future perfect: *will have established*

3b Complete by a point in the future: *will have established*
Still in progress at a point in the future: *will be having*

4 1 will have found
2 will be travelling
3 will have discovered
4 will be living
5 will have taken over; will be providing
6 will be making; will be going

5a Very certain: 1
Fairly certain: 3, 5
Not very certain: 2, 4

7 After I ~~will~~ finish the last year of university I am definitely going to have a long holiday. I expect I ~~am going~~ *will go* with my friend, Luis, to a place where we will ~~be doing~~ *do* lots of sport and relax~~ing~~ in the sun to recover from all our hard work.
But before that there is a lot of work. My exams ~~will~~ start on the 15 June and they ~~are lasting~~ *last* two weeks. The results will not ~~have been~~ *be* here before the end of August, so I ~~am having~~ *will have* a long time to wait. For the next month I will *be* study*ing* for two hours every evening and I ~~am not~~ *won't be* going out during the week.

Writing p.72
2 1 The museum's groups organiser.
2 You are interested in organising a group visit to the museum.
3 Who you are, your intention and the four questions.
4 Formal (no direct questions, contractions, etc.).

3a 1 introducing yourself
2 saying why you're writing
3 asking about booking
4 asking about numbers
5 asking about eating
6 asking about photos
7 asking about video cameras
8 conclusion

3b **Paragraph 1**: introducing myself; saying why you are writing
Paragraph 2: asking about booking; asking about numbers
Paragraph 3: asking about eating
Paragraph 4: asking about photos; asking about video cameras
Paragraph 5: conclusion

4b Opening: I am the secretary of my college Science Club. I saw your advertisement for the exhibition 'The Next 100 Years' and I was wondering if I could ask you some questions about it.
Closing: I look forward to hearing from you.

4c Yours faithfully

5   **Sample answer:**

Dear Sir or Madam

I am the secretary of my college Science Club. I saw your advertisement for the exhibition 'The Next 100 Years' and I am interested in organising a group visit. I was wondering if I could ask you some questions about it.

I would be grateful if you could let me know whether we need to book, and if so, how far in advance do we need to say that we will be coming? Our group is quite large, so I would also like to know if there is a maximum size for a group.

Since we will probably be coming for the whole day, I would like to know if there is anywhere to buy snacks, or if there is a picnic area where we can eat our own food.

Some members would like to bring cameras to record the trip for their project work. Could you let me know if they can use flash photography or video cameras?

I look forward to hearing from you and visiting your museum.

Yours faithfully

Toni Hidalgo

Toni Hidalgo (Ms)

(179 words)

LANGUAGE SPOT: polite questions

1   Do you think you could tell me where we can/could leave our bags?
2   Could you tell me whether there is a toilet on this floor?
3   I would be very grateful if you could tell me how much we will have to pay.
4   I wonder if you could tell me when the museum closes?
5   Could you please tell me where the cloakroom is?
6   I would be grateful if you could tell me what time the museum closes.
7   Could you tell me whether we can pay by credit card in the museum shop?
8   I wonder if you could tell me who is in charge?

Unit 10 Invention

To set the ball rolling ...

With books closed, ask students the difference between a discovery – something that existed but was not known before, such as penicillin – and an invention – something new that did not exist before, such as the telephone. See if they can think of any other examples of either.

Listening p.74

1a Ask students what the cartoon shows, and point out/elicit the connection to the title of the unit (see Key, p. 40).

1b Point out the task strategy. Emphasise that at this stage students should only read the questions, not the answers. Students probably won't have heard of Trevor Baylis, but from reading the questions in the listening task they learn that he is an inventor, he possibly had another job before becoming an inventor, he invented a wind-up radio, and he gains satisfaction from his work. Check that students understand *wind-up radio* – one with a handle that you turn to make it work, like an old clock or watch – from the verb *to wind s.th. up*.

Background

Trevor Baylis is an Englishman who became famous after inventing the wind-up radio in 1991. He is an interesting character who often appears as a guest on TV shows. He has set up a foundation to encourage individual inventors, raise their profile and help them receive proper rewards for their inventions.

2a Go through the task strategy before students listen.

2b Ask students to remember any phrases that justify their answers. Remind them that in part 4, the questions will often ask about feelings and opinions as well as facts.

3   You could put students in groups and get each to think of one invention, with reasons, and present their ideas to the class.

Speaking p.75

Here, students see how Part 3 leads into Part 4, when the examiner joins in and it becomes a three-way discussion.

1a You may need to provide the words *sticky notes* and *highlighter*. Check students understand these by asking what they are used for.

1b This is to help prepare students for the sample answers that they are going to listen to. It doesn't matter if they can't think of advantages **and** disadvantages for every invention.

2a Once you have checked students' answers, tell students that it is important in Paper 5 that they know what to do in each part. If they have any doubts, they should check with the examiner. They will not be penalised for this at all. The candidate in the recording summarises the examiner's instructions, which is a good way to check you have understood.

3a These are typical Part 4 questions, extending the topic from Part 3. Students could consider why some are easier to answer than others, e.g. is the language difficult, or would they find it hard to come up with ideas and opinions?

4 If the class is not equally divisible by three, have one or two groups of four, so that each group has at least an examiner and two candidates.

5 Students should discuss their own and the others' performance.

▶ **Student's Resource Book page 47**

Use of English 1 p.76

1 Start by asking students if they have ever felt like the person in the picture when using a computer, then go on to discuss the question about modern technology.

2b Students read the task strategy and refer back to the notes in Unit 8 if they need to.

2c This draws students' attention to some of the language tested in Paper 3 Part 4.

3 You could give a brief example of your own to get students started, then get them to discuss the question in groups.

Language development 2 p.77

LOOK As you go through the box with students, you could use simple drawings on the board to illustrate differences, e.g. *He hurt himself* – a man sitting on a chair with an arrow pointing down to indicate *fell off. He hurt his sister* – a man and a woman with an arrow pointing from the man towards the woman to indicate *bumped into. They talked to each other* – two people facing each other, with speech bubbles. *They talked to themselves* – two people with speech bubbles, but further apart, not facing each other, and with a line between to indicate that they are in separate rooms and talking to themselves!

1a Students could discuss their answers in pairs, referring to the box, before class feedback.

1b Point out that students will need to use object pronouns here, as well as language from the box.

2 After question 1, as a contrast you could ask *What things do you prefer to do by yourself?*

3a Look at the box with students before they start the exercise, pointing out that the word order in *B Question word + clause* is as in a statement, not as in a question. The first two examples are from the Use of English text on the opposite page.

3b If students can't think of anything true to write, they should try to invent interesting sentences.

▶ **Student's Resource Book page 48**

Use of English 2 p.78

1 You could do this exercise with books closed. Write the names of the people on the board, and in groups students try to name each one's discovery. Check that students know *penicillin* – today, a medicine known as an antibiotic because it kills bacteria and so helps cure infections.

Background

Sir Isaac Newton discovered gravity in 1687, stating that gravity is the force of attraction between two objects, and that greater objects, such as the earth, pull smaller objects, such as people, towards them. He is said to have discovered this watching an apple fall from a tree to the ground.

Fleming, Hale and Bopp – see texts on p.78

In the first century BC, Archimedes discovered that an object placed in water 'loses' an amount of weight equal to the weight of the water that it has displaced. He is said to have discovered this when he got into a full bath and it overflowed.

2a Remind students not to focus on the gaps. They should only need a minute or so to do this exercise.

3 When students have finished, ask them which of the four discoveries in Exercise 1 they think are the most and least important.

Language development 3 p.79

1a Nouns can be formed from verbs or adjectives. This exercise focuses on nouns formed from verbs.

2a Before students do the exercise, ask if they know of any famous explorers.

3a This exercise focuses on nouns formed from adjectives.

4 Encourage students to guess the formation of nouns not given in the tables by comparing them to similar words, e.g. *describe/description* is similar to *decide/decision*.

5a Point out that the phrasal verb is in the fourth line of the second Use of English text.

5b Students could use their dictionaries to check.

6 Remind students to put the verbs in the correct form. You could provide personalised practice by giving students sentence stems to complete, e.g.:

1 The biggest problem I've come up against is/was … .

2 I once tried … but it didn't come off.

3 Once when I was looking for … I came across … .

4 Recently I came up with … .

. . . .
Photocopiable activity
Photocopiable activity 10 (p. 147) would work well here. It is a game of dominoes in which students form nouns by joining suffixes to verbs.
. . . .

▶ **Module 5 Review CB page 80**

▶ **Module 5 Test: How much do you remember? TRB page 181**

Unit 10 Key

Listening p.74

1a The cartoon shows how people have been inventing things for a long time, and inventions are often the result of trying to solve a problem or a need.

2a 1 B (*as a child … he was fascinated by machines … taking things apart, seeing how they worked …*)
2 B (*the company pays you to go to college on the fifth (day)*)
3 C (*… most of Trevor's inventions start as a problem (that he sees)*)
4 C (*… people had machines long before there was electricity*) Not B because he didn't examine a piece of outdated technology, he only dreamt about it.
5 A (*… think that's how they're going to make their fortune.*)
6 B (*… you need to have faith in it if you're going to convince anyone.*)
7 C (*… things to help disabled people … these inventions … they're the ones that Trevor says he's proudest of.*)

2b Facts: 1–4
Feelings and opinions: 5–7

Speaking p.75

1a computer, pen, highlighter, CD player, sticky notes, TV and video, phone

2a 1 First, talk to each other about the advantages and disadvantages of each invention. Then decide which two are the most important.
2 So we have to discuss <u>all</u> the photos and then choose the two most important?

2b Yes, but they tend to interrupt each other quite frequently.

2c 1 So, we think the computer and the phone are the most important inventions.
2 Thank you.

3b 1, 3, 4

Use of English 1 p.76

2a 1 T
2 F – the college had copies of everything
3 F – he didn't use a computer for weeks

2b 1 own – *a video recorder* (any) or *his own video recorder*
2 ✓
3 himself – *to be like somebody*
4 the – usually a possessive with parts of the body; no article with possessives
5 by – *get into* – phrasal verb meaning *to enter*
6 been – active not passive
7 ✓

8 it – *delete* is the object, so not possible to have the object pronoun *it*.

9 one – *other* is the determiner, can't be followed by a number.

10 ✓

11 for – *what to do* (*what* + *to* + infinitive)

12 ✓

13 him –*to use* + something

14 ✓

15 to – *make someone do something* (without to)

HELP Line 3 – Yes: *he, himself*
Line 4 – we don't use an article with a possessive
Line 8 – *Enter, Delete*

2c reflexives – question 3
question word structures – question 11

2d reflexive – *He was furious with himself* (line 10)
question word structure – *They never found out why it had happened* (lines 12–13)

Language development 2 p.77

LOOK He was working *on his own* …
Everything disappeared from *his own* screen …
He was furious with **himself** …

1a **1** I used to work ~~myself~~ abroad. – in this case *work* is intransitive
2 ✓ – reflexive
3 Can you help ~~myself~~ me? – subject and object are different people, so reflexive not possible
4 Robots can't talk to ~~each~~ one another. – *each other* or *one another*
5 ✓
6 Have you enjoyed ~~you~~ **yourself**? – subject and object are the same person, so the reflexive is needed
7 ✓ subject and object are the same person, so the reflexive is needed
8 Relax ~~yourself~~ ! – *relax* not a reflexive verb
9 I built the model **on** my own.
10 Clare and Rob met ~~themselves~~ **each other** last year – you can't meet yourself, you have to meet somebody else

1b **1** its own – a bird
2 themselves – a fly and an eagle
3 myself – same subject and object
4 myself – for me
5 them – robots
6 us – relates to *we* in the previous sentence, and *our* in this sentence
7 themselves –without the help of others
8 me – relates to the object pronoun
9 themselves – without the help of others

3a **1** know how to use a
2 you've done what I
3 where to find the/where we can find the
4 know who to/know who I should

Use of English 2 p.78

1 **1** d; **2** a; **3** b; **4** c

2a penicillin, mould, bacteria, important

2b **1** unexpected – negative adjective
2 possibility – noun
3 puzzling – adjective
4 accidentally – adverb
5 excited – adjective
6 discovery – noun
7 effective – adjective
8 infection(s) – singular or plural noun possible here
9 scientists – plural noun
10 successfully – adverb

HELP Question 1 – no
Question 2 – *-ity*
Question 4 – adverb

2c **1** four – 2, 6, 8, 9
2 4, 10
3 1

3 It was named after two people because they both discovered it, simultaneously but independently.
1 astronomers – plural noun
2 pleasure – noun
3 discoveries – plural noun
4 combination – noun
5 professional – adjective
6 unusually – adverb
7 supervisor – noun
8 construction – adjective
9 observer – noun
10 equipment – noun

HELP Question 3 – plural
Question 6 – negative
Question 7 – *-or*
Question 9 – *-er*

Language development 3 p.79

1b *-ment*: equipment
-ure: pleasure
(t/s)ion: infection; combination
-y: discovery
-er: astronomer; observer
-or: supervisor

2a **1** b; **2** a; **3** c; **4** a
2b **1** assistance; organisation
2 existence; achievement
3 sailors; equipment
4 explorer; failure

3a *-ness*: kindness; darkness; sadness; illness
-th: length; strength
-ity: ability; generosity; equality; reality; popularity

3b possibility

4 1 popularity
   2 descriptions
   3 ability, importance
   4 observations, loneliness

5a c – happen

5b 1 b; 2 d; 3 f; 4 a; 5 g; 6 h; 7 e; 8 c

6 1 come up against; 2 come up; 3 came round;
   4 come out; 5 came across; 6 come in for;
   7 come off; 8 come up with

Coursebook
Module 5 Review p. 80

1 1 'm going to study; 'll go
   2 don't think I'll find; get; 'll see
   3 'll come; won't be; 'll be; can
   4 will be / is going to be; 'm not working; shall
   I book

2a 1 will go / will be going
   2 will be living (will be working)
   3 will be studying
   4 will have moved
   5 will have
   6 will have bought (will have)
   7 will be working
   8 will have retired

3 1 his own; 2 each other/one another; 3 him;
   4 on his own; 5 on his own / by himself;
   6 himself; 7 on his own; 8 itself

4 1 strength; 2 ability; 3 assistance; 4 decisions;
   5 generosity; 6 loneliness; 7 failure;
   8 achievement

5 1 C; 2 D; 3 A; 4 C; 5 B

Teacher's Resource Book
Module 5 Test: How much do
you remember? p.181

1 1 B; 2 D; 3 C; 4 A; 5 B

2 1 himself; 2 own; 3 what; 4 if; 5 where

3 1 Jackie didn't want to do all *the cooking on
   her* own.
   2 We did all the *work ourselves to keep* costs
   down.
   3 Could you *let me know whether/if* you will
   have a room available next month?
   4 I *will have moved house by* the end of the year.
   5 It won't be *long before someone discovers* a
   cure for cancer.

4 1 ✓; 2 himself; 3 will; 4 ✓; 5 it

5 1 pride; 2 unscientific; 3 specialist; 4 equality;
   5 longest

Module 6 The arts

Units 11 and 12 are linked by the theme of 'The arts', in a broad sense, and include topics such as ballet dancing, children in movies, favourite books/films, art and pop music.

Lead-in p.81

With books closed, get students to compare *art* (painting, drawing, sculpture, etc.) and *the arts* (more general). Brainstorm different types of arts, e.g. music (classical, pop, folk, opera), theatre, musicals, dance (ballet, contemporary), cinema, art (modern, different periods/media), literature. Build up a spidergram on the board, then ask students what 'arts' are shown in the pictures on page 81. Get them to discuss the questions. In the first question, *important to you* could be interpreted either as something that you personally spend time on, or that you consider to be important in general.

Unit 11 A dream come true

> **Photocopiable activity**
>
> Photocopiable activity 11A (p. 148) could be used either as a lead-in to the unit or as follow-up to the reading. It is a questionnaire designed to find out how ambitious you are.

Reading p.82

1a Ask if anyone has ever studied ballet or another type of dance. If anyone has, they could briefly describe what it is like to be a dancer. Then students discuss the question in pairs or small groups.

2 Students should be quite familiar with skimming by now, but you may want to set a time limit of a minute if you feel they still need it.

3a This text and task are in the format of Paper 1 Part 2 – seven multiple-choice questions, each with four answers. Encourage students to follow the task strategy.

4 Encourage students to give examples of under what circumstances they would do, or have done, each of the things listed.

5 If there is time after the vocabulary exercise, you could ask students to think of any dreams they have had that came true (not necessarily on the same scale as Alina) and to tell the class about them. Give them an example of your own first.

▶ **Student's Resource Book page 52**

Language development 1 p.84

1a With books closed, ask students how many films they can think of with children in the leading roles. Then see if any of theirs are on page 84, before matching the photos to the titles.

1b There is no need to spend too long on this; students should just talk about the films they know and pool their knowledge. Supply any answers that the students are unable to give.

2a When students have read the text and answered the questions, you could ask them to deduce the meaning of some of the vocabulary, e.g. *destined, auditions, role*.

2b It would be useful to find the first example of each type of clause with the whole class and to highlight its structure before students look for the rest.

3 Review what each relative pronoun refers to, such as *who* for people, *whose* for possession, etc., before students do the exercise.

4, 5 This exercise requires students to think a little more about both the type of clause to create and how to do it. Point out that it is exactly the same when they are planning compositions for Paper 2.

6 It can be difficult for students to grasp that a participle clause can be used to refer to different times. Point out that the time reference is usually clear from the second part of the clause, e.g.: *The woman singing that song **is** … . The car going round the corner **was** … .*

7 This exercise will require some planning, which could be done for homework.

> **Photocopiable activity**
>
> Photocopiable activity 11B (p. 149) would work well here. It is a game in which students use relative clauses to define vocabulary associated with the arts.

▶ **Student's Resource Book page 53**

Writing p.86

1 Some discussion here on types of film, e.g. science fiction, comedy, action, would generate some useful vocabulary.

3a In the list, *title* refers to the book/film title, not the title of the student's article.

3b Point out that a good article should attract the reader's attention with a catchy title.

4 Point out how a strong opening engages the reader and a strong ending has a positive effect on the reader.

4c One way to look at the functions table would be to go through it first as a whole class using a film that most students are familiar with, e.g. *Titanic*, as an example.

5 Review the outline and content of the article before students choose a book/film of their own to write about.

6 Remind students to check their writing thoroughly.

LANGUAGE SPOT: avoiding repetition

You could give students an example of writing with a lot of repetition in it to highlight why it is important to avoid it, e.g. *My favourite film is* Titanic. Titanic *is about a ship called* Titanic. Titanic *sinks* … .

▶ **Student's Resource Book page 55, exercises 1–3**

Unit 11 key

Reading p.82

1a Possible answers:
Strength to perform a lot of the steps in ballet; discipline, to keep training, rehearsing and improving; stamina to keep going through many performances; a 'thick skin' to cope with negative criticism, from coaches and from reviewers.

1b The title suggests she achieved her ambition to become a principal dancer with the Royal Ballet.

2 1 A family friend suggested ballet lessons to quieten her down.
2 Kiev and London
3 Her work is very tiring and she hasn't much time for friends.

3a 1 B (*the news took time to sink in. … 'I couldn't speak.'*)
2 D (*'I was a very lively little girl … A family friend thought ballet would quieten me down.'*)
3 A (*'I had to show the others how the steps should be done and I always got top marks.'*)
4 C (*… she became determined to stay there and become a dancer.*)
5 A (*'I felt I needed to be stretched.'*)
6 A (*A principal dancer became ill and Alina was asked to replace her.*)
7 B (*'I'm fine as I am.'*)

5 1 (to be) in tears (1.8–9)
2 to sink in (1.16)
3 to get under (my mother's) feet (1.24)
4 to pay off (1.52)
5 a big fish in a small pond (11.67–68)
6 the rest is history (11.81–82)

Language development 1 p.84

1a 1 D *E.T. the Extra-Terrestrial* (Drew Barrymore and Henry Thomas)
2 F *Harry Potter and the Philosopher's Stone* (Daniel Radcliffe and Rupert Grint)
3 A *The Wizard of Oz* (Judy Garland)
4 E *Oliver!* (Mark Lester and Jack Wild)
5 B *Billy Elliot* (Jamie Bell)
6 C *Home Alone* (Macauley Culkin)

1b 1 *Oliver!* (From Oliver Twist by Dickens), *Harry Potter and the Philosopher's Stone* by J. K. Rowling, *The Wizard of Oz* by L. Frank Baum.
3 A *Wizard of Oz*: a girl is taken by a tornado to a strange land called Oz – she has to find the wizard to help her get back home again.
B *Billy Elliot*: in a poor mining town, a boy's father wants him to be a boxer, but he wants to become a ballet dancer – succeeds and becomes famous.

C *Home Alone*: an eight-year-old boy whose parents forget to take him on holiday defends his home against bungling burglars.
D *E.T.*: an alien left behind on Earth by his flying saucer is looked after by a group of children.
E *Oliver!*: A boy escapes from an orphanage in Victorian London and falls in with a group of pickpockets led by an elderly man.
F *Harry Potter*: adventures of a boy who goes to a special school to learn to be a wizard.

2a 1 He loves all the Harry Potter books.
2 He made a video and wrote a rap song.
2b **A** 1 The boy who plays Harry Potter's best friend Ron Weasley
2 a dream that had come true
3 a rap song in which he explained …
B 1 For Rupert Grint, who looks like Ron, being chosen was …
2 Rupert, whose family all have red hair like the Weasleys, felt he was destined …
3 … a video, which he says was terrible.
C 1 the letter he sent, …

3 1 *Billy Elliot* is set in an English mining town **where** there is high unemployment and poverty. It tells the true story of a boy **that/who** wants to become a ballet dancer, but **whose** father wants him to become a boxer.
2 *Oliver!*, **which** is a musical based on Charles Dickens' novel *Oliver Twist*, is set in London, **where** there was a lot of poverty in the nineteenth century.
3 The alien *E.T.*, **whose** most famous line was 'Phone home', was later used in an advertising campaign for a telephone company. Drew Barrymore, **who** co-starred as Gertie in *E.T. the Extra-Terrestrial*, is now an established Hollywood actress.
4 Judy Garland, **whose** daughter Lisa Minnelli is also an actress, starred as Dorothy in *The Wizard of Oz*. It is basically the story of a girl **that/who** has a vivid dream.
5 *Home Alone*, in **which** parents leave their young child at home on his own, touches on a theme **that/which** is not uncommon in real life today.
6 In the book *Harry Potter and the Philosopher's Stone*, Harry does not want to return to his cruel uncle and aunt, **which** motivates him to succeed in the tasks (**that/which**) the school sets him. But this is not so obvious in the film version, for **which** it has been criticised.

4 1 I saw a poster which/that was advertising a new dance show.
2 I phoned the box office, which was in London.

3 There was an answering machine which/that was telling me to call another number.
4 I spoke to a man on the other number who/that told me there were only expensive seats left.
5 I booked two tickets which/that cost €60 each.
6 I paid by credit card, which is a very convenient way to pay.
7 On the day, we went to the theatre, which overlooks Leicester Square in London.
8 We couldn't get into the theatre, which had been closed because of technical problems.
9 I went home with my friend, who was very disappointed.
10 Next day I phoned the theatre, who were very helpful and offered replacement tickets.

5 1 The 1976 film *Bugsy Malone*, **in which all the actors are children**, is a musical satire of 1930s gangster movies.
2 Director and writer Alan Parker had the idea for *Bugsy Malone*, **which was only the second film he wrote**, when he was watching *The Godfather*.
3 14-year-old Scott Baio, **who played/(playing) the leading role of Bugsy Malone**, was acting in his first film.
4 Co-star Jodie Foster, **who was 13 when the film was made**, had appeared in seven films already.
5 The cast of more than 40 children, **whose acting and dancing made the film a success**, didn't actually sing in the film themselves.

6 1 I saw a poster **advertising** a new dance show.
3 There was an answering machine **telling** me to call another number.
5 I booked two tickets **costing** €60 each.
7 On the day, we went to the theatre, **overlooking** Leicester Square in London.

Writing p.86
2 1 to inform, to entertain
2 Two: which film/book, why you like it
3 facts in the first part, opinion in the second part
4 lively

3a **Paragraph 1**: attention-grabbing introduction; title
Paragraph 2: brief description of the story
Paragraph 3: what you like
Paragraph 4: what you don't like
Paragraph 5: recommendation; conclusion

3b **B** is the most eye-catching – it makes you want to know more about the novel.
A is a little dull, and doesn't really attract you to the article.
C isn't very enthusiastic.

4a B

4b A

5 Sample answer:

The film of the decade

I have to tell you about my favourite film, *Fellowship of the Ring*. It's the best film I've seen for a long time.

The film is based on the first of three books called *The Lord of the Rings*. It's set in an imaginary place and it's about a special ring. A character called Frodo has to take the ring to a place far away and destroy it, to stop a bad person called Sauron getting the ring and having its power.

The actors are perfect for their roles and the special effects for the battles and fights are very exciting. I was on the edge of my seat.

I must admit that the story is a bit slow in places, but it's never really boring. Some people find it a little confusing, too, if they haven't read the book.

A good story, great actors and special effects. It's got everything. If you like fantasy and adventure, you'll love this film.

(160 words including title)

LANGUAGE SPOT: avoiding repetition

a their – good musicals
   they – the audience
   this – *Fame*
   their – the actors
   the show – *Fame*
   they – the actors
   ones – actors
   You – the reader
   their – the young actors'
   they – the young actors
   these – the acting and singing
   It – the plot
   this – the thin plot
   we – the audience
   them – the characters

b 1 They; 2 It; there; 3 it/to; 4 then; 5 ones

Unit 12 Sound and vision

Unit 12 continues the arts theme with speaking and listening activities about different aspects of art, and Use of English texts about the Tate Modern, the Dutch artist Vermeer, the musician Stevie Wonder and a music festival.

To set the ball rolling …

Ask general questions about art: *Do you ever look at art or sculptures? Do you prefer modern or traditional art? Why?* If students are not very interested in art, keep this discussion brief.

Speaking p.88

1 Reassure students that in the exam they won't be required to have any expert knowledge, but in Paper 5 they could be asked a question like this about their personal preferences.

2a Elicit the format of Paper 5 Part 2, i.e. individual long turn followed by a short response from the other candidate.

2c Tell students that the expressions may not be in the same order as they are in on the page. Play Alice's response up to *I really don't know what it is.*

2d Play the rest of Alice's response.

3 It is important that students remember this short phase of Paper 5, are prepared for the examiner's question, and listen to it carefully.

4a Both students practise an individual long turn and give a short response. Point out the task strategy.

4b/c Allow enough time for students to give each other constructive feedback.

Listening p.89

1 This is the first time students look at Paper 4 Part 1 in detail. The format is the same here as in the exam, except that there are six questions here, not eight as in the exam.

2a Students first read the task strategy.

If there is time, students could have a discussion based on the arts. They should each choose one of the following topics and prepare to speak about it by making notes. Then put them into groups for the discussion.

- Your favourite film of all time.

- The type of music you most enjoy listening to.

- A play you have enjoyed (at the theatre, on the radio, on TV).

- A novel you have read more than once.

• The painting you would most like to have hanging on your bedroom wall.

▶ **Student's Resource Book page 57**

Use of English 1 p.90

1 As with the Lead-in on page 88, reassure students that they don't need to be art experts, but they should be prepared to give opinions. The two pictures are Vermeer's *Guitar player* and Picasso's *Weeping Woman*.

Background

The guitar player was painted in 1670 by Dutch artist Johannes Vermeer (1632–1675). The guitar player is one of few smiling women in Vermeer's paintings. There is more about Vermeer on page 91.

The Spanish artist Pablo Picasso (1881–1973) painted *Weeping Woman* in 1937. It is a portrait of his mistress Dora Maar. She was also a painter and had helped him complete his famous work *Guernica*.

2a Students should ignore the gaps as they skim the text to answer the questions.

Background

The Tate Gallery opened in 1897 and was named after its major financial backer, Henry Tate, a sugar merchant. In May 2000 the gallery split, with the old building (now called Tate Britain) retaining 18th and 19th century British art and the new building, Tate Modern, housing modern art.

2b As you check students' answers, point out that in questions 3 and 5, *at* and *about* can both be used but there is a difference in meaning when used with people. *At* goes with the object of the action or feeling (*laugh/get angry at someone*) whereas *about* goes with the cause (*laugh/get angry about someone/something*).

2c Tell students that dependent prepositions are frequently tested in the exam, but there would not be so many in one text as there are here, where the aim is to test/practise dependent prepositions.

3 Remind students of the importance of learning dependent prepositions, and find out if they have a particular method. Compare their methods with those given.

Language development 2 p.91

LOOK Go through the box with students. If they have just done Exercise 2c on page 90, they will have no difficulty remembering the adjective + preposition combinations in the text. Point out that these phrases are followed by nouns, pronouns or -*ing* forms.

1a Tell students to record the whole phrase, not just the two words. E.g., question 1 *the result of*, question 2 *feel sorry for*.

1b See the background notes on Vermeer in the teaching notes for page 90 Exercise 1.

2 Students could discuss these personalised questions in pairs or small groups.

3 Highlight for students the difference between the state, expressed by *be used to*, and the action, expressed by *get used to*. You could use a simpler example to help, such as *Paul is married* (state). *Paul got married in 2001* (action).

4 Students should do this in pairs or small groups before class feedback. You could ask each group to discuss just one of the bullet points, then report back to the class.

Photocopiable activity

Photocopiable activity 12 (pp. 150–151) would work well here. Students play a version of the game 'Battleships' to practise adjective/noun + preposition combinations.

▶ **Student's Resource Book page 58**

Use of English 2 p.92

1a Possible further questions: *What type of music is popular now? What used to be popular? Are some types of music hard to get used to?*

2a Before students do the task, ask what they know about Stevie Wonder.

Background

Stevie Wonder (born 1950) is one of the greatest Motown artists of all time. He has sold more than 70 million albums and has had as many Top Ten hits as Elvis Presley and The Beatles. His later, more political, music includes protests against racism, nuclear weapons and third world poverty.

3 Get students to look at the photo and identify the group, The Jacksons. See if they can recognise which one is Michael Jackson (he is the one on the right).

Background

'The Jackson Five' were five brothers born in the USA between 1951 and 1958. The group formed in 1964, when Michael was six. They joined Motown in 1969 and were a huge success, competing with The Beatles in the music charts for two years. In 1971 Michael started his solo career, and in 1975 the group left Motown and became The Jacksons. The boys' three sisters, Rebbie, Janet and La Toya, and their younger brother Randy, are also successful singers.

4 Possible further questions: *Have you ever studied/did you use to study a musical instrument? If you could join any group which would it be?*

Language development 3 p.93

1a Note the endings for occupations (*-er, -or, -ist*). Check pronunciation, especially the changes of stress in *piano* – *pianist*, *music* – *musician*.

2b Encourage students to draw a table big enough to add other negative adjectives in future. Elicit patterns such as *im-* and *il-* adjectives, but emphasise that they are only patterns, not rules.

3b Encourage students to answer honestly! If they know each other well they could be asked to agree or disagree with what people say about themselves.

4a *Say, tell, speak, talk* are often confused. Tell students that, rather than worry about meaning, they should focus on collocation, as in the box.

4b Remind students to use the correct form of each verb.

5 Get students in pairs to tell each other what they have written. Encourage them to ask questions about each other's sentences and explain them further if necessary.

▶ **Module 6 Test: How much do you remember?**
   TRB page 182

▶ **Exam practice 3: Papers 1 and 3 CB pages 94–96;**
   Papers 2 and 4 TRB pages 183–184

Unit 12 Key

Speaking p.88
2a … type of art you think is more interesting.
2b 1 Yes, she spends equal time on both parts.
   2 Yes, she keeps talking for a minute, then the examiner stops her when she pauses.
2c The statue could be … .
   I get the impression that … .
2d Well, I like some modern art but if you ask me to choose, I think I would choose classical art because I understand it.

3a Robert, are you interested in art?
3b I'm not really very keen on art. I prefer listening to music.

Listening p.89
1 1 a function – What, doing, when speaks
   2 an arts topic – What, speaker, talking about
   3 a place – Where, taking place
   4 a feeling – How, boy, feel
   5 a person – Who, talking about
   6 an aspect of an exhibition – What, criticise

2a/b 1 B (*So do they give the exact dates?*)
   2 C (*… until the very last page … it would probably transfer very well to stage or screen.*)
   3 B (*move to the back … if I'd known how much noise there'd be … might as well put my bed on the motorway.*)
   4 A (*… better to stick to the plot of the original … it just didn't hold my attention.*)
   5 B (*… see him in the canteen … someone new like that.*)
   6 A (*It's just the way it's been put together that I don't like.*)

Use of English 1 p.90
2a 1 True; 2 False; 3 False
2b 1 its – possessive
   2 than – *more than* – comparative
   3 at/about/by – *surprised* + preposition
   4 in – *interested* + preposition
   5 at/about – *angry* + preposition
   6 on – *spend money on* s.th.
   7 in – phrasal verb *bring in* = attract
   8 has – auxiliary verb for present perfect
   9 about – *talk about* s.th.
   10 rather – *rather + than* comparing the gallery and contents
   11 was – auxiliary verb for past simple passive
   12 who/that – relative clause defining the architects
   13 instead – *instead + of* comparing two ideas
   14 which – non-defining relative clause
   15 to – *get used to* s.th.

2c   adjectives + prepositions – 3, 4, 5
verbs + prepositions – 6, 7, 9
verb forms – 8, 11

Language development 2 p.91

LOOK … some people were *surprised at/about/by* its success.
A lot of people in Britain are not *interested in* modern art, and even get *angry about/at* the large sums of money which are spent on it.

1a **1** of – *the result of* something
2 for – *feel sorry for*
3 in – *have success in* + -*ing*
4 between – *no comparison between* two people/things
5 of – *be tired of* + -*ing*
6 in – *get involved in* + noun
7 in – *have difficulty (in)* + -*ing*
8 about – *be excited about* + -*ing*
9 with – *be annoyed with someone*
10 of – *have no hope of* + -*ing*

1b **1** for – *be famous for something*
2 at – *be good at* + -*ing*
3 for – *be usual for someone to do something*
4 of – *be capable of* + -*ing*
5 for – *be responsible for something*
6 about – *be puzzled about something*
7 to – *be similar to something/someone*
8 about – *have no doubt about something*
9 of – *a means of* + -*ing*
10 about/of – *be suspicious about/of something/someone*
11 about – *be right about something*
12 for – *lose respect for someone/something*

3   **1** used to live
2 get used to living
3 wasn't used to filming
4 get used to hearing
5 didn't use to print
6 aren't used to watching
7 get used to people staring
8 'm not used to going

Use of English 2 p.92

2a **1** artistic – adjective
2 singer – adjective + noun (person)
3 impressive – adjective + noun
4 extraordinary – adjective (= very unusual) + noun
5 recording – compound noun
6 extremely – adverb + adverb
7 disappointing – adjective
8 uninterrupted – adjective, describing *run of hit records*
9 freedom – noun
10 political – comparative form more + adjective

HELP Question 4 – prefix
Question 5 – -*ing*
Question 8 – both

3   **1** ambitious – adjective
2 ability – noun
3 greatness – noun
4 incapable – adjective *incapable of* + -*ing*
5 development – noun
6 curiously – adverb
7 incredibly – adverb
8 underestimate – verb
9 importance – noun
10 astonishing – adjective

Language development 3 p.93

1a **1** pianist; **2** drummer; **3** trumpeter;
4 composer; **5** conductor

1b **1** dancers; **2** musicians; **3** singers;
4 performers;
5 violinists; **6** cellist; **7** traditional; **8** guitarist;
9 singer; **10** performance

2a uninterrupted, incapable

2b *un-*: untidy, unfair, unfit, unsatisfactory
in-: inexperienced, insecure
dis-: disloyal, dishonest
im-: impolite, impatient, impractical
il-: illiterate, illogical

3a **1** untidy; **2** impractical; **3** dissatisfied;
4 unsatisfactory; **5** illiterate; **6** inexperienced;
7 unfit

4a **1** The teacher ~~spoke~~ **told** us a horror story.
2 I can't stand it when artists ~~say~~ **talk** politics.
3 We all ~~talked~~ **said** a prayer together.
4 Excuse me, could you ~~say~~ **tell** me the time?
5 My brother ~~talks~~ **speaks** three languages.
6 ~~Tell~~ **Say** hello to Rosie for me.
7 Mike ~~said~~ **told** the police what he had seen.
8 Don't trust him. He's always ~~speaking~~ **telling** lies.

4b **1** speak; **2** say; **3** say; **4** talks; **5** told; **6** telling;
7 say; **8** speak; **9** tell

Teacher's Resource Book
Module 6 Test: How much do you remember? p.182

1   1 C; 2 B; 3 A; 4 D; 5 B

2   1 in; 2 used; 3 of; 4 between; 5 whose

3   1 Sarah is slowly *getting used to living on* her own.
2 I stayed in a *flat that/which belonged to* my uncle.
3 Luke *must have made* the mess in this room.
4 I g*et the impression/feeling(that) Pat* can't drive.
5 Brenda is *too inexperienced to* work in this office.

4   1 that; 2 ✓; 3 who; 4 to; 5 is

5   1 impatient; 2 descriptive; 3 friendship;
4 dissatisfaction; 5 illogical

Coursebook
Exam practice 3 p.94

Paper 1 Reading
Part 3 1 G; 2 A; 3 B; 4 D; 5 E; 6 C

Paper 3 Use of English
Part 1 1 B; 2 D; 3 C; 4 D; 5 A; 6 C; 7 A; 8 B;
9 A; 10 D; 11 C; 12 B; 13 C; 14 A; 15 B

Part 3 1 It won't *be long before John has* finished his work.
2 What's the name of the man *whose nose was/got broken* in a fight?
3 I *have (great) difficulty (in) believing* anything he says.
4 It took me several years *to get used to driving* on the left.
5 Excuse me, *I wonder if you could/would* tell me the time.
6 I think that *what he* did *was* very stupid.
7 I saw him take the money *with my own* eyes.
8 I don't think there's *any/much hope of us/our* finishing this crossword.
9 The woman who is *brushing her hair is called* Kate.
10 The band *will already be playing* when the Queen comes in.

Part 5 1 annoying; 2 unnecessary; 3 patience;
4 badly; 5 pleasure; 6 reflection; 7 amusing;
8 easily; 9 ambitious; 10 variety

Teacher's Resource Book
Exam practice 3 pp.183–184

Paper 2 Writing
1   Style:
Neutral.
Content:
Say where Danny is and why a lot is expected of him (e.g. what is the sport/what type of event is it/why do people think he will do well?).
Explain what happens next and say how Danny feels about it.
You could make some reference to 'everybody's expectations' at the end of the story: does Danny do as well as everybody expected? Why (not)?

2   Style:
Semi-formal or neutral.
Content:
1 Describe the resort e.g. location, facilities.
2 Say what young people can do there.
3 Say what young people will especially like about it.

3   Style:
Formal letter.
Content:
Say why you are interested in the job.
Explain in detail the things you could do with the children, mentioning any experience you have of this sort of work and saying why you are a good candidate for the job.

Paper 4 Listening
Part 2
1 Presentation Skills
2 actress/actor
3 conference
4 (rich) uncle
5 department store
6 £2500/two thousand, five hundred pounds
7 computers/computer equipment
8 theatre/theater
9 read (from/their) notes
10 angry

Module 7 What's in fashion?

Units 13 and 14 are linked by the theme of fashion in food and clothes. Topics include the history of McDonald's, food and eating, restaurants, describing clothes and designer labels.

Lead-in p.97

Get students to look at the photos in pairs and briefly describe each one. Then go onto the lead-in questions. If students need help with ideas for the first question, give them prompts such as where we eat, what we eat, who we eat with, who prepares the food; what people wear, level of formality of clothes, what clothes are/aren't acceptable in different situations, where we get our clothes. In the second question, the quote means that no fashion is really new; it's just the return of an old fashion. (Geoffrey Chaucer, 1342–1400, was the greatest English writer before Shakespeare's time. His most famous work, *The Canterbury Tales*, was written in the last ten years of his life.)

Unit 13 Fast food

To set the ball rolling ...

You could introduce the topic with books closed. Ask students to decide in groups where they can go for something to eat if they only have 45 minutes before their film starts at the cinema. Groups report back to the class and explain their decisions.

> **Photocopiable activity**
>
> Photocopiable activity 13A (p. 152) could be used as an introduction to the topic, or after the reading activity. It is a quiz on the subject of the global food and drinks market.

Reading p.98

1 Students may notice the difference between *fast food*, the two-word noun in the unit title and *fast-food*, the hyphenated adjective in the title of the article. *Fast food* usually refers to hot food served quickly from a service point in restaurants, which may be 'eaten in' or taken away. Some famous international chains are McDonald's, Burger King and KFC.

3a Use the task strategy to remind students of good exam technique for multiple matching. Look at the example in paragraph 0 together, highlighting the links between the key phrases in the text and the main words in the heading.

3b You could do number 1 together first if you think it necessary.

4 *Junk food* is a negative way to refer to *fast food*. It reflects the fact that such food is often highly processed and high in fat, sugar, carbohydrate and additives.

▶ **Student's Resource Book page 62**

Language development 1 p.100

1a With books closed, ask students how often they eat in restaurants, what type they most enjoy going to and on what occasions. Or ask them to talk briefly about the last time they went to a restaurant (who with, why, where, who paid, etc.)

Tell students not to worry about the exact meanings of the sentences in the exercise at this stage. As they do it, they could identify who the pronouns refer to and/or how waiters traditionally refer to customers – *sir* or *madam*.

1b First check students' understanding of the terminology in the table. Giving permission –you can do something; Prohibiting –you cannot do something; Obligation – no choice because of a duty to do something. When students have completed the table, elicit the form (i.e. all are followed by verbs in the infinitive). It may be necessary to highlight the fact that while *must* and *have to* both express obligation, the negative forms are quite different.

2a Do question 1 together as an example.

2b Students could go on to describe school rules or rules in a job that they do (or once did).

3a See how many different ways students can express the answer to question 2.

3b Consolidate *needn't have* with concept questions: *Did he wear a suit? Yes. Was it necessary? No.* You could add further examples, such as *I needn't have taken any money to the restaurant. Did I take it? Yes. Was it necessary? No. Why? Maybe someone else paid the bill. Did I know that before I went? No.*

4a Encourage students to think about what the two options express.

4b If students find it hard to think of food and eating rules, ask them to think of any rules they had in other areas, such as clothes, going out, use of the bathroom, tidying up.

Advice and recommendation

The mistakes are all to do with form. All these forms express advice and recommendations.

5 Students skim the letter to get the gist. Ask *Who is writing to who?* and *Why?*

6 Give students time to think and write before comparing sentences in groups. Alternatively, this could be a homework writing activity.

> **Photocopiable activity**
>
> Photocopiable activity 13B (p. 153) could be used here. It is a pairwork activity that gives further practice of this language.

▶ **Student's Resource Book page 64**

Writing p.102

1 First get students to look at the photo of the cruise boat, asking them what type of boat it is, where you would find one and what people do on them. Then they discuss the questions in the book.

2 Remind students that the transactional letter in Paper 2 Part 1 is compulsory. It is important to understand the task fully and then to select all the information to be included.

4c When students have matched the expressions to the functions, elicit which function is needed in each of the four points to be covered in the letter. E.g.: Directions – referring to questions; No time – apologising.

4d Elicit ways to finish each of the phrases, e.g. *We should manage to get to the pier in five minutes from the town centre.*

4e First think about what to include in the final concluding paragraph: *We are all looking forward to meeting you next month.* Then establish how students should open the letter. It is a reply, so we know the name of the person we are writing to, but it should be formal, e.g. *Dear Ms/Miss/Mrs* + name. From this, elicit a suitable closing, i.e. *Yours sincerely*.

5 The letter can now be written in class or for homework. Suggest a time limit of 15 minutes.

6 Remind students to use the checklist in the Writing reference on page 206.

> **LANGUAGE SPOT:** giving directions
>
> **a** Prepositions of place and direction, although often considered quite basic, still cause problems for students at FCE level.

▶ **Student's Resource Book page 65**

Unit 13 Key

Reading p.98

2 2 – In the USA in the 1930s and 40s, because people wanted to eat in their cars.
3 – because of their reliability and consistency
4 – Possibly not, as people are returning to traditional healthy food.

3a surprising – astonished
amount – how much
evidence – what they come across

3b 1 E (... *people were becoming so attached to their cars ... waitresses ... carry trays of food out to those customers ... eating in their vehicles*)
2 B (*The business was not without its problems ... decided to look again ... find a way round drawbacks*)
3 A (... *streamline the process ... as straightforward and as uncomplicated as possible.*)
4 C (... *uniformity ... reliability ... order a 'Big Mac' at any McDonald's on the planet and know exactly what they will get.*)
5 D (... *the influence of the McDonald approach can be seen throughout the service economy ... businesses which benefit from being organised according to the same principles.*)
6 F (... *there are some people who question its long-term appeal. ... a new attitude towards food in the western world.*)

5 Suggestions:
staff – chef, cook, wine waiter, kitchen porter
crockery – dinner plate, side plate, bowl, cup, saucer
cutlery – fork, spoon, teaspoon, chopsticks
ways of preparing food – cooking: boil, fry, roast, bake, steam, casserole, stew; cutting: slice, chop, dice. mixing: stir, whisk

Language development 1 p.100

1a 1 customer – we = customer
2 customer – them = staff
3 waiter – you = customers
4 waiter or customer
5 waiter
6 customer
7 waiter
8 customer
9 waiter
10 customer
1b **Giving permission:**
1 You're allowed to smoke in this area.
2 You can choose any table on this side, madam.

Prohibiting:
1 We're not allowed to smoke, are we?
2 I'm afraid you can't sit there – it's reserved.
3 Children over 12 mustn't use the play area.
4 You're not supposed to use your mobile phone here.
Expressing obligation:
The speaker feels it's necessary:
1 I must try one of those desserts.
The rules or situation make it necessary:
2 I'm sorry, but you have to wear a tie to eat here.
3 I think we're supposed to leave a tip.
Expressing lack of necessity:
You don't have to give them a tip.

2a **1** must book
2 can't wear
3 's/is allowed to come
4 're/are supposed to wait
5 don't have to have
6 mustn't bring
7 aren't allowed to drink
8 can pay

3a **1** No.
2 He/She wasn't allowed to smoke/Smoking wasn't allowed/They couldn't smoke/They weren't allowed to smoke. But <u>not</u> They mustn't smoke as *must* is not used in the past.

3b **It was permitted:**
They were allowed to use the play area.
It was prohibited:
1 The children couldn't play in the restaurant.
2 I wasn't allowed to smoke.
It was necessary:
We had to pay by credit card.
It wasn't necessary:
We didn't have to book a table.
It was done but it wasn't necessary:
He needn't have dressed so smartly.

4a **1** didn't have to pay – not necessary and not done
2 were allowed to – permission not obligation
3 had to – obligation not permission
4 could – permission not obligation
5 couldn't keep – prohibited
6 had to – obligation not permission
7 have to cook – obligation
8 needn't have worried – 'not necessary but done' – not prohibition
9 didn't have to – not necessary and not done

Advice and recommendation
1 You ought *to* complain about that soup – it's cold.
2 You shouldn't ~~having~~ **have** a dessert if you're full up.
3 If you don't like pasta, you'd better *to* have a pizza.
4 You must ~~have~~ try that new restaurant in Castle Street.

5 **1** You have to; **2** you mustn't; **3** can; **4** You don't have to; **5** can; **6** You must; **7** You'd better

Writing p.102
2 **1** Who are you writing to? The leader of a group of students coming to your school.
2 What is the purpose of the letter? To reply and to give information requested.
3 How many pieces of information should you include? four: directions, there is no time for a walk, they can get the 14:45 coach to London, and you will check about the vegetarian option.
4 What style are you going to use? – Quite formal but friendly. The group leader is important and you probably have not met her before.

3a/b The letter could have five paragraphs:
1 Response to the leader's letter
2 Directions
3 Time – no time for a walk; coach stops at pier so can catch the 14.45
4 Will check vegetarian option
5 Conclusion

4a Thank you very much for your letter. Here are the answers to your questions/queries.
4b First go straight ahead.
When you get to … .
Go round … .
Take the … turning on the …
Follow the road until … .
Keep going until …
4c **Referring to questions:**
You asked about … .
You wanted to know whether … .
Talking about possibilities:
We should manage to … .
We might be able to … .
Apologising:
I'm afraid there won't be … .
Unfortunately, I don't think … .

5   Sample answer:

Dear Ms Sato

Thank you very much for your recent letter. Here are the answers to your questions.

You asked about directions to the pier from the town centre. I have enclosed a simple map showing the best route. It shouldn't take you more than five minutes on foot.

As for getting off for a walk at Tower Island, I am afraid that, there won't be enough time. However, there will be plenty of time to get the 14.45 coach to London as it stops to pick passengers up at the pier.

You wanted to know whether the meal includes a vegetarian option. At present, I don't know but I am going to check with the cruise boat company on Monday and I will let you know.

If you have any other questions please do not hesitate to contact me. We all look forward to meeting you next month and hope that you will enjoy the cruise.

Yours sincerely

Aldo Addler

(162 words)

LANGUAGE SPOT: giving directions

a   1 on – outside
2 at – location point in the city
3 to – next to
4 past – beyond
5 on – on the right/left
6 across – from one side to the other
7 at – the crossroads is an exact point
8 past – the front of it

b   1 been to; tell me the way
2 Where do we go
3 You should; find the way OK.
4 There's no need; you might; a bit
5 get there; 'll see

Unit 14 How do I look?

The fashion theme continues with activities about clothes people wear, deductions from appearance, designer labels, fashion week, and Royal Ascot.

To set the ball rolling ...

With books closed, students brainstorm items of clothing in groups for two minutes. Or they could talk about their favourite item of clothing, saying why they like it, where they got it, when they wear it.

Listening p.104

1a This would best be done in small groups. Emphasise that students should modify the statements as in the example.

1b There are no 'right' answers here – students may find more than one statement that matches each person. Encourage them to speculate, and to explain their choices.

2a Remind students of the strategy for multiple matching in listening.

2b After checking answers, ask students which of the five speakers they are most similar to.

3   1 A *fashion victim* is someone who wears what is fashionable even if it doesn't look good on them. Ask students if they know any fashion victims.

2 Explain *dress code*: a standard of what clothes should be worn in a particular situation, e.g. at work.

4a Khaki /kɑːki/ is a dull green-brown or yellow-brown colour and is a colour often worn by soldiers.

Speaking p.105

1   Check that students know the names of the clothes in the photos.

2a Elicit the format of Paper 5 Part 3. If the class it not divisible by three, you could have four people in some groups (3 candidates and an examiner). Remind 'examiners' that they will need to give some feedback on the others' performance at the end.

2b 'Candidates' should give their own assessment of how well they did before getting feedback from the 'examiners'.

3   This exercise introduces the types of question the examiner might ask. It is obviously important in this part that students listen carefully to the question and respond accordingly.

4a Students should look at question 3 again before listening to the sample answer.

4b Encourage students not just to decide who gives a better answer, but also to think about why it is better.

4c Let students discuss this in pairs or small groups before checking with the whole class.

4d Here, Julia's answer is better as it picks up on what Paul has said and expands the same point.

5a The 'examiner' should give both students a chance to answer the questions, and try to ensure that both 'candidates' get an equal chance to speak.

▶ **Student's Resource Book page 67**

Language development 2 p.106

1a Point out that being modals, all the verbs are followed by the infinitive without *to*.

1b As students look at the bags, encourage them to think about what is certain and what is possible.

2 From the examples in the table, highlight the past modal form (modal + *have* + past participle) and point out that *have* here is weak and contracted in spoken English. Practise the contracted forms such as *must've* /mʌstəv/ before students do the exercise.

3 First elicit what type of word they should use after *looks/feels/seems* (an adjective). Encourage students to use both present and past modals. When they have completed the sentences, get them to compare in groups.

▶ **Student's Resource Book page 68**

Use of English 1 p.107

1a The aim here is to revise the strategy for key word transformations in Unit 2. Elicit the correct answers to the three example transformations for practice.

2b Students could answer the questions about the task before checking their answers to the task.

Photocopiable activity

Photocopiable activity 14 (p. 154) would work well here. It is a mingling activity where students use modals of deduction to correct or respond to other students.

Use of English 2 p.108

1 With books closed, check/teach *designer label*, if possible by pointing out one that a student is wearing, and *counterfeit* – an illegal copy designed to make someone believe it is the real thing. Then students discuss the questions in pairs followed by class feedback.

2b Set a time limit of about 15 minutes to do the task.

Language development 3 p.109

1a Point out that all the phrases in this exercise are correct in themselves, but that they aren't all correct in this context. As you check the answers, make sure students understand both phrases in each pair, by eliciting synonyms for each one (see Unit 14 Key).

Background

Fashion weeks are when a number of designers come together to show their latest collections to other people in the fashion industry. They usually take place twice a year in places like Paris, New York, London, Milan, Tokyo.

1b One way to learn the phrases is by preposition. Check students know the meaning of all the phrases listed and can provide the correct preposition where needed.

2 Explain that *do harm, buy clothes, spend money* are simply different collocations, but *hope/expect* are actually different in meaning. These may need further explanation and examples:
hope = you want something to happen in the future but you don't know if it will – *When I buy a lottery ticket, I hope to win.*
expect = you think something will happen because it should – *When I work for a company, I expect to get paid.*
In the examples from the Use of English text, young children want to be able to buy designerwear in the future, but they don't know yet if they will be able to afford it. Followers of designer labels think they should be able to buy the companies' products.

3 As you check the exercise, discuss the difference between the verbs and check that students know all forms of the verbs.

5

Background

Royal Ascot is a four-day horse racing festival which takes place in June each year in Ascot, near Windsor. Members of the Royal Family always go and it is a big social event with a strict dress code. Women have to wear dresses and hats – the hats are famously lavish and outrageous – and men have to wear morning suits – a jacket with long 'tails' at the back and striped trousers.

6 Possible further questions to practise the language:
How do you make a good impression in an interview?
What do you expect to do in the next class?
What do you enjoy doing from time to time?

▶ **Module 7 Review CB page 110**

▶ **Module 7 Test: How much do you remember? TRB page 185**

Unit 14 Key

Listening p.104

1 A (*I lend to wear fairly elegant clothes at work … clothes that are businesslike*)

2a 2 F (*… it's always sports stuff. … What matters is feeling relaxed*)
3 E (*At the moment, the trend is … I wouldn't dream of wearing anything old-fashioned.*)
4 C (*I'll wear anything …*)
5 B (*I do tend to spend quite a lot on my clothes … they don't drop to pieces.*)

4a opinion – scruffy, old-fashioned
size/shape – baggy, tight, high-heeled, fitted
colour – navy
pattern – checked, patterned, flowery
origin: Scottish
material – linen, cotton, viscose

Speaking p.105

3 1 give personal information
2 describe an experience
3/4 give an opinion
5 make a comparison
6 make a prediction

4b Paul's answer is better as he expands his ideas and gives examples.

4c Paul used 2. It gives him time to think about what to say, but avoids a long hesitation, which the examiner could interpret as searching for language, rather than ideas.
1 This answer is very negative and defeatist. There is no attempt at keeping communication going.
3 This answer is obviously too short and cuts off the conversation.

4d Julia was agreeing.
She uses *Apart from that …*
To add her opinion, she could have used *And there's another thing …* or *Not only that … .* She could not have used *Actually …* as that would introduce a difference of opinion rather than an additional point.

Language development 2 p.106

1a 1 Marlie's in her pyjamas. She ~~can~~ **must** be going to bed.
2 It ~~mustn't~~ **can't** be his jacket – it's too small.
3 That ~~might~~ **must** be Kate. I recognise that voice.
4 I think that's John's case, so he ~~couldn't~~/**might** be here.
5 She's decided not to buy those shoes. She ~~could~~ **may not**/**might not** have enough money.
6 Mike ~~must~~ **can't** work in a clothes shop – he knows nothing about fashion!

1b Suggested answers:
1 A It must belong to a woman. She must be rich because she has a Visa card. She must like to look nice, because she's got a mirror, lipstick and perfume in her bag.
2 C It could belong to someone on holiday or a working tour because there is a map in the rucksack.
3 B It could belong to either a man or a woman because there's nothing like make-up or aftershave. I think he/she works in a high-powered job because of the computer and calculator.

2 1 can't have left
2 may/might/could have been stolen
3 must have cost
4 may/might/could have been; may/might/could have bought
5 can't have been
6 must have had

Use of English 1 p.107

1a 1 The candidate has changed the keyword *been* to *be* and therefore incorrectly changed the tense. Correct answer: *must have been pleased*
2 The candidate has written more than five words. Correct answer: *wish I could go to*
3 The candidate has changed the second sentence, removing the word *in*, and has changed the keyword *spite* to *despite*. Correct answer: *spite of the fact that*

2a 1 it can't be Kate
2 must be tired
3 haven't eaten for
4 must have just been on
5 too unfit to
6 may have been in the
7 as long as you
8 can't have left
9 he could have heard
10 Lucy if she had finished

2b 1 1, 2, 4, 6, 8, 9
2 Present: 1, 2. Past: 4, 6, 8, 9
3 3 present perfect simple
5 *too/enough, un-* prefix
7 conditional with *as long as*
10 reported speech

Use of English 2 p.108

2a 1 They are very keen on it.
2 The media tells us what is in fashion.

2b 1 C – claim – state something is true
2 D – expect – + *to*
3 B – effort – *in an effort* + *to* = phrase
4 B – used – use a symbol
5 A – recent – not long ago, recent survey = collocation

6 D – admit – admit + *that* (*consent to, permit someone to*)

7 C – latest – most recent but not final

8 B – revealed – surveys reveal (*make known something previously unknown*)

9 A – amount – of money (U)

10 D – argue – state (with reason) that they believe something is true

11 C – whole – phrase *on the whole* = generally

12 B – item – piece

13 A – real – real (genuine) choice

14 D – in – *in fashion* = fashionable

15 C – look = appear

2c 11 – *on the whole*, 14 – *in fashion*

Language development 3 p.109

1a **1** at all times = always (at the moment = now, currently)

2 in danger of = at risk (in favour of = supporting)

3 (go) from bad to worse = deteriorate (from time to time = occasionally)

4 at first = initially (at least = as a minimum)

5 by mistake = accidentally (by the way = to change the subject …)

6 to my surprise = surprisingly (to my advantage = good for me)

7 in a bad mood = unhappy (in a loud voice = loudly)

8 From then on = subsequently (from time to time = occasionally)

9 to a certain extent = partly (to the point = short and concise)

1b **1** (in/at) the beginning

2 (in) conclusion

3 (from) time to time

4 (on) purpose

1c **1** in the end; **2** in fashion; **3** out of date; **4** on purpose; **5** for a change; **6** in luck

2 **1** hope; **2** expect; **3** spend; **4** do; **5** buy

3a **1** do; **2** make; **3** make; **4** do; **5** do; **6** make; **7** make; **8** do; **9** make; **10** do; **11** make; **12** make

3b **1** an Armani suit; **2** a lot of money on it; **3** in cash; **4** trying it on; **5** it would be comfortable; **6** feel so good; **7** to show my friends

4 **1** rise – rise [I], raise [T]

2 became

3 earned – earn money from work, win money in a competition

4 damaged – damage something, injure someone

5 resign – resign = quit a job, retire = stop work for ever.

6 healed – heal wounds, cure an illness

5 **1** retired; **2** spend; **3** expect; **4** made; **5** do; **6** bought; **7** make; **8** made

Coursebook
Module 7 Review p. 110

1 **1** grill; **2** cutlery; **3** scruffy; **4** old-fashioned; **5** baggy; **6** elegant; **7** linen; **8** patterned

2 **1** don't have to; **2** have to; **3** can; **4** are allowed to; **5** has to; **6** are not allowed to; **7** needn't; **8** had to; **9** wasn't allowed to; **10** could; **11** had to; **12** didn't have to

3 **1** might be/could be

2 may be/might be/could be

3 can't be

4 must have stolen

5 could (the thieves) have got in

6 can't have broken in

7 may have had/might have had/could have had

8 may have left/might have left/could have left

9 may have hidden/might have hidden/could have hidden

10 must be

4 **1** At; **2** from; **3** to; **4** In; **5** for; **6** for; **7** at; **8** on; **9** to; **10** in; **11** to; **12** from; **13** At; **14** at; **15** in; **16** on

5a **1** do; **2** do; **3** spend; **4** raise; **5** become
a resign; **b** make; **c** makes; **d** expect; **e** earn

Teacher's Resource Book
Module 7 Test: How much do you remember? p.185

1 **1** C; **2** B; **3** A; **4** D; **5** A

2 **1** for; **2** on; **3** if/whether; **4** all; **5** my

3 **1** Gill *can't have left (yet)* because her computer is still on.

2 I agree with you *to a certain extent/to an extent*, but you have forgotten one thing.

3 Jack *wasn't allowed to buy* a drink at the club because he wasn't a member.

4 Karen *needn't have gone to* work as there was nothing to do.

5 You *are not/aren't supposed to eat* in here.

4 **1** ✓; **2** like; **3** to; **4** do; **5** ✓

5 **1** worldwide; **2** unfashionable/old-fashioned; **3** comparison; **4** healthily; **5** living

Module 8 The important things in life

Units 15 and 16 are linked by the theme of 'The important things in life' and include love, relationships, family, living alone or with others, hobbies and free time.

Lead-in p.111

Get students to look at the photos in pairs and briefly describe each one. Then they should go on to discuss the lead-in questions, followed by class feedback. The quote by Thoreau means that if you are alone you are independent and can make all your own decisions; you don't have to compromise with a companion.

Background

The American essayist, poet, and philosopher Henry David Thoreau (1817–1862) lived the doctrines of Transcendentalism as recorded in his masterwork, *Walden* (1854). He was a vigorous advocate of civil liberties, as evidenced in the essay *Civil Disobedience* (1849). He once spent a night in jail for refusing to pay his taxes, which he had done in protest at the American Government's support of slavery and its war on Mexico.

Unit 15 Relationships

To set the ball rolling ...

Put students into pairs or groups to brainstorm different types of relationship, e.g. father–son, teacher–student, husband–wife.

Photocopiable activity

Photocopiable activity 15A (p. 155) could be used as an introduction to the reading text, or after Exercise 5 on CB page 112. It practises prepositional phrases describing stages in a romantic relationship.

Reading p.112

1a Point out that the places listed are examples, and students might think of other places were people meet. You could also ask if any students want to tell the class where and how they met their partner.

2 Get students to give you a signal when they have finished, such as putting their pen down, so you can get an idea how long it is taking them.

3 Paper 1 Part 3 has two variations. In Unit 7, students practised the variation with sentences removed; here it is whole paragraphs that have been removed.

4 1 The story of Wendy and Dennis is true.

    2 A *soul mate* is someone you are naturally close to, as you share the same emotions and interests and you understand each other.

▶ **Student's Resource Book page 72**

Language development 1 p.114

1a Focus students on the photos first, and ask them to imagine how life was different when the first photo was taken. Then students discuss question 1a. If they need prompting, get them to think about going out together, living together, getting formally engaged, asking parents' permission to get married.

1b You could get students to guess the answers first, then read and check.

1c Point out that all the reported sentences on the right come from the text. You may want to do the first one or two with the class to get them started.

1d The aim here is to show students that we don't always change tenses in reported speech. First point out that in 1–6, there is the usual change of tense for reported speech, then ask them to discuss the question. If they find it hard, prompt with clues, e.g. *What was the secret 50 years ago? What is the secret now? What has changed?*

1e Students need to be aware of changes to time expressions and some verbs, as well as tenses. Explain that these changes do depend on context though, e.g. *I'll do it this afternoon,* reported a few minutes later, would be *He said he would do it this afternoon.* Reported the next day, it would be *He said he would do it yesterday afternoon.*

2 Tell students that they will also need to change pronouns. You could do the first one or two with them.

3a This exercise provides freer, more personalised practice. Give students a little preparation time, then get them to work in pairs. They should try to ask each other one or two questions too.

3b This would work well in groups of four. Students should report what their partner said, e.g. *She told me her favourite place is the beach,* and also any questions they asked, e.g. *I asked her when she had first gone there.*

4a Demonstrate the effect of just reporting the exact words: *I said … and he said … so I said … then he said … .* Explain that the exact words are not usually important, so we can use reporting verbs to summarise and add variety. Check meaning and pronunciation of the verbs after they have completed the sentences.

4b You may want to do this with the class, so that they can clearly see how each of the verbs fits into the table.

4c Get students to do this in pairs, using a dictionary when necessary. When students have completed the table, elicit the negative construction for each verb, e.g. verb +(object) + *not* + *to*; verb + *not* + *-ing*.

4d The aim here is to show that the structure verb (+ object) + *that* + clause is common, but not possible for all verbs.

5 Transformations from direct to reported speech are common in Paper 3 Part 3. Encourage students to look at the table in 4b for help, and remind them to think about pronoun changes.

6 Give the class a little time to prepare the sentences before they compare them in groups. You could get them started by giving some examples about yourself.

7 Point out that here the verbs are being used to report general statements about the present and so the present simple is used. After you have checked the sentences, students could discuss them, saying whether they agree with each one and giving their personal opinion.

> **Photocopiable activity**
> Photocopiable activity 15B (pp. 156–157) would work well here. It uses film quotes to practise reported speech and reporting verbs.

▶ **Student's Resource Book pages 73–74, exercises 1–4**

Writing p.116

1 Get students to do this in pairs or small groups, followed by class discussion.

2 As you go through students' answers, advise students that they should only choose the discursive composition in the exam if they are sure they have something to say about both sides of the argument.

3a Elicit why the composition should have two points for both sides – it ensures the writing is balanced, and gives students the opportunity to link their ideas coherently within the word limit.

3b This is a standard format for a discursive composition of this type. Tell students that each point should be backed up with a reason and an example.

4a/b For pairs A, C and D, style is the important issue. For pair B, it is more a question of which is a more 'open' and interesting introduction to the composition.

4c This could be done in pairs or with the whole class.

5 Give students 30 minutes to write the composition.

> **LANGUAGE SPOT:** linking expressions
> This focuses on other linking expressions which would be useful in discursive compositions and are tested in Paper 3.

▶ **Student's Resource Book page 75**

Unit 15 Key

Reading p.112

1b **1** They met on the tube (the London Underground) by chance. Perhaps they bumped into each other.
2 *Meant to be* means destined or fated to happen.

3c **1** G (*Although Dennis had noticed Wendy* links to *gave me a little nod* in para. 3)
2 C (*Seeing this* links to *the businessman's head … resting on her arm* in para. 5; *gave the man's briefcase a kick to wake him up* links to *as he fell into a deeper sleep* in para. 5)
3 B (*the scrap of paper* links to *Dennis pushed a note into her hand* in para. 7; *It was Dennis* links to '*I'm sorry,' he said* in para. 9)
4 D (*When Dennis left* links to *Wendy's flat* in para. 9; *He asked Wendy to call* links to *he hadn't given her the right number* in para. 11)
5 E (*Wendy saw the funny side of this* links to *giving her the number of his ex-girlfriend* in para. 11; *Dennis proposed* links to *too soon to think about … that.* in para. 13)
6 A ('*So … my Mister Right*' links to '*I had fallen in love with him.* in para. 13; *Fate must have been on my side* links to *stunned by her good fortune* in para. 15.)

HELP **1** G; **2** C; **3** B; **4** D

5a go out **with** someone – to date, to be a couple
get on **with** someone – have a good relationship (could be with friends, parents, teacher, neighbour, etc.)
fall in love **with** someone – start to love
5b **1** packed; **2** drop off (to sleep); **3** get to (your) feet; **4** flustered; **5** scribble; **6** dash

Language development 1 p.114

1a **Possible answer:**
Everything would probably be more formal then – there might be strict rules about going out together and not being left alone together at home. Engagement might be a very formal step, requiring parents' permission, and a couple probably wouldn't live together at all until they were married.
1b **1** They'd only met the previous summer and hadn't known each other very long.
2 The husband has to be in charge.
1c **1** love you; **2** 've only known; **3** met last; **4** Ask; **5** Will you; **6** 's; **7** 's; **8** 's changed
1d Because what is reported is still true in the present.

1e

today	that day
tomorrow	the next day/the following day
yesterday	the day before/the previous day
last week	the week before/the previous week
next month	the following month
this	that
here	there
come	go
bring	take

2 **1** what I was; **2** I was; **3** that was; **4** to come/go out; **5** I'd/I had nearly; **6** had; **7** 'd/had been to; **8** it was; **9** to pick me/if he could pick me; **10** 'd/would be; **11** had to be (*must* becomes *had to*)

4a **1** accused; **2** persuaded; **3** agreed; **4** suggested; **5** explained
4b verb + *to*: agree
verb + object + *to*: persuade
verb + *-ing*: suggest
verb (+ object) + prep + *-ing*: accuse
verb (+ object) + *that* + clause: explain
4c verb + *to*: decide, offer, refuse
verb + object + *to*: advise, remind, warn
verb + *-ing*: admit, deny, recommend
verb (+ object) + prep + *-ing*: apologise, insist
verb (+ object) + *that* + clause: decide, advise, remind, warn, admit, deny, recommend, insist
4d verb (+ object) + *that* + clause: agree [I], persuade [T], suggest [I], decide [I], advise [T], remind [T], warn [I/T], admit [I], deny [I], recommend [I], insist [I], explain [I]

5 **1** advised her not to get married yet./advised her that she shouldn't get married yet.
2 admitted starting the argument./admitted that she had started the argument.
3 insisted on cooking dinner that night./insisted that he was cooking/would cook dinner that night.
4 warned her sister not to go out with Mike./warned her sister that she shouldn't go out with Mike.
5 apologised to his girlfriend for hurting her feelings.
6 suggested staying in that weekend./suggested that they (should) stay in that weekend.
7 offered to carry the bag for her mother.
8 refused to listen.

7 **1** Sometimes people suggest that marriage is an old-fashioned idea.
2 Parents often persuade their children to get married.
3 Some people insist on getting married while they are still teenagers.
4 One couple admits getting married for financial reasons.

5 Some couples refuse to have a religious wedding.

6 A few women decide not to change their surname.

Writing p.116

2 **1** a teacher; to summarise a discussion and give an opinion.

2 both sides

3 fairly formal

4 a balanced discussion, good organisation and clear linking of ideas.

4a/b A – 1 – Paragraph 4

B – 2 – Paragraph 1

C – 2 – Paragraph 3

D – 1 – Paragraph 2

5 **Sample answer:**

> *Nowadays more people are deciding to live by themselves. Some people claim this is more enjoyable, whereas others disagree.*
>
> *The main advantage of living alone is that there is nobody to tell you what to do, so you can live your life your own way. What is more, you can organise or decorate your house as you want. There is no one else to disagree with.*
>
> *On the other hand it can be quite lonely for some people. Secondly, it is more expensive because you have to pay all the rent and bills yourself, so you have less money to enjoy yourself. Last but not least, it can be hard to find a nice flat for one person so you might not be able to live in the best area.*
>
> *To sum up, there are strong arguments on both sides. In conclusion I believe that living alone is better for older people who have more money and like privacy, but not for young people, who need to share the costs.*

LANGUAGE SPOT: linking expressions

1 In fact – reinforcing a point, perhaps with an example. *In addition* is used to add a further point.

2 In addition – adding a further point. *In other words* is used to rephrase, to say the same thing in a different way.

3 For instance – to introduce an example. *That is to say* is used to rephrase or explain a point.

4 Moreover – adding a further point.

5 Besides – adding a further point.

6 Nevertheless – introducing a contrasting point. *On the other hand* is used to introduce the opposite point of view.

7 Even so – introducing a contrasting point.

8 On the other hand – introducing the opposite point of view.

Unit 16 Hobbies

Unit 16 continues the theme of 'The important things in life' with texts and activities on the topic of hobbies.

To set the ball rolling ...

Start by getting students in groups to think of two popular hobbies and two more unusual ones. Then compare and vote on which group has thought of the most unusual hobbies.

Listening p.118

1a First check that students know who the people in the photos are: Julia Roberts, American actress; Kate Moss, English supermodel; Jarvis Cocker, English lead singer of the band Pulp; Rod Stewart, Scottish rock singer.

Also, check that they know the names of the hobbies in English: model trains, indoor wall climbing, bird-watching, knitting, jigsaw puzzles. Then students in groups discuss who does which hobby. Clarify that there are only four people, so there is one extra hobby that doesn't go with any of them.

2a This listening is the same format as Paper 4 Part 2 of the exam. For the first part of the task strategy, do one with students to get them started. E.g., question 1 must be a noun or noun phrase, it is followed by the preposition *on* and Mick Jagger sees it as a good thing.

2b For question 2, students may not find it easy to remember the wording in the recording. You could give them a copy of the tapescript.

3 As students discuss the questions, you could elicit/teach other expressions similar in meaning to some of the idioms, e.g. *keen on – into/mad about, all the rage – fashionable/in, wind down – unwind/chill (out)*.

> ### Photocopiable activity
> Photocopiable activity 16 (p. 158) would work well here, or later in the unit whenever you feel a speaking activity is needed for a change of pace. It is a Paper 5 Part 3 type discussion in which students have to choose a leisure activity.

Speaking p.119

1a You could start this section with books closed and elicit areas that might be covered in Paper 5 Part 1. Help students with their questions by asking what they like to know about someone that they have just met. Emphasise that they should just make notes for the answers and not write full sentences.

1b This could be done in pairs or with the whole class mingling, each student moving on to a different partner after they have answered a question.

2a Before students listen, elicit what you would need to do to create a good first impression, e.g. being positive and attentive, speaking clearly and with reasonable accuracy and fluency, giving extended answers but not going on for too long, listening carefully to the examiner and the other candidate. After listening, point out that the two candidates may be asked the same questions or different questions, as in this example.

2b You could ask students to shout *Stop!* each time they hear Anna or Giorgio dealing with a word they don't know.

3a Give the assessors some guidance on things to look for, such as accuracy, fluency, expanding answers appropriately, making a good first impression.

3b You could do this after each turn if you have plenty of time available. If time is short it will probably be more efficient to do it when everybody has had their turn.

▶ **Student's Resource Book page 77**

Use of English 1 p.120

1 Students discuss the questions in pairs or small groups before brief class feedback.

2 Students should be quite familiar with error correction by now. You could give them a gist question to read quickly for, such as *Where did origami originate?* (no one really knows) before they do the task.

3 1 If anyone in the class does origami, you could get them to make something for the class and/or show the class how to make a simple model.

Language development 2 p.121

You could start with a quick competition to see who can think of the most words formed from the stem *able* (unable (adj.), ability (n.), disability (n.), ably (adv.), enable (v.), disable (v.), disabled (adj.), inability (n.)).

LOOK Check that students understand the distinction made in B between general ability (i.e. long-term) and specific ability (i.e. on one occasion). Also, in D, you could compare *I don't know how to* (lack of knowledge) with *I can't* (maybe lack of knowledge, maybe physical, maybe just temporary). Highlight the grammar of the alternative verbs: *know how +to* + infinitive, *manage + to* + infinitive, *succeed + in + -ing*)

1a For each question, get students to think about the time – past, present or future – and whether it is general or specific. Highlight some of the vocabulary in the exercise, e.g. *get away* = have a break, *over* = finished.

1b First get students to look at the sentences on their own, then discuss them with a partner.

3

Background

Meccano is a construction toy with pieces of metal in various sizes and shapes with holes in. They can be joined together with nuts and bolts to create cars, cranes, etc.
Robot Wars is a TV programme in which remote control 'robot' warriors compete against each other. A robot wins by immobilising its opponent or pushing it out of the ring. The robots are constructed and controlled by teams made up of friends or family members.

▶ **Student's Resource Book page 78**

Language development 3 p.122

1a You could begin by brainstorming, with books closed, any phrasal verbs with *get* that students know. Note them on the board and tick them off as they come up in the exercises. If students aren't sure, get them to work it out, based on what time people start and finish work.

1c The *True/False* statements are intended as be a guide to what the phrasal verbs mean. Elicit meanings or get students to check in a dictionary.

1d One way to conduct the discussion would be to divide the class and get each to think of the disadvantages from one aspect (the worker, the employer, the government, etc.). Some possible disadvantages: workers may not get paid so much; productivity might be reduced; prices of products might go up if companies cannot get their workers to do extra hours unpaid.

2 This exercise introduces more phrasal verbs with *get*. Again, if the meaning is not clear, students should check in a dictionary.

3b Encourage students to expand their answers and develop them into a conversation.

Use of English 2 p.123

1 The aim here is to focus on some of the more lexical areas frequently tested in Paper 3 Part 3.

2a Identifying the type of language being tested in each case will help students towards the right answer.

2c Encourage students to add the preposition combinations, fixed phrases and phrasal verbs to their vocabulary books.

▶ **Module 8 Test: How much do you remember?**
TRB page 186

▶ **Exam practice 4: Papers 1 and 3 CB pages 124–126; Papers 2 and 4 TRB pages 187–188**

Unit 16 Key

Listening p.118
1b see Coursebook page 219.

2a 1 bad influence; 2 stamp collecting/collecting stamps; 3 image; 4 football; 5 video; 6 (old) coins/(old) matchboxes (in any order);
7 (playing) board games; 8 indoor climbing;
9 dancing; 10 gardening

Speaking p.119
2a 1 Anna: home town, house, job, free time activities
Giorgio: home town, family, career, music.
2 They both create a good first impression. They are positive, they speak accurately and fluently, they extend their answers and they listen carefully.

2b colleagues (Anna) (*… the other people who work with me …*)
eclectic (Giorgio) (*… how do you say it, I like many different kinds of music.*)

Use of English 1 p.120
1 Possible answers:
1
Similarities:
They are all quiet activities.
You can do them all on your own at home.
Differences:
Painting and model making are more creative.
You mainly use your hands for painting and model making.
You use your head for reading and doing puzzles.

2 1 to – *can* + infinitive without *to*
2 of – *appreciate* something – no preposition
3 many – *know how to* = ability (*how many* = quantity)
4 ✓
5 no – double negative

6 it – *it* is a pronoun and so should replace something, but here it does not replace anything
7 being – simple past passive for a single completed action, not a past activity in progress
8 ✓
9 for – *for* + noun, *to* + infinitive
10 ✓
11 a – *what is* + adjective *is* … (no article)
12 can – *were able to* = past ability
13 ✓
14 lots – quantifier *lots* not possible with a number
15 ✓

Language development 2 p.121
LOOK A: models that can be made
you can decide on a model
B: the Japanese were able to turn it into a decorative art
D: you know how to copy other people's designs

1a 1 can – present, general
2 was able to – past, specific
3 could/have been able to – past, general ability/past up to now, general ability
4 couldn't – past, general negative
5 have managed to – present perfect, achieved something difficult
6 will be able to/can – both forms possible to talk about the future
7 managed to – past, specific and hard, surprising
8 managed to find/succeeded in finding – past, specific, difficult

2 1 won't be able to finish – future
2 manage to stay – you stay slim (present) and it must be difficult
3 succeeded in passing – very difficult
4 can't come – future, known now
5 couldn't win – past/specific
6 don't know how to play – present/we haven't learnt
7 wasn't able to stay – past/specific
8 couldn't swim – past/general

3 1 can use – present, general
2 could put together/was able to put together – past, general
3 succeeded in building/managed to build – past, specific
4 could/was able to reach – past, general
5 couldn't fly/wasn't able to fly – past, general
6 managed to get – past, specific, difficult
7 succeeded in winning – past, specific, very difficult
8 can/will be able to carry on – future, general

Language development 3 p.122

1b The average working week was reduced to 35 hours.

1c 1 T – get someone down – make someone feel unhappy
2 F – get together – meet each other
3 T – get away with – avoid trouble, not get caught
4 F – get across – succeed in communicating
5 T – get round – find a way to deal with or avoid
6 F – get off to a good start – start successfully
7 T – get off – finish and leave (work or school/college)
8 F – get away – leave (for a holiday)
9 T – get back to – return to
get down to – start doing

2 1 A; 2 A; 3 B; 4 B; 5 A; 6 B

3a 1 get together; 2 get away, get off to; 3 get (you) down; 4 got away with; 5 get on; 6 get by; 7 get round; 8 get off

Use of English 2 p.123

1 1 a fixed phrase
2 a phrasal verb
3 a preposition following a noun

2a 1 phrasal verb
2 fixed phrase
3 phrasal verb
4 fixed phrase
5 phrasal verb
6 fixed phrase
7 verb + preposition
8 phrasal verb
9 noun + preposition
10 phrasal verb

2b 1 get away with cheating
2 in case we want to
3 got down to some
4 's/is unlikely (that) there will
5 had to be called off
6 pay any attention to what
7 didn't succeed in persuading
8 was let off with/got off with
9 had trouble (in) writing
10 get the truth out of

Teacher's Resource Book
Module 8 Test: How much do you remember? p. 186

1 1 B; 2 A; 3 C; 4 B; 5 D

2 1 with; 2 be; 3 other; 4 in; 5 that

3 1 The boy *denied having broken* the window.
2 We *might be able to do* it for you tomorrow.
3 She said that *she had to go that* afternoon.
4 I *know how to put* petrol in my car but that's about it.
5 She asked me *if I would lend her* some money.

4 1 it; 2 ✓; 3 the; 4 much; 5 you

5 1 impression; 2 unfortunately; 3 employers; 4 recommendation; 5 incredibly

Coursebook
Exam practice 4 p.124

Paper 1 Reading
Part 2 1 C; 2 D; 3 B; 4 C; 5 A; 6 A; 7 C

Paper 3 Use of English
Part 2 1 would/will; 2 were; 3 to; 4 when 5 out; 6 for; 7 has; 8 be; 9 every; 10 from; 11 the; 12 been; 13 how; 14 better; 15 it

Part 3 1 Amy really *need not/needn't have gone to* the doctor's.
2 Lucy's *father told her to stop* running.
3 Our football team *got off to a good* start this season.
4 Harry didn't get a place at university so he *must have been very* upset.
5 Holly *had better not go to* work because she doesn't look well.
6 Emily *denied hitting the man's* car deliberately.
7 The man *managed to escape by diving* into the river.
8 I had dinner with Luke at home last night, so he *can't have been staying* in London.
9 Alexis warned *Tom not to touch the* hot plate.
10 Teachers *ought not to use* bad language in front of their classes.

Part 4 1 and; 2 at; 3 ✓; 4 have; 5 for; 6 hand; 7 be; 8 to; 9 a; 10 ✓; 11 the; 12 much; 13 ✓; 14 what; 15 who

Teacher's Resource Book
Exam practice 4 pp. 187–188

Paper 2 Writing

1 Style:
Formal or neutral.
Content:
Talk about the importance of fashion and clothes in today's world.
Write in favour of the statement, perhaps talking about the aspects of character which might be reflected in clothes (e.g. shyness, liveliness, etc.).
Write against the statement, perhaps saying that many people have little choice (e.g. uniforms, social pressures, fashion, etc.).
Say whether you agree with the statement and give your reasons.

2 Style:
Neutral.
Content:
Give the name of the programme and what type of programme it is.
Say what you like about the programme.
Say why the programme will be good for people of all ages.

3 Style:
Neutral.
Content:
Describe the text message; why was it mysterious?
Say what happened as a result of the message.
Say how the mystery was resolved.

4 Style:
Informal.
Content:
Say which course you chose and why.
Mention things you do on the course and how you feel about it.
Talk about the other people on the course – have you made friends? What are they like/what do you do with them/why not?

Paper 4 Listening
Part 4 1 C; 2 B; 3 B; 4 A; 5 C; 6 A; 7 A

Module 9 The consumer society

Units 17 and 18 are linked by the theme of 'The consumer society' with topics including starting a business, TV quiz shows, money, complaining, shopping and supermarkets, a professional shopper, customer relations and banking.

Lead-in p.127

With books closed, write *consume* on the board and ask what it means (to use time, energy, goods). Elicit related words and write them on the board: *consumer* (buys and uses products and services), *consumer goods* (that people buy to use in the home), *consumer society* (in which buying products and services is important), *consumerism* (the idea that buying and selling products is the most important activity for a person or society), *consumption* (the amount that is used).

Get students to look at the photos and ask how each one represents consumerism. Then discuss the lead-in questions.

Unit 17 Making money

To set the ball rolling ...

Ask students if they prefer making, spending or saving money, and why.

Reading p.128

• •
Photocopiable activity

Photocopiable activity 17A (p. 159) could be used as an introduction to the unit, to pre-teach vocabulary or as a follow-up to the reading. It is a board game in which students make or lose money at each turn.
• •

1a You may first need to pre-teach *funding* (money given or lent for a specific purpose).

1b First check that students understand the title, i.e. *How to get rich **when you are** young.* Encourage students to guess, rather than look for 'right' answers at this stage.

2 When students have finished, ask how many they guessed correctly, and if they are surprised about any of the people.

3a/b Set a time limit of 15–20 minutes. Students could compare and justify their answers in pairs before you go through it with them.

4 This is best done in groups of three or four students. Pre-teach *innovative* – using clever new ideas and methods.

5 All these expressions come from the reading text. You could point them out, or get students to find them (1: lines 7–8; 2: line 20; 3: line 33; 4: lines 87; 5: line 97).

▶ **Student's Resource Book page 82**

Language development 1 p.130

1a With books closed, ask students if they like TV quiz shows and if so, whether they have a favourite. Then they go on to discuss the question in the book, giving reasons.

1c/d Students should look carefully at the context. They may know these conditionals as zero, first, second and third.

2a This practises the first three structures in 1c and shows how the choice of structure is a personal one, depending on how likely the speaker thinks the *if* part is to happen. Do the first question together as an example. Compare two people who have entered a competition and believe they have a good chance of winning – *If you win a lot of money, what will you spend it on?* – with two people who have not entered a competition and are just imagining – *If you won a lot of money, what would you spend it on?*

2b Encourage students to expand their answers, giving reasons.

3 This practises the last structure in 1c (unreal past). Do the first one as an example, asking concept questions: *Did he set his alarm?* (no) *Did he oversleep?* (yes)

4a Students discuss this together before you check with the whole class. Explain that in example 1, 'now' is not just 'at this moment'. It is a present situation that was also true at the time of the past action.

4b If necessary, give two more examples about yourself: 1 *I trained to be a teacher (in the past). I am a teacher (now). So ... If I hadn't trained to be a teacher (in the past), I wouldn't be a teacher (now). 2 I am your teacher (now). I marked your homework last week. So ... If I weren't your teacher (now), I wouldn't have marked your homework last week.*

5 Tell students to think about the time in each part of the sentences – is it in the past or now/generally true? Do the first one with them and ask concept questions to check: *Do I earn more money?* (no) *Did I go for a job interview?* (yes).

6 Point out that these conjunctions are alternatives to *if* in certain situations. You could get students to look at the Grammar reference before or while they do the exercise.

7 This is a final practice of the different conditionals and conjunctions. Ask students to justify their answers.

▶ **Student's Resource Book page 84**

••
Photocopiable activity
Photocopiable activity 17B (p. 160) would work well here. It is a card game in which students ask and answer questions about real, imaginary and past situations.
••

Writing p.132

1 First ask students what kinds of things people complain about, e.g. poor service, unreliable transport, poor quality goods, unfulfilled promises. These ideas could act as prompts when students discuss the questions.

3 Get students to answer the basic planning questions: who, what, why and how.

4a The opening phrase *I am writing to* + verb is always useful. Point out the different construction following each verb.

4b Elicit why the phrases in A are inappropriate (they are too informal).

4c First ask students if the phrases are in the order they would be used in a letter (they are). Let students complete as many as they think necessary for their letter.

┌───┐
LANGUAGE SPOT: spelling

a Tell students that as a general principle, if they are unsure of the spelling of a word they should avoid using it in the exam. But knowing which words they commonly misspell will help when they check their work.

b These are all common students' spelling errors. Students could check answers with each other, in a dictionary, or in the Spelling section of the Writing reference on page 216.

c You could follow this up in a later lesson with a short dictation of the words, either in isolation, in these sentences, or in different sentences.
└───┘

▶ **Student's Resource Book page 85**

Unit 17 Key

Reading p.128

2 A Organising parties
B Sports coaching
C Making and selling jewellery
D Internet and technical support
E Writing

3a/b 1 B (*At first, the administrative side was a struggle …*) (ll. 39–40)
2 E (*… working for myself, rather than … working for someone else.*) (ll. 114–116)
3 D (*Tom mainly reinvests his money*) (ll. 93–94)
4 E (*she does not splash her money around.*) (ll. 119–120)
(3 and 4 – answers could be in any order)
5 B (*I got a grant and an office from Mencap, a charity …*) (ll. 37–38)
6 D (*But what really keeps me going is the thought of all the cash I'm making.*) (ll. 84–86)
7 E (*… my business aim. This was to write 'popular' books that would earn me a fortune.*) (ll. 112–114)
(6 and 7 – answers could be in any order)
8 C (*I have decided not to go to university because I don't feel it has anything more to offer me.*) (ll. 62–65)
9 B (*Everyone warned me … I took no notice of them.*) (ll. 28–34)
10 C (*Work excites me. I can work all day every day without a break and never get bored.*) (ll. 65–67)
11 A (*It all began when Justin … was turned away for being too young.*) (ll. 1–7)
12 E (*After she'd written her first book … a publisher … advised her to tear it up and start again.*) (ll. 101–107)
(11 and 12 – answers could be in any order)
13 A (*What gets me excited is coming up with new ideas.*) (ll. 19–21)
14 D (*I think it's worth giving up a few nights out …*) (ll. 86–87)
15 B (*… the company I set up won an award …*) (ll. 42–43)

5 1 on – keep on at someone = talk to someone a lot (possibly annoying)
2 up – come up with = think of
3 of – take (no) notice of = (not) observe/follow/listen to
4 up – give up = stop doing/using
5 up – keep up with = maintain knowledge/understanding of

Language development 1 p.130

1b **1** By answering fifteen questions correctly.
2 He got the last question wrong.

1c/d Always true: *If they answer fifteen questions correctly, they win a million pounds. If + present + present*
Possible and likely: *if you watch it now, you'll soon learn the rules. If + present + future*
Unlikely or imaginary: *if I went on the show, I wouldn't win a million! If + past + would*
Unreal in the past: *If he had got it right, he would have won a million. If + past perfect + would have*

2a Possible answers:
1 If you won a lot of money, what would you spend it on?
2 If a classmate asks you to lend him/her a small amount of money, what will you do?/If a classmate asked you to lend him/her a small amount of money, what would you do?
3 If a classmate asked you to lend him/her a large amount of money, what would you do?
4 What do you do if you need change for the phone?/What would you do if you needed change for the phone?
5 If you found a lot of money, what would you do?
6 What would you do if you lost a/your wallet or purse?
7 What would you say if you received a present you didn't like?/What do you say if you receive a present you don't like?
8 What will you buy if you go shopping at the weekend?/What would you buy if you went shopping at the weekend?

3 **1** If James had remembered to set his alarm, he wouldn't have overslept.
2 If he hadn't been late for work, he wouldn't have got the sack.
3 If he had been able to find another job, he wouldn't have started his own business.
4 The business wouldn't have been a great success if it hadn't been such a good idea.
5 If James hadn't worked very hard he wouldn't have become a millionaire.
6 So, he wouldn't have become very rich if he had set his alarm!

4a **1** now, last week
2 last week, now
4b A 2
B 1

5 **1** earned (present – imaginary); wouldn't have gone (unreal in the past)
2 would be able (present – imaginary); hadn't spent (unreal in the past)

3 had invested (unreal in the past); would be (present – imaginary)
4 were (present – unlikely); would have reduced (unreal in the past)
5 would be (present – imaginary); hadn't missed (unreal in the past)
6 couldn't have bought (unreal in the past); weren't (present – imaginary)

6 **1** provided that
2 Unless
3 Even if
4 as long as

7 **1** Unless; hurry up 'll miss/'re going to miss (possible and likely)
2 give; as long as/if/provided that; spend (always true)
3 If; hadn't lent; would have (mixed – unreal in the past/present imaginary)
4 'll come; as long as/if/provided that; pay (possible and likely)
5 If; didn't run; would have (present imaginary)
6 Even if; had asked; wouldn't have been (unreal in the past)
7 If; didn't work; wouldn't feel (present imaginary)
8 If; were/was; wouldn't have spent (mixed – present imaginary/unreal in the past)

Writing p.132

1 **2** Possible answers:
a shopping website: overcharging; goods not delivered or delivered late; wrong, faulty or damaged goods delivered.
an airline: delays, cancellations, overbooking, lost luggage, poor service.
a hotel: overbooking, facilities missing or not working; room dirty, noisy, too hot, too cold.

2 **Who**: The Director of a lottery game company
What: Complaining about misleading advertisements
Why: see the four handwritten notes on the advert
How: Formal letter of complaint

3 **1** B – introduction
2 D – first two complaints
3 C – further two complaints
4 A – conclusion

4a **1** complain + about
2 object + to
3 express + noun
4 draw your attention + to
4b **1** d; **2** b; **3** a; **4** c
4d **1** d; **2** c; **3** e; **4** b; **5** a

4e Example answers:

I hope that in future you will be more honest in your advertising.

If I do not get a satisfactory reply, I will have no alternative but to contact the media.

Please can you assure me that you will look into these matters.

5 Sample answer:

Dear Sir or Madam

I am writing to complain about the advertisement for your new game. Having just played the game, I realise that the advertisement is misleading.

My first complaint is that you say there are big cash prizes and everyone can win. In fact, there is only one big prize so the chance of winning is quite small. You also say that the game is cheap, but I think £5 for a game is expensive.

Furthermore you claim that the game is easy to play whereas it is actually quite complicated. Even worse, you say that all the money goes to charity but, to my horror, I have discovered that half the money goes on administration.

I am very disappointed. I hope that in future you will tell the truth in your advertisements. If I do not get a satisfactory reply I will report your company to the government.

Yours faithfully

Carlos Cazador

Carlos Cazador

(155 words)

LANGUAGE SPOT: spelling

b surprised, separate, recommend, unnecessary, committee, immediately, sincerely, receive, beginning, embarrassed, advertisement, writing

c 1 tried, loose
2 cassette, foreign, pronunciation
3 principal, their, accommodation, address
4 Unfortunately, medicine, effect
5 definitely, until, developed, responsible

Unit 18 Spending money

Unit 18 continues the theme of 'The consumer society' with the topics of shopping, money and banks.

To set the ball rolling ...

With books closed, put a line on the board with a smiley face at one end and a miserable one at the other and ask students where they would put shopping on it and why. They could draw their own line and put different types of shopping on it as you call them out, e.g. shopping for clothes, shoes, presents; shopping in traditional shops, in supermarkets, by mail order; Sunday shopping, late night shopping. Then they explain their line to a partner.

Speaking p.134

1a At this stage students should just give a general answer rather than describe the photos in detail.

1b You could suggest that students think of two advantages and two disadvantages of each type of shopping.

2 Remind students that if they don't know a word they should try to explain or define it. Use the photos to elicit objects/ideas to explain, using the expressions in the box, e.g.: *It's a kind of staircase that moves.*
It's like a huge supermarket but with many different shops.
It's something you need/can use when you haven't got any cash.
It's when you buy things using the Internet.

3a/b Before students begin, elicit ways of checking the examiner's instructions and asking the examiner to repeat them. Point out the list of expressions for this in the Functions reference on page 224. Remind 'candidates' to try and keep going for the full minute, and remind 'examiners' to time 'candidates' and stop them after approximately one minute.

3c Encourage students to discuss their own and others' performance, and not to be too critical!

Listening p.135

1 Remind students of the type of task, and elicit the strategy. Do question 1 together as an example. Key words: What, advertised, television, computer, board game.

2 You could let students compare and discuss their answers, both between the first and second playing of each extract, and after the second playing of each one.

3 First check that students understand the words in italics. They are all in the listening extracts, which you could use to help with context and examples. Then students discuss the questions in groups, followed by class feedback.

▶ **Student's Resource Book page 87**

Use of English 1 p.136

1 You could introduce some useful vocabulary here, such as *shop around, wait for the sales, buy in bulk, get good value for money*.

2a Encourage students to recall as much of the strategy as possible before checking on page 30.

2c Give students a time limit for the task, e.g. 12–15 minutes. Don't discuss questions 1, 4, 7, 9, 13 in too much detail, as they are dealt with in Language development 2 on page 137.

3 Possible further question: *Would you use the Good Deal Directory? Why/Why not?*

Language development 2 p.137

LOOK With books closed, write some sentences on the board and get students to decide if they are correct or not, e.g.: *The results are good. The news are good. Most people likes shopping. Everyone likes shopping. The majority of people likes shopping. A few people likes shopping. Clothes are interesting. Politics are interesting. Some of the customers were complaining. More than one of the customers were complaining. There were many cafes. There were more than one cafe. A couple of people was waiting. Two weeks are not long to wait.* Students can then check which are right and which are wrong by referring to the box. Concord here means agreement in terms of number (i.e. plural verb form with plural subject).

1 Students refer back to the table to check their answers.

2 Tell students that they don't need to choose a tense – all the verbs are in the present simple – but they need to decide which verbs are singular and which verbs are plural. Students could have further practice by conducting a class/group survey into shopping habits/opinions and then reporting back the summary using quantity expressions such as *a large number, the majority of, hardly anyone*. It would be better if each student asked a different question.

3 Although this is a relatively basic grammar point, it can still cause difficulty for some students at FCE and is often tested. Students should use the information in the box to help them with the exercise.

4 This exercise gives further practice of empty subject *it* in questions 1 and 2, and both *it* and *there* in question 3 (*There are …/It's a good idea to …*).

▶ **Student's Resource Book page 88**

Use of English 2 p.138

1 You could give your own answers to the questions as an example. Get students to give examples in their discussion. They could also name their favourite and least favourite shops.

2 Elicit the strategy for word formation before students do the task.

3 Possible further questions: *Is it worth paying more to go shopping where the staff are knowledgeable and helpful? Do you prefer supermarkets with a good choice and poor service, or small specialist shops with less choice but good personal service?*

4

Background
On 1 January 2002, euro notes and coins were introduced into twelve European Union countries: Austria, Belgium, Finland, France, Germany, Greece, Ireland, Italy, Luxembourg, The Netherlands, Portugal and Spain. The remaining three members of the European Union at that time – Denmark, Sweden and the UK – did not adopt the currency then, and continued to use their own national currencies.

5 Students should give reasons for their answers.

Language development 3 p.139

1 Students complete the quiz in pairs and/or with a dictionary. You could get them to do one section at a time, so that you can check answers and focus on differences in meaning within each section.

2 Discuss how this money vocabulary could be recorded and what other things students will need to note, such as prepositions, which verb to use with the word, whether it is formal or informal.

3 First make sure students understand all the statements. Students could discuss them in small groups. They should give reasons for their answers, and examples from their own experience if possible.

4a Students looked at forming adjectives in Unit 4 and forming nouns in Unit 10. Here they look at forming verbs. Draw students' attention to the change in stress in the two-syllable 'no change' noun/verb: *'record* (noun) */re'cord* (verb).

4b Check students' pronunciation of *blood* /blʌd/, *bleed* /bliːd/, *choice* /tʃɔɪs/, *choose* /tʃuːz/, 'import (n), im'port (v).

• •
Photocopiable activity

Photocopiable activity 18 (p. 161) could be used here. It is a split crossword which practises money vocabulary and word formation.
• •

▶ **Module 9 Review CB page 140**

▶ **Module 9 Test: How much do you remember? TRB page 189**

Unit 18 Key

Speaking p.134

1a A shopping centre or shopping mall; Internet shopping

Listening p.135

1 1 What advertised? television, computer, board game
2 What doing? faulty goods, money back, goods delivered
3 What doing? blaming, advice, suggestion
4 Where? bus station, shop, library
5 What complaining about? attitude of staff, accuracy of information, arrangements changed
6 Who talking to? hotel receptionist, conference organiser, secretary
7 Which sector? service successful, travel, health, entertainment.
8 What about? e-commerce disadvantages, new idea, research into success.

2 1 C (*Throw the dice and race round the board.*) (Based on the hit TV programme)
2 B (*I can't give you a cash refund unless the product is faulty in some way.*)
3 B (*I just wondered if you had any ideas on what I could do.*)
4 A – ... mark the bus routes on it ... that uniformed man over there ... (Why don't we go to a shop ... take it next door to the library ...)
5 B – Had I known that there was a midday flight ... she said there was only one flight a day ...
6 C – ... it's probably on my desk somewhere – can you have a look? (Or perhaps you could check with the organisers)
7 A – The idea has caught on fastest when there's something to be picked up, especially holiday documents.
8 B – ... fortunately, it looks like a solution is at hand.

Use of English 1 p.136

2b 1 The Good Deal Directory tells you where to buy ~~expensive, high quality~~ *the cheapest* items.
2 Noelle Walsh ~~doesn't visit many~~ *visits a lot of* shops, ~~but~~ *and* she knows where to buy the cheapest things.
3 She hates shopping at weekends, ~~but she always does~~ and her family ~~do~~*does the family* shopping.
4 Noelle believes her work makes a ~~big~~ *small* difference to people.

2c 1 is – singular subject *An amazing total*
2 No one/Nobody – subject, negative (*not even*)
3 as – comparative *as many as*
4 is – singular subject *One of her main strengths*
5 much – before uncountable *effort*
6 else – *anyone else* = all other people
7 have – plural subject *The majority of people*
8 who/and – relative clause or adding information
9 do/does – singular or plural verb with *family*
10 to – according + *to*
11 about – (preposition) before *-ing*
12 there – *there are* = they exist
13 is – singular subject *no one*
14 what/things/information
15 some/many/other – plural determiner

Language development 2 p.137

1 1 Everyone think*s* it's a good idea. (singular)
2 The majority of us agree*s*. (plural)
3 ✓
4 Neither of them know*s* what to buy. (singular)
5 These jeans ~~doesn't~~ *don't* fit. (plural)
6 ✓
7 Ten euros ~~aren't~~ *isn't* very ~~many~~ *much*. (singular)
8 ✓
9 ~~This~~ *These* scissors ~~doesn't~~ *don't* cut very well. (plural)
10 The United States ~~have~~ *has* a new President. (singular)

2 1 sells (singular); 2 feel (plural); 3 causes (singular); 4 wants (singular); 5 seem (plural); 6 is (singular); 7 say (plural); 8 admit (plural); 9 confess (plural); 10 wants (singular)

3 1 There are – existence, plural
2 it is – empty subject
3 there is – existence, singular
4 It is – It = the set meal
5 there are – existence, plural
6 it is – empty subject

Use of English 2 p.138

2 **1** smallest – *the* + superlative + noun
2 exhausted – *be* + adjective
3 impatient – *become* + adjective
4 extremely – adverb + adjective
5 stressful – *find something* + adjective
6 friendliness – noun and noun
7 satisfaction – noun
8 flight – *take a flight*
9 sight – noun (*catch sight of* something)
10 amazement – to someone's *amazement*

4 **1** currency – noun
2 nearest – *the* + superlative + noun
3 designer – adjective
4 failure – noun
5 confusion – noun
6 unbelievable – adjective
7 Naturally – adverb
8 winnings – plural noun
9 receipts – noun
10 investigation – noun

Language development 3 p.139

1 **1**
1 B; **2** B, B; **3** A; **4** B, B; **5** A; **6** B; **7** A
2
1 from – borrow something from somebody
2 to – *lend something to somebody*
3 to – owe something to
4 on – spend money on something
5 on – waste money on something
6 into – pay money into an account
7 into – change money into something else
8 from – make money from something
9 on – have money on you
10 to – leave money to someone
3a
1 (buy, get) the tickets, (make) a big profit, (ask for, get, receive) a discount
2 (pay, repay) a refund, (get, obtain, receive) a receipt, (get, take out, pay back) a loan
3b
1 discount; **2** profit; **3** refund; **4** interest; **5** bill; **6** a good salary; **7** fine; **8** loan

4b No change: dry, import, calm, name
Internal change: choose, bleed
Prefix: endanger
Suffix: criticise, strengthen, fatten, widen, lengthen

5a **1** criticise; **2** import; **3** endanger; **4** choose
5b widen; modernise; calm; strengthen

Coursebook
Module 9 Review p. 140

1 1e; 2c; 3a; 4f; 5d; 6b

2 **1** it wasn't/weren't so expensive.
2 had known the computer had a fault; wouldn't have
3 hadn't spent so much money on a holiday; would have enough to buy
4 you pay; won't reserve the bike.

3a **1** do; it; **2** has; **3** everyone; hardly; **4** There; it; **5** It; there; **6** is

4 **1** A hard up   B from
2 A discount   B pay
3 A interest   B profit
4 A into   B on
5 A loan   B pay

5 **1** modernise; **2** lengthen; **3** enlarge; **4** strengthen; **5** endanger; **6** widen; **7** clean; **8** choose; **9** criticise; **10** calm

Teacher's Resource Book
Module 9 Test: How much do you remember? p.189

1 **1** A; **2** C; **3** B; **4** D; **5** C

2 **1** on; **2** with; **3** has; **4** there; **5** by

3 **1** We must avoid anything that *puts the children in danger/at risk* at school.
2 'I'll come at six unless *I hear from you* before then,' Keith said.
3 I'll cook for you *as long as you're* not a vegetarian.
4 If Judith's car *had started, she would/might have* been on time.
5 *Hardly anyone seems* to be polite these days.

4 **1** a; **2** the; **3** not; **4** ✓; **5** in

5 **1** creativity; **2** financial; **3** innovative; **4** advertising; **5** bleed

Module 10 Out and about

Units 19 and 20 are linked by the theme of 'Out and about'. They include topics such as travelling, holidays and hotels, public transport, going out for the evening, going clubbing and Internet cafés.

Lead-in p.141

With books closed, write *Out and about* on the board and ask students what they understand by it. It can mean both 'not home and busy' and 'away travelling'. Then get students to identify the means of transport in the photos and discuss the questions.

Background

The American novelist and travel writer Paul Theroux (b.1941) taught English in Malawi, Uganda, and Singapore for eight years before settling down in England and beginning a career as a writer. His novels include *The Family Arsenal* (1976), about a group of terrorists in the London slums, and *The Mosquito Coast* (1982), about an American inventor who attempts to create an ideal community in the Honduran jungle. He first achieved commercial success with a best-selling travel book, *The Great Railway Bazaar* (1975), describing his four-month train journey through Asia. Other travel books include *The Old Patagonian Express* (1979) and *The Happy Isles of Oceania* (1992).

Unit 19 Travel

To set the ball rolling ...

With books closed, get students to write the word *travel* vertically on a piece of paper and then write words across it that they associate with the topic. Demonstrate on the board how to start, e.g.

> T I M E
>
> T R A I N S
>
> A
>
> A D V E N T U R E
>
> E
>
> P L A N E

In pairs, students then explain the significance of their words, e.g. *time – you need a lot of time to really enjoy foreign travel; trains – my favourite way to travel.*

....
Photocopiable activity
Photocopiable activity 19A (p. 162) can be used at the start of the unit or as a follow-up after the reading text. It is a light-hearted questionnaire to discover what students consider important when travelling.
....

Reading p.142

1 First check that students understand the title: *go = travel; go for it* is an expression of encouragement.

2 Tell students to read quickly, and to ignore the gaps in the text.

3 Elicit the task strategy. Look at the example together: *an idea* in the heading matches a *new kind of cheap extended holiday* in the text and *is established* in the heading matches *became a must* in the text.

4 If you didn't use Photocopiable activity 19A at the start of the unit, you could use it before this discussion to help pair like-minded students. Allow time for the discussion.

▶ **Student's Resource Book page 92**

Language development 1 p.144

1a With books closed, brainstorm places to stay while on holiday. Check/Pre-teach *self-catering* – when you arrange your own food and cooking, e.g. staying in an apartment rather than a hotel. Then get students to discuss the question, giving reasons for their preferences.

1b First students use the picture to identify the type of text (a holiday brochure). Explain that the answers to question 1 are in the text, whereas they will have to think of the answers to question 2 themselves.

1c Elicit the form of the passive (*be* + past participle) and why it is used. Point out that not stating who has done something has the effect of making the statements more impersonal and so more formal. Highlight the use of *by* when we want to say who has done something: *They were built … by a team of highly skilled workers …*

1d As you check students' answers, elicit why each tense is used. Explain that the passive is not a tense, and the rules of tense use are exactly the same as for active verb forms.

2a This exercise focuses mainly on forming the passive. Get students to work together identifying the correct tense in each case and establishing how to form that tense correctly.

2b Here, students have to think about both form and use, changing the sentences from active to passive to make them more formal. You could do the first one or two together as an example.

3 Start by writing two sentences on the board: *Fleming discovered penicillin. It is an important medicine.* Ask students to rewrite the sentences, emphasising the medicine: *Penicillin is an important medicine. It was discovered by Fleming.* Students then read the information in the box and answer the questions.

5 Point out that reports are often more formal and less personal, and consequently often contain a lot of passive forms.

> **Photocopiable activity**
>
> Photocopiable activity 19B (pp. 163–164) would work well here. Students write travel-related news stories based on notes.

▶ **Student's Resource Book page 94**

Writing p.146

1 With books closed, brainstorm forms of public transport and ask students which they use most. Then discuss the questions in the book.

2 This exercise focuses on task completion, style and effect on the reader, which all contribute towards the general impression mark in the exam.

3a Elicit the two problems mentioned in the task, poor public transport and the small car park. Get students to look at the examples under these two headings, and ask them what other things they could say, e.g. Public transport: expensive, slow, unreliable. Car park: too small, difficult to park. Then get them to think about possible solutions for each problem, e.g. improve public transport and make it cheaper, encourage students to use public transport rather than drive, make the car park bigger.

3b Remind students to use all seven pieces of advice, and that some go with more than one paragraph.

3c Once students have matched their notes to the paragraphs, point out that they now have the basic structure of the report. Explain that they don't have to come up with a lot of complex ideas in the exam, just clear, well-organised points.

3d Encourage students to discuss the strengths and weaknesses of each of the three subject headings before deciding on the best.

3e Explain that the paragraph headings should be short but should say clearly what the paragraph is about.

4a Elicit what a topic sentence is – one sentence which summarises the main point.

4b Point out that the expressions in the table are useful for any report, but obviously it is important to use them correctly.

4c Do this with the whole class as a quick check.

5/6 Give students 20 minutes to write their report and 10 minutes to check it. They could check each other's reports, to see if they find it easier to spot other people's mistakes than their own. This may help them to look at their own writing more objectively.

> **LANGUAGE SPOT: passive report structures**
>
> This focuses on different ways of using passive structures to add emphasis when writing a report. Point out that *be supposed to* here means *be generally said to*.

▶ **Student's Resource Book page 95**

Unit 19 Key

Reading p.142
2 1 students and working people (ll. 11–15; ll. 31–34)
2 get new gear, book flights and copy documents (ll. 45–62)
3 they work, especially on farms (ll. 67–80)

3 1 E (*exotic long-distance destinations have now become commonplace.*)
2 H (*A growing number of working people are opting to clear their desks and head for the open road.*)
3 A (*All trips will require a certain amount of money up front …*)
4 G (*… in case they were lost or stolen. … if you lose any vital documents …*)
5 D (*… this will only be possible if you apply for work permits and other documents.*)
6 B (*The days are often long and the work physically demanding.*)
7 F (*… arriving at the right moment could be essential.*)

Language development 1 p.144
1b 1 They stay cool, they are well decorated, there is a buffet breakfast, a barbecue area is being constructed.

2 You have to share facilities with others, the shops are not very close, breakfast is not included, and it could get too hot.

1c are grouped; were built; have been designed; have all been decorated; is served; is now being constructed; will soon be completed; can be found

The passive is used here because what has been done/is done is considered more important than who did it or does it.

1d 1 are grouped
2 is served
3 have been designed
4 have all been decorated
5 were built
6 is now being constructed
7 will soon be completed
8 can be found

2a 1 are situated (present simple)
2 were redecorated (past simple)
3 can be supplied (modal)
4 will be installed/will have been installed (future simple/future perfect)
5 are being built (present continuous)
6 has been given (present perfect)
7 must be checked (modal)
8 will be asked (future simple)

2b 1 Our facilities are always being improved.
2 All our flats have been modernised in the last two years.
3 Our kitchens have been equipped to the highest standards.
4 The beds will be made daily (by maids).
5 The holiday village can be found two kilometres outside the town.
6 A full programme of sports activities is offered (by the village).
7 Very few complaints were received last year.
8 Extra people may be accommodated (by guests) on the sofa beds.
9 The maximum number of people allowed in each caravan is indicated by/in our brochure.
10 Keys must be returned to reception on departure.

3 A by – to specify the agent (the one that does the action)
B 1 – person + passive verb + thing + *by* + agent
C thought (doesn't matter who thinks), said (doesn't matter who says)
D to cheer, to empty

4 1 it was composed by Schubert.
2 were given two tickets
3 was seen to steal/seen stealing
4 is believed the Prime Minister will call
5 's/has been promised a place
6 it was discovered by Fleming.
7 is thought to have hidden

8 'll/will be made to pay

5 Suggested answer:
The town has changed a lot in the last 30 years. *All the old factories have been pulled down and replaced with* hi-tech science parks. *It's felt to be* unfortunate that *one of the older schools was also demolished, as children will have to be sent* by bus to the next town. *It is said that a brand new school will be built* in the town in the next few years when *extra funding is provided by the Government. That will be appreciated by the newer residents in particular.*

Writing p.146

2 1 two parts – analysis of problem and recommendations
2 formal and impersonal – it's for the Principal of the college and represents the recommendations of the committee
3 good organisation, clear analysis, logical recommendations

3b **Paragraph 1**: b, d, g
Paragraph 2: a, e, g
Paragraph 3: a, e, g
Paragraph 4: c, f

3d C is the best. It is formal, short and clear, telling the reader immediately what the report is about.
A is too general, mentioning transport but not students.
B is slightly informal, and doesn't mention students.

3e **Suggested answers:**
Paragraph 1 – Background/Introduction
Paragraph 2 – Public transport
Paragraph 3 – Parking/The car park/Cars
Paragraph 4 – Possible solutions/Recommendations

4a **Example answers:**
Paragraph 1: … the problems students have with transport to and from college.
Paragraph 2: … has become less reliable and more expensive.
Paragraph 3: … more students have cars.
Paragraph 4: … the college writes to the bus company.

4b The aim of this report is to …2
In order to prepare this report …6
It appears that the majority of students …7
The only problem is that …9
Most students seem…1
Not surprisingly, …3
According to …5
All things considered, …4
We have no hesitation in recommending …8

4c passive
more
less

5 Sample answer:

Student transport

Background

The aim of this report is to analyse difficulties that students face travelling to college. In order to prepare this report we interviewed a number of students at the college.

Public transport

The following points were mentioned.
• It appears that the majority of students find the bus service unreliable and expensive.
• Most students seem unwilling to walk or cycle to college.

Parking

Not surprisingly, most students prefer to drive to college. However:
• The car park is too small.
• It quickly becomes full.
• It is expected that more students will want to use cars in future.

Possible solutions

Two possible solutions were suggested:
1 Improve the bus service. It would be used more if there were a better service.
2 Extend the car park. Most students would rather have parking space than a sports field.
All things considered, we recommend asking the bus company to improve the service.

(155 words)

LANGUAGE SPOT: passive report structures

a **1** that the Principal is in favour.
2 that about 50 students will attend.
3 that many of the students (have) had difficulties getting a visa.
4 that some of them (have) left early.

b **1** is supposed to reduce the number of private cars.
2 is supposed to be becoming easier and cheaper.
3 are supposed to travel further on holiday these days.
4 is supposed to broaden the mind.

Unit 20 Going out

Unit 20 continues the theme of 'Out and about' with the topics of leisure facilities, cinema, dancing, clubbing and Internet cafés.

To set the ball rolling ...

With books closed, get students to talk briefly in groups about their last good night out, e.g. where they went, who with, what they did.

Listening p.148

1a First elicit the names of the activities in the pictures – bowling, clubbing, eating out. Remind students to give reasons for their answers in the discussion.

1b These questions encourage students to read the rubric and task carefully, and to use them to predict before they listen, e.g. *discussing facilities* – the focus is on buildings or organised activities; *small town* – if the town is small, are the facilities likely to be good or poor?

2a Point out that students have to listen for views expressed by either speaker. Read the task strategy together. They may hear views which sound similar to those in the statements, but which are the opposite. This is why students should first decide if the statements are negative or positive (e.g. 2 is positive, 4 is negative).

3 Check some of the vocabulary (e.g. *food hall, multiplex, multi-media*) before the discussion. Remind students to give reasons for their choices.

Speaking p.149

1a This is a review of the format of Paper 5 Part 2. Students discuss the statements in pairs before you go through them with the class.

1b First remind students of the meaning of *speculate* (to talk about possibilities) and *paraphrase* (to explain a word in another way).

1c Keep this fairly brief to avoid creating endless lists!

2a/b Divide the class into groups of three. If your class is not equally divisible by three, have one or two groups of four with an extra assessor. Give the examiners time to check the instructions and prepare the material.

2c Encourage everyone in each group to discuss the candidates' performance.

▶ **Student's Resource Book page 97**

Language development 2 p.150

1 With books closed, you could act the part of a bored teenager, eliciting the person's age and what he/she is thinking, before students open their books and discuss the questions in pairs. Explain that in question 1 they need to think of the time referred to rather than the verb forms. Verb forms are focused on in question 2.

When going through the answers together, remind students that, as with conditionals, the wish contrasts with reality, so we use a positive verb form for a negative situation and vice versa, e.g. *I wish there was something…* (but there isn't); *I wish we hadn't moved here* (but we have).

We often use *wish + would* to describe situations over which we have no control and where we see no likelihood of change. If necessary give more examples, eliciting the wish each time:

He smokes – I wish he didn't smoke (but he does).

He can't give up – I wish he could give up (but he can't).

He won't give up – I wish he would give up (but I don't think he will).

I smoke – I wish I ~~would~~ could give up (but I can't).

2 Students will need to think about the time reference and a possible change/regret in each situation.

3 This exercise provides personalised practice of the grammar. Look at the first two questions and get students to think about what would fit. In question 1 *be* could be a main verb, e.g. *I wish I were rich*, or an auxiliary verb, e.g. *I wish I were lying on the beach now, I wish I were going to the party tonight*. Similarly, in question 2 *have* could be a main verb, e.g. *I wish I had more time*, or an auxiliary verb, e.g. *I wish I had done my homework*.

4 The aim here is to check students' understanding of the grammar in the box. First go through the examples in the box with students, pointing out how these expressions use the tense shift backwards to express hypothetical situations.

5 Remind students to think carefully about the time (present or past) and the choice of verb form (present or past).

6 Encourage students to write true sentence endings where the sentences are true for them.

⋯⋯⋯⋯⋯⋯⋯⋯⋯⋯⋯⋯⋯⋯⋯⋯⋯⋯⋯⋯
Photocopiable activity

Photocopiable activity 20 (pp. 165–166) would work well here. It gives further practice of *wish/if only*, as students imagine what people are thinking in various leisure situations.
⋯⋯⋯⋯⋯⋯⋯⋯⋯⋯⋯⋯⋯⋯⋯⋯⋯⋯⋯⋯

▶ **Student's Resource Book page 98**

Use of English 1 p.151

Begin with a quick review of Paper 3 Part 3, asking: *How many questions are there?* (ten) *How many marks per question?* (two) *How long should you spend on part 3?* (20 minutes) *How many words should you write?* (between two and five)

1 This question aims to revise some of the task strategy. Get students to discuss it in pairs first.

2a Point out that students shouldn't rush key word transformations. They should work slowly and carefully to avoid unnecessary mistakes.

2b Remind students that in the exam the ten questions test a wide range of structures and vocabulary.

Use of English 2 p.152

1 First check that students know *clubbing* – going to nightclubs. You could also ask whether students themselves go clubbing.

2a This is a review of the task strategy for Paper 3 Part 2.

2b Remind students that skimming the text will not only give them a general understanding; it will also help them identify the style, time frame and possible source of the text, all of which could help them complete the task.

2d Verb + preposition combinations are commonly tested in Paper 3 Part 2.

3 Get students to reread the text before the discussion. If they disagree with question 2, ask them to suggest better places to meet people.

Language development 3 p.153

1 With books closed, read out the examples in the box, stopping as you get to each preposition and eliciting it. Then get students to look at the examples before doing the exercise.

2 As you go through the answers, check that students understand the different meanings of the verbs.

3 First ask students if they use Internet cafés and if they have heard of *easyEverything*.

Background

Stelios Haji-Ioannou also started *easyJet*, the European low-cost airline whose flights can be booked on the Internet, *easyCar*, the Internet-only car hire company, and the *easyMoney* credit card. His philosophy is to provide a cheap, uncomplicated service for customers.

4 Verbs of perception can be easily confused because two different verbs in English may translate as just one verb in the students' language. Encourage students to use dictionaries, and when you go through the answers check that they understand the differences:

look – a deliberate action; *see* – not deliberate; *watch* – a deliberate action over a period, e.g. a football match or TV programme

gaze – look at something for a long time because it is so interesting; *peer* – try to look at something but with difficulty; *stare* – look in a very fixed way for some time

hear – could be deliberate or not; *listen* – a deliberate action

feel – could be deliberate or not; *touch* – a deliberate action

▶ **Module 10 Test: How much do you remember? TRB page 190**

▶ **Exam practice 5: Papers 1 and 3 CB pages 154–156; Papers 2 and 4 TRB pages 191–192**

Unit 20 Key

Listening p.148
2a 1 YES (*unemployment is actually rising*)
2 NO (*it's not so handy when it comes to using its leisure facilities*)
3 NO (*… the centre caters more for people our age. But for older teenagers, … there's not much for them really*)
4 YES (*bus services to other towns round here aren't exactly the most frequent or reliable*)
5 YES (*In my day, we used to have a disco here as well as two cinemas*)
6 NO (*the solution is to build a new shopping complex on the outskirts of town*)
7 YES (*when large numbers of kids get together like this, you're just inviting trouble*)

4 **1** travel; **2** becoming; **3** meet; **4** becoming

Speaking p.149
1a 1 True
2 True – first, compare and contrast, then give an opinion or reaction.
3 False – you should deal with them together, comparing and contrasting.
4 True
5 False – it's an individual long turn!
6 True – only about 20 seconds.
1b 1 a; **2** d; **3** b; **4** g; **5** c; **6** e; **7** f

Language development 2 p.150
1 **1** the present: 1, 3
the past: 2
the future: 4, 5
2 the present: *wish* + past; *if only* + *could*
the past: *wish* + past perfect
the future: *wish* + *would*; *if only* + *would*
3 *if only* is stronger/more emphatic

2 **Suggested answers:**
1 I wish/If only I hadn't dyed my hair bright red. I wish/If only I'd kept it blonde.
2 I wish/If only he didn't/wouldn't borrow my car. I wish/If only he would stop borrowing my car.
3 I wish/If only I could afford a taxi. I wish/If only I didn't have to take the bus.
4 I wish/If only I hadn't come to see this. I wish/If only I were/was watching something else.
5 I wish/If only he/she would hurry up. I wish/If only he/she didn't/wouldn't take so long in the bathroom. I wish I could get into the bathroom.

4 1 A – … but you should.

2 B – … but it's too late to change the situation now.

3 B – … someone else did.

5 1 learnt – present time, past verb form

2 was/were – present time, past verb form

3 phoned – present time, past verb form

4 had met – past time, past perfect verb form/has met – present time (i.e. he knows her) present perfect verb form

5 had bought – past time, past perfect verb form

Use of English 1 p.151

1 1 Leave it and come back to it when you've done the ones you can do.

2 Make sure you write something for every question. Don't leave any gaps.

2a 1 wish I'd gone – past; negative reality, positive verb form

2 'd rather you phoned – present situation, past verb form

3 were you, I'd book – unreal conditional (I'm not you)

4 isn't (very) far from

5 wish I had told – past; negative reality, positive verb form. Note *truth* in answer opposite to *lying* in question

6 was hardly anyone/anybody at/in

7 (just) in time to see/for

8 is supposed to be

9 (high/about) time you stopped going

10 you mind not using – *mind* + *(not)* + *-ing*

2b 1 1, 2, 5, 9

2 I'd rather you = Would you mind if you didn't use = not using

Use of English 2 p.152

2a 1 after – you should read the text right through first for a general understanding

2 short – if you get stuck with one answer, you will have less time for the rest of the task and the rest of Paper 3

3 one – if you put more than one word, it will be marked as incorrect, even if one of the words is correct. If you can't decide between two possible answers, you should always choose one rather than put both.

2b 1 They have become much more popular with young people.

2 Because they are a good way to meet new people, as we become more wary of our neighbours and people around us.

2c 1 to – *change from one thing to another*

2 of – *hear + of + something*

3 is – singular verb

4 were – past passive, plural (Superclubs)

5 up – phrasal verb *set up* = to start

6 to/with – *compare + to/with*

7 which/that – defining relative clause

8 about – *think + about* something

9 it – = what he does

10 on – *depend + on*

11 be – passive; modal + infinitive (*must be linked*)

12 in – *believe + in*

13 our – possessive adjective, agrees with *we*

14 from – *differ + from*

15 even – *even if* = *in spite of the fact*

HELP Question 3 **singular**

Question 11 **passive**

2d Questions 1, 2, 8, 10, 12, 14

Language development 3 p.153

1 1 to; 2 in; 3 from; 4 to; 5 with; 6 from

2 1 for (something); on (= served in a restaurant)

2 about (= consider); of (= invent)

3 to (= forced to accept); from (= leave a job)

4 as (= what he is); for (= why he is famous)

5 of (= didn't know); from (= received a call or letter)

6 to; for (apologise to someone for something)

3 1 in – believe in someone/something

2 in – succeed in + *-ing*

3 with – communicate with someone

4 with – agree with someone/something

5 with – crowded with

6 to/with – compared to/with someone/something

7 for – pay for something

8 about – complain about something

9 of/about – think of/about something/someone

10 on – depend on someone/something

11 on – concentrate on something

12 to – look forward to + *-ing*

4 1 a – looked (deliberate); seen (not deliberate)

b – watch

2 a – stare (long fixed look)

b – peered (difficult to see)

c – gazed (interesting)

3 a – listened; (deliberate), hear (not deliberate)

b – listen (deliberate)

c – hear (deliberate)

4 a – feel (not deliberate); touch/touching (deliberate)

b – Feel (deliberate)

c – touch (deliberate)

Teacher's Resource Book
Module 10 Test: How much do you remember? p.190

1 1 C; 2 D; 3 A; 4 B; 5 C

2 1 It; 2 about/high; 3 had; 4 of; 5 in

3 1 You will *be shown some pictures by* the examiner.
2 People *asking/who ask questions make Nigel* nervous.
3 I *would rather you had told* me earlier.
4 Someone *is thought to have been* rescued.
5 If *only my girlfriend would call* me tonight.

4 1 in; 2 ✓; 3 one; 4 ✓; 5 is

5 1 clubbing; 2 unexpected; 3 unrealistic;
4 hesitation; 5 resigned

Coursebook
Exam practice 5 p.154

Paper 1 Reading
Part 1 1 F; 2 B; 3 D; 4 A; 5 G; 6 C

Paper 3 Use of English
Part 1 1 C; 2 B; 3 D; 4 B; 5 A; 6 D; 7 B; 8 A;
9 A; 10 D; 11 D; 12 B; 13 C; 14 A; 15 C

Part 3 1 I *was taught everything I know* about music by my music teacher.
2 I really think it's *time you got/time for you to get* a new car.
3 I *was made to wear* a uniform when I was at school.
4 The new computer program *is said to be* very easy to use.
5 If I *had not/hadn't had your* help, I couldn't have cooked such a big meal.
6 Mary *wished she hadn't (had not) sold* her house.
7 I *'d (would) rather you didn't* get up if you are ill.
8 There's *hardly anyone/anybody who thinks* he is a good president.
9 If Sarah had got the job, *she would be living* in London now.
10 They *didn't/wouldn't let us* go into the club.

Part 4 1 myself; 2 and; 3 was; 4 ✓; 5 been;
6 have; 7 ✓; 8 the; 9 these; 10 seem; 11 kind;
12 is; 13 any; 14 so; 15 ✓

Part 5 1 irritating; 2 unpleasant; 3 failure;
4 highly; 5 widen; 6 restrictions; 7 realistic;
8 incredible; 9 refusal; 10 naturally

Teacher's Resource Book
Exam practice 5 pp.191–192

Paper 2 Writing
1 Style:
Formal report style with headings.
Content:
Talk about the economic situation in your country.
Say how easy it is for young people to get jobs – give examples.
Describe the career opportunities open to young people, mentioning qualifications needed, recruitment methods, competition for jobs, etc.

2 Style:
Formal.
Content:
Talk about public transport in your country.
Discuss the advantages and disadvantages of using public transport. Mention other reasons why people use public transport.
Say whether you agree with the statement and why (not).

3 Style:
Informal.
Content:
Tell your friend about the weather and give an idea of what activities you could do, and what to bring for them.
Tell your friend the sort of gift that would be appropriate, or you may prefer to say that it is not necessary to bring a gift.

4 Style:
Neutral/semi-formal.
Content:
Talk about the advantages and disadvantages of zoos in general – mention education, endangered species, conditions in which animals live, etc.
Talk about whether zoos should be in city centres, mentioning any alternatives.
Give your opinion and your reasons.

Paper 4 Listening
Part 3 1 E; 2 C; 3 B; 4 F; 5 A

Module 11 Well-being

Units 21 and 22 are linked by the theme of 'Well-being' and include topics such as happiness, relaxation, avoiding stress, health and spas.

To set the ball rolling ...

With books closed, ask students what they do to make themselves feel good. You could give one or two examples of your own to get them started, e.g. go for a walk, have a big cream cake …!

Lead-in p.157

Elicit the meaning of the module title, 'Well-being' – a feeling of being healthy, happy and comfortable with life. Then get students to discuss the questions.

If you think it necessary, you could do an example of your own for the second and third questions. Choose three of the photos yourself and start explaining how they are related. Then give a brief example of what is most important to your well-being.

Unit 21 Happiness

::: Photocopiable activity

Photocopiable activity 21A (p. 167) can be used at the start of the unit to introduce the topic, or as a follow-up to the reading exercise. It is a group discussion on factors in life that affect happiness.
:::

Reading p.158

1a Students discuss the questions in pairs. It's usually said that an optimist will describe the glass as half full, whereas a pessimist will describe it as half empty.

1b If students have already done the photocopiable activity, their answers from it would be relevant to question 1. Question 2 implies that when you know the secrets, it is possible to control happiness.

3 Remind students of the strategy. This task is designed to focus on text structure, so students need to recognise the links between removed sentences and those that precede and follow them.

3a Give students a couple of minutes to do this, then go through it with them.

3b Pre-teach *temperament* – the emotional part of someone's character, how likely they are to be happy, angry, etc. Give students about 15 minutes

to do the task. Then get them to compare which parts of the text helped them.

5a Point out that these words are all used in the text, either as nouns or adjectives.

5b Give one or two examples of your own to get students started. Let them choose which emotions they want to discuss, as they may not want to discuss unhappy experiences.

▶ **Student's Resource Book page 102**

Language development 1 p.160

With books closed, put the class into groups and see which group is first to come up with a specified number of ways to relax (e.g. five to ten).

1a Give prompts if necessary to encourage ideas: How do you relax at the weekend?/at home?/with friends?/after a long day at work?

1b Ask students if they recognise the woman in the photo. If so, what do they know about her? If not, what can they guess about her? E.g. She's an athlete, she's British, she competed in Barcelona in 1992, she probably won. Get them to try and guess the answers to the questions, then read to check their guesses.

Background

Sally Gunnell is the only woman to have held the European, Commonwealth, World and Olympic 400 metre hurdles titles at the same time. Her greatest victory came at the 1992 Olympic Games in Barcelona when, as captain of the British women's team, she won a gold medal for the hurdles (in a world record time) and a bronze for the relay. She now commentates on athletics for BBC TV.

1c Begin by eliciting the function of the expressions in italics in the text extracts: Ask *What do the expressions explain?* – the reason for something. Tell students that the six expressions operate in three different ways grammatically. Then look at sentence 1 as an example, and ask *What did Mark do?* – he left his job. *Why?* – because it was stressful. When you check students' answers, make sure they understand that *as, because, since* all operate in the same way, and so do *because of, due to, owing to*. But these last three can operate in two different ways, i.e. followed by a noun or *the fact that* + subject + verb.

2a Point out that there are three possible answers for each sentence, and students should list them all.

2b Here students need to think about the form that follows each expression.

3a Go through the box with students before they do the exercise. Point out that *in order that* and *so that* operate in the same way as each other, as do *in order to*, *so as* to and *to*.

3b Remind students to look at what follows the options in italics, as that tells them what fits grammatically.

4 As you go through the box, draw students' attention to *despite* (one word) and *in spite of* (three words) which are often confused.

5 This exercise practises all three types of clause: reason, purpose, contrast. Tell students that for each one they should identify the type of clause first, then think of a logical ending.

> **Photocopiable activity**
>
> Photocopiable activity 21B (p. 168) could be used here. It is a card game in which students use the three types of clause to make sentences about themselves from prompts.

▶ **Student's Resource Book page 103**

Writing p.162

1 With books closed, write *polite* on the board. Ask students what it means for them and ask them to give examples of polite behaviour before going on to discuss the question in the book.

2 This question encourages students to read the task carefully and helps them focus on the attitude of the writer. Ask them to say where in the task they found the answer.

3a/b Students should be well practised in planning letters now, so you could either give them ten minutes to start planning the letter then compare what they have done, or elicit what they need to do to plan the letter and then let them do it.

4 First get students to read the letter and comment on content, organisation and style. Elicit that the content and organisation are good, but the style is too informal.

6 Encourage students to produce a checklist from memory first, then check the Writing reference on page 206 if necessary.

> **LANGUAGE SPOT:** attitude phrases
>
> This practises a number of phrases that can be used in this type of writing. As you check answers, make sure they know the meaning of the alternatives.

▶ **Student's Resource Book page 105**

Unit 21 Key

Reading p.158
2 1 Having the right genes, contentment, giving and receiving affection, mental and physical activity.
2 Yes

3a Such people: the cheerful type of person … as a result. (ll. 2–6)
health*ier*: happ*ier* (l. 6)
happiness: But what is the secret of happiness? (l. 7)

3b 1 D (*someone else with more than you, so trying to compete* links to *try to keep up with others* in lines 13–14; *frustration and anxiety* links to *dissatisfied* in line 15).
2 F (*this is just a temporary state* links to *a level we always return to, whatever happens to us in life* in lines 21–22)
3 C (*The latter* links to *their character* in line 27. This contrasts with *The former* line 27)
4 B (*Such people* links to *happy people* in line 31; *They* also … in line 32)
5 A (*being part of a social group* links to *tend to relate to other people* in line 36; *a community or a club* links to *sports teams, choirs, political parties* in lines 38–39.
6 E (*To avoid this* links to *stress results in unhappiness* in line 47; *it is important to pick a sport* links to *But mental activity can be just as important* in line 48)
7 G (*The key* links to *to recognise happiness* in lines 49–50; *learning to celebrate them* links to *One way of doing this* … in line 51)

5a 1 contented; 2 satisfied; 3 frustrated;
4 anxious; 5 depressed; 6 stressed; 7 miserable

Language development 1 p.160
1b 1 They lead busy lifestyles: they have to travel to compete and do promotional work.
2 She does yoga.
1c 1 as, because, since
2 because of, due to, owing to
3 because of, due to, owing to

2a 1 as, because, since
2 because of, due to, owing to
3 because of, due to, owing to
4 as, because, since
5 Because of, Due to, Owing to
6 because of, due to, owing to
2b 1 a was snowing
b the snow/the fact that it was snowing
c the snow/the fact that it was snowing
2 a was raining
b the rain/the fact that it was raining
c it was raining

3a **1** in order to, so as to, to (+ verb)
2 in order that, so that (+ subject + verb)
3 in case (+ subject + verb)
3b **1** to (+ verb)
2 in case (precaution)
3 so that (+ subject + verb)
4 in order to (+ verb)
5 In order that (+ subject + verb)
6 in case (precaution)
7 so as to (+ verb)
8 so as not to (+ verb)

4 **1** e – contrasting but not contradicting
2 c – *despite* + *-ing*
3 h – *although* + subject + verb (very active + not feeling well)
4 a – *even though* + subject + verb (not getting better + appetite returned)
5 g – *despite* + noun
6 b – *in spite of the fact that* + subject + verb
7 f – contrasting but not contradicting
8 d – *in spite of* + *-ing*

5 **Example answers:**
1 … I have tried many times/ways. Contrast.
2 … the noise of the cats outside. Reason.
3 … he knows where to pick me up. Purpose.
4 … the glorious spring sunshine … . Contrast.
5 … find out whether they open on Sundays. Purpose.
6 … the fact that we reminded him to take it. Contrast.

Writing p.162

2 An older person (When we were young …)

3a **1** Most young people are polite.
2 People have to hurry.
3 Children have always been noisy.
4 I've seen old people get aggressive and impatient.
Points 1 and 2, or 2 and 3, or 3 and 4, could be grouped together.
3b **Example answer:**
Paragraph 1: Introduction; reason for writing
Paragraph 2: Points 1 and 2
Paragraph 3: Points 3 and 4
Paragraph 4: Conclusion

4 I am writing in response to the letter about young people's behaviour in last week's *Courier*. I have to disagree with the points the writer makes.
Firstly, it is simply not true that all young people are noisy and aggressive. In my experience, most young people are polite. And whereas it may be true that they are sometimes in a hurry, we have to accept that they need to get to work, school or college.
I also disagree with the generalisations about younger and older people. Children are no noisier today than they used to be. They have always had to play. And do you really think older people are   more polite? I have seen older people being aggressive and impatient in shops, for example.
In conclusion, while we should all have consideration for others, I think we should all try to be more patient and tolerant of each other. We were all young once!

5 **Sample answer:**

Dear Sir or Madam,

I am writing in response to the letter in today's newspaper about young people and the way they behave. Some of the points the writer makes are simply ridiculous.

Firstly, I cannot accept that young people today are noisier than in the past. Young children like to play and have always been like that. Secondly, young people nowadays have busy lives so it is not surprising that they are in a hurry to get to work.

It is also unfair to say that all young people are aggressive. Most are polite and friendly. It might be true that a few young people get aggressive at times because of the pressures they face but the same is true for older people. I have seen them lose their patience and temper in shops.

In conclusion, we should all realise that we were all children once. It is the world that has changed, not young people.

Yours faithfully,

(159 words)

LANGUAGE SPOT: attitude phrases

1 To be honest – What I really think is (As far as I know = I may be wrong but I think it's true that …)
2 Presumably – I imagine (Actually = I know this is true)
3 As a matter of fact – polite contradiction (Clearly = it is evident that; Naturally = Of course)
4 Certainly – I accept the fact that (Frankly = What I really think is; Surely = I don't know but I imagine it must be true that)
5 Generally speaking – as a generalisation (Roughly speaking = approximately; Strictly speaking = If we follow the rules exactly)
6 Admittedly – I admit this is true (In my opinion = I think; At least = As a minimum)
7 As far as I'm concerned – In my opinion (According to me = The facts as I have explained them are that)
8 Personally – in my opinion (Truly = honestly; In person = Not by letter or on the phone)

Unit 22 Health and fitness

Unit 22 continues the theme of 'Well-being' with the topics of health and spas.

To set the ball rolling ...

Ask students how healthy they think their lifestyle is on a scale of 1–10. Ask them how healthy they were a few years ago, and how healthy they think they will be in ten years' time. What has changed, and what do they think will change?

> **Photocopiable activity**
>
> Photocopiable activity 22 (p. 169) is designed to be a lead-in to the unit and to pre-teach some of the vocabulary. It is a light-hearted questionnaire in which students find out how healthy they are.

Listening p.164

1a Don't discuss the pictures at this stage as they are part of the Speaking task on p.165. Students should answer the statements about themselves then compare answers in pairs/groups, giving examples.

1b The listening task is similar to that already practised in Units 6 and 16, but here the format is slightly different as students have to complete a set of notes. Remind them that, before they listen, they should try and guess what type of information might be missing, based on the context. E.g. number 1 is something positive, that helps our capacity to breathe, and it must be food or drink because it is under that heading.

3 Possible further questions:

Do you think the government should tell people how to live healthily? Is it right for a government to tax cigarettes and alcohol so much that it puts people off smoking or drinking?

4 If students need help with ideas, tell them to look again at the information in 2a and come up with ideas that are the opposite of those expressed in the programme.

Speaking p.165

1a First ask students what they remember about Paper 5 Parts 3 and 4.

2 Divide the class into suitable groups. The examiners need to read the rubric on page 223. If possible it would be good to record one or more of the groups doing the task now that they are more familiar with the format and the exam is getting closer, then play it back when students do the analysis at the end.

3a To ensure that all students have an opportunity to practise, you could tell students to change roles after every two questions.

3b Students should discuss their own performance and that of other members of their group. Encourage them to be constructive.

▶ **Student's Resource Book page 107**

Language development 2 p.166

1a With books closed, you could introduce the language point by writing on the board:

My problem is that I eat ..... much chocolate. It's ..... nice that I can't say 'No'. I don't have ..... will power to stop and it's costing me ..... a lot of money!

Ask students to think of the missing words (*too, so, enough, such*) and explain why. Then get them to look at the grammar box.

2 Students should do this in pairs, then refer back to the grammar boxes to check.

3 *As* and *like* are commonly confused by some students, partly because they both translate as the same word in some languages, and partly because of the number of different uses of *like*. Go through the examples in the box with students.

4 When students have completed the exercise, ask them if they would like to do something similar.

▶ **Student's Resource Book page 108**

Use of English 1 p.167

1a Get students to discuss the question in pairs first.

1b Students discuss this in pairs. As you go through it with them, elicit what has led to the mistakes in each case, and how they could have been avoided by following the instructions and checking carefully.

2a Students should be able to do this without too much help from the task strategy.

Use of English 2 p.168

1 You could also ask students if they have ever visited any Roman baths and if so, where.

2a Remind students that they should always read the text for a general understanding first, and tell them that these questions are to help focus their reading.

Discussion

Ask if students have ever visited a 'day spa', and if so what it was like. Similar things that people do today might include going to a sauna or going to stay on a 'health farm'.

Language development 3 p.169

Look The topic of health is rich in idiomatic expressions and phrasal verbs. You could begin with books closed, brainstorming any words or phrases students already know. Then get them to do the task in the box.

1a First get students to read the text and answer the question: *Is George now more or less healthy than he used to be?* (more). Then you could do the first one with them as an example, so that they can see how the exercise works. Draw students' attention to the image of the human body as a piece of electrical equipment, with expressions like *run-down, recharge his batteries, still going strong.*

1b Point out that some of the expressions (e.g. *recharge your batteries*) appear in two places in the dictionary.

2a If students are unsure of any of the phrasal verbs, get them to use dictionaries.

3 This is an opportunity for personalised discussion. When students have finished, you could get them to think of more questions to ask each other, using both the idiomatic expressions and phrasal verbs on the page.

▶ **Module 11 Review CB page 170**

▶ **Module 11 Test: How much do you remember? TRB page 193**

Unit 22 Key

Listening p.164

1b **1** A type of food or drink
2 A problem in a part of the body (e.g. lung) or a function of the body (e.g. breathing).
3 After *your*, again it must be a part of the body or a function.
4 After *treating* it must be a type of health problem.
5 The question is followed by *a night* so it must be an amount (e.g. 2 hours) or a frequency (e.g. twice). 'Enough' suggests a minimum amount required.
6 This could be a type of exercise (e.g. jogging), a place (e.g. in the gym), an amount (e.g. an hour), or a frequency (e.g. daily).
7 After *up to* this must be a number.
8, 9, 10 These must be either a positive activity (e.g. join a club), or stopping a negative activity (e.g. give up smoking).

2a/b **1** apples (*… if we eat around seven apples a week.*)
2 heart (*… it also contains a chemical that actually helps in the prevention of heart disease.*)
3 teeth (*… there is something in tea which does help to prevent holes forming in teeth.*)
4 headache(s) (*… coffee is a better and faster painkiller than a lot of stuff you buy at the chemist's to get rid of headaches.*)
5 six/6 hours (*There's no need to sleep longer than six hours …*)
6 outdoor(s) (*… this is better for you if it takes place outdoors.*)
7 80/eighty (*… we use as many as 80 muscles when we have a really good laugh.*)
8 dog walking/walking a dog (*… it's a good way to make friends – everybody stops to speak to you.*)
9 (take/taking up) a hobby/hobbies (*… they tend to devote more time to that hobby and this keeps their brain active.*)
10 get(ting) married/marriage (*… getting married is one way of increasing your likelihood of a long life.*)

Speaking p.165

1a **1** F – they speak **together** for about 3 minutes.
2 T – e.g. discuss and choose
3 F – it should be an open discussion – expressing your ideas is more important than agreeing.
4 T – probably between three and six questions will be asked, between the two candidates.
5 F – you should develop your answers beyond a simple 'yes' or 'no'.

6 T – the examiner may ask you to respond to something the other candidate says.

1b 1 b; 2 c; 3 d; 4 a; 5 f; 6 e

Language development 2 p.166

1a 1 so – e.g. so difficult, so many, so fast
2 such – e.g. such bad behaviour
3 such, a – e.g. such a nice person

1b 1 noun (e.g. enough sleep); adjective (e.g. warm enough)
2 1c (e.g. too much, too expensive), 2a (e.g. very tired), 3b (e.g. enough sleep)

2 1 Jim's ~~so~~ **such** a good doctor that everybody likes him.
2 My yoga class is great; I'm always ~~too~~ **so** relaxed afterwards.
3 Paul has bought such ~~an~~ expensive fitness equipment! (uncountable)
4 The food is too spicy for me to eat ~~it~~.
5 ~~The~~ **There aren't enough** vegetables in your diet ~~aren't enough~~.
6 I'm ~~very~~ **too** tired to go jogging now.
7 John is so unfit ~~so~~ **(that)** he can't even run for a bus.
8 ~~The~~ **There isn't enough** money ~~isn't enough~~ for us to buy a drink.
9 You should be pleased with yourself for losing so **much** weight.
10 I'm not **old** enough ~~old for~~ to join that club.

3 1 like/such as – example
2 as – role/function
3 like – *sound + like*
4 like/such as – example
5 as if/as though – *look* + clause
6 As – *as* + clause

4 1 as; 2 like; 3 As; 4 like/such as; 5 like; 6 as

Use of English 1 p.167

1b 1 meeting my wife for **the** – article needed before *first time*
2 in case ~~of~~ the tickets are – *in case of* + noun, *in case* + subject + verb. Six words in the answer should have alerted the candidate to the mistake.
3 was ~~too~~ **so** tired (that) he – *too tired* + to, *so tired* + that
4 as long as we ~~will~~ arrive – *as long as* + present when referring to future time. Again, six words in the answer should have alerted the candidate to the mistake.

2a 1 explained to us what the
2 I get back to you
3 wasn't fit enough to
4 put you up
5 weren't/wasn't so hot we
6 such a delicious
7 Judy whether she wanted
8 isn't enough room/space
9 n't/not like Tom to be
10 is not so/as popular as

Use of English 2 p.168

2a 1 a place with a mineral water spring
2 because they were cheap
3 read, talk, play sports, eat, have a massage

2b 1 C – cure a disease
2 D – living a long time ago
3 A – contain, have enough space for
4 B – fees can be high or low
5 D – time sequence
6 C – collocation
7 B – have a massage
8 A – get pleasure from doing something
9 A – cool down = phrasal verb
10 B – go for a swim (take a swim)
11 D – a bite to eat = a small meal (idiomatic)
12 C – event
13 A – as people call them
14 B – have time on your hands = not busy (idiomatic)
15 D – don't mind doing something

Language development 3 p.169
LOOK 2

1a 1 middle-aged; 2 unwell; 3 didn't want to eat; 4 was very tired; 5 get back his energy; 6 was physically fit; 7 healthy; 8 fit and healthy

2a 1 put on; 2 cut down on; cut out; 3 picked up; 4 give up; 5 coming down with; get over; 6 take up

2b 1 6; 2 4; 3 5; 4 2; 5 1; 6 3

Coursebook
Module 11 Review p. 170

1   1 A satisfied   B depressed
     2 A anxious   B stressed
     3 A contented   B miserable

2a   **(Example answers)**
     1 Even though I don't laugh very much, I'm a very cheerful person.
     2 I drink a lot of water so as not to get dehydrated.
     3 In spite of getting plenty of sleep, I always seem to feel tired.
     4 I warm up before doing any serious exercise, in case I pull a muscle.
     5 Despite the many warnings about eating animal fat, I still eat too much of it.
     6 I often listen to classical music in order to relax.
     7 I try to avoid shopping as much as possible, since it makes me stressed.
     8 Owing to my busy work schedule, I don't have much time to take holidays.
     9 I like a big breakfast so that I don't feel hungry in the middle of the morning.
     10 I like to go swimming to keep fit, whereas a lot of my friends prefer to go jogging.

3a   1 such a nice young man
     2 considerate enough
     3 as
     4 Just like
     5 like / such as
     6 far too loud
     7 so much noise
     8 seems like / seems as if
     9 so friendly
     10 as if

4   1 B; 2 A; 3 D; 4 C; 5 B; 6 A; 7 D

5   1 going down with; 2 picked up; 3 get over;
     4 put on; 5 cut down on; 6 take up

Teacher's Resource Book
Module 11 Test: How much do you remember? p. 193

1   1 B; 2 D; 3 A; 4 C; 5 A

2   1 in; 2 off; 3 as; 4 case; 5 such

3   1 These shoes *are not big enough* for my feet.
     2 There were *such a lot of* people there that Ellen couldn't get in.
     3 It looks *as if England are going* to win, they're 3–0 up.
     4 Neil can't get a job *in spite of the fact* that he did well at university.
     5 It *smells as if lunch is* ready.

4   1 in; 2 ✓; 3 of; 4 ✓; 5 my

5   1 anxiety; 2 financially; 3 laughter; 4 healthier;
     5 frustration

Module 12 Getting your message across

Units 23 and 24 are linked by the theme of 'Getting your message across' and include an extract from a novel, ways of connecting ideas, describing fiction, an interview with a journalist, advertising, celebrities, paparazzi and spin doctors (political advisers).

To set the ball rolling ...

With books closed, brainstorm ways in which we receive information, e.g. newspapers, magazines, TV, radio, books, post, Internet, email, phone, text messages, advertising, direct mail.

Lead-in p.171

Get students to look at the photos and discuss the questions. Tell them that there are no hard and fast answers for the second question. You might want to discuss one or two of the photos with the class to give them an idea of the kind of answers required. Some examples of what students might come up with (clockwise from top left): Email: to communicate about work and with friends; Mobile phone text messaging: to communicate in short chatty messages with friends, sometimes with business colleagues; Books: to inform, entertain or educate; Magazines: mainly to entertain, also sometimes to inform; Billboard advertising: to advertise and promote products; TV: to inform and entertain; Newspapers: to inform.

Unit 23 Bookworm

To set the ball rolling ...

With books closed, you could put students into groups and see how many types of book they can think of in three minutes, or get them to draw two columns, headed 'fiction' and 'non-fiction', and write the genres into the correct column as you dictate them. Then they discuss the differences between the genres.

Fiction	Non-fiction
novels, horror, romance, short stories, crime/thrillers, contemporary, historical, best seller, blockbuster, science fiction, adventure, classics, children's, etc.	biography, autobiography, history, science, travel, sport, art, food and drink, health, philosophy, home and garden, etc.

Reading p.172

1a Get students to expand with examples of what they have read recently or what they are reading at the moment.

1b Elicit as much as you can from the book cover and ask if anyone has read the book or seen the film.

Background

Patricia Highsmith's crime thriller *The Talented Mr Ripley* was first published in 1956. The 1999 film was directed by Anthony Minghella. Tom Ripley, a poor young man, pretends that he is a friend of Dickie Greenleaf, a spoilt millionaire playboy who has gone to Italy. Dickie's father offers Tom money to convince Dickie to come home but when the errand fails, Tom kills Dickie and assumes his privileged life.

2 When students have skimmed the article (give them a minute or two), discuss the question.

3a/b Give students 15 minutes to complete the task and then let them compare their answers, explaining where they found them in the text.

4a Put students into groups to discuss the questions. Ask anyone that has read the book or seen the film not to 'give the game away' until others have expressed their opinions. Encourage students to give reasons for their answers.

4b In the set book option of Paper 2, students may be asked a question like this. You could specify a number of advantages and disadvantages that each group should think of, or you could get some groups to think of just the advantages and others to think of just the disadvantages and then compare.

Remind students to give examples of films that they have seen which were based on books.

5a If appropriate, use the list of words to revise pronunciation of stress patterns, e.g. comparing *enthusi'astic* with *en'thusiasm*.

5b If students can't guess the meanings, get them to look up the words in a dictionary, deciding each time what the key word is.

Photocopiable activity

Photocopiable activity 23A (p. 170) could be used here. Students write a story based on a series of pictures.

▶ Student's Resource Book pages 112–113

Language development 1 p.174

1b This revises different ways of connecting ideas covered earlier in the book. Get students to compare their answers before you go through them with the whole class.

2 Students should discuss the sentences in pairs and then use the table in 1b to check their answers.

3 When students have looked at the information in the box, elicit why it might be useful to make sentences shorter, e.g. to make your writing more interesting, to give it more impact, to reduce repetition. For each sentence, students need to identify whether both parts of the sentence occur at the same time or one occurs earlier, and whether the sentence is active or passive. Do the first one together as an example.

4 For each group of sentences, students should produce one longer sentence using the connecting devices given in brackets. Look at the example together to show how it has been constructed: the first sentence is reduced to a participle clause – *Written by a woma*n – and combined with the second using a relative pronoun – *who has lived in India for many years,* – resulting in some small changes to the third sentence – *the book tells us a lot about India.* If you think students are not too confident with this, do question 2 with them, then get them to work in pairs, and check their answers as they complete each one.

Background

The author of *Heat and Dust*, Ruth Prawer Jhabvala, was born in Germany in 1924. She emigrated to England and went to university in London. She moved to India in 1951 after marrying an Indian architect, and since then has written many novels set in India. She wrote *Heat and Dust* in 1975, and in 1983 the famous producer–director partnership of Ismail Merchant and James Ivory made it into a film.

Photocopiable activity

Photocopiable activity 23B (p. 171) would work well here. Students use a variety of connecting words and phrases to tell a story, working towards a specified ending.

▶ Student's Resource Book page 113

Writing p.176

1 If students have read different books get them to discuss all three questions. If they have all read the same book they should just discuss question 3.

2 Although students are writing about a set book, it is important in the exam that they establish what sort of writing is required. They will still need to follow the style and conventions of that sort of writing.

3a You could group students who have decided to do the same writing task and get them to do the preparation together. Alternatively, you could ask the whole class to focus on one of the tasks in this lesson, and set the other task in a subsequent lesson or for homework.

3b As students do this, monitor and check that they are just writing notes rather than whole sentences, and that the notes relate to the question.

4a You could work through this together with students, checking understanding where necessary, or they could do it in pairs or with dictionaries to help with meaning.

4b Limit this activity, either by specifying how long students have to think of other adjectives, or how many they should think of in each category. Once they have thought of some words, they could ask others to decide if they are positive or negative.

4c Go through these with the whole class, focusing on what type of word or clause could come next, e.g. *This is a story about* + a/the person/time/place who/when/where … . *It is set in* + time/place.

6 Remind students of the checklist to use when checking their work. They also refer to the checklist in the Writing reference on page 206.

LANGUAGE SPOT: avoiding repetition

Start by giving students an example of language with a lot of repetition in it, to show them why it is important to avoid, e.g. *Mike writes stories about a group of teenagers. The teenagers in Mike's stories live in a big city. The teenagers have a lot of problems in the city. Mike writes about the problems the teenagers have in the city and how the teenagers overcome the problems of city life.*

▶ Student's Resource Book page 115

Unit 23 Key

Reading p.172

2 It is a crime thriller.

3a/b 1 B – see highlighted text
2 A (*He had offered Dickie friendship, companionship and respect … and Dickie had replied with ingratitude and now hostility.*) (ll. 23–26)
3 D (*… receive Dickie's cheque every month and forge Dickie's signature on it.*) (ll. 35–36)
4 C (*The danger of it … only made him more enthusiastic.*) (ll. 39–41)
5 A
6 B (*… the only way to keep Dickie from seeing what must have been a very strange expression on his face.*) (ll. 60–62)
7 C

5a Nouns: impatience, frustration, anger, disappointment, impulse, shame, failing friendship, companionship, respect, ingratitude, hostility, irritation, attention, rudeness
Adjectives: enthusiastic, ashamed, amused

5b 1 *It crossed Tom's mind* – he thought – the idea came into his mind suddenly for a short time.
2 *shoving him out in the cold* – rejecting/abandoning him
3 *step right into Dickie's shoes* – become Dickie – to adopt the life and position that Dickie had
4 *eating out of his hand* – having control over – getting him to do exactly as he wanted

Language development 1 p.174

1a 1 To find out more about the American way of life.
2 The humour. Not knowing anything about the USA before reading it.
3 Because they're too tired to look for a hotel.

1b a in order to; b As; c before; d If; e who; f While; g and; h because; i When; j so … that; k However
1 who; 2 While; 3 before; 4 before; 5 so … that; 6 If …; 7 and; 8 However; 9 in order to; 10 As; 11 Because

2 1 The part ~~what~~ *(that)* I liked best was the ending.
2 The main character is an old man who ~~he~~ has never left his home town.
3 It was ~~a~~ such *a* good book that I couldn't stop reading.
4 ~~During~~ *While* the police look for the main suspect, Holmes makes other enquiries./During the police *search* …
5 It is set in a town where there are a lot of factories ~~in~~.

6 It can be helpful to see the film before ~~to~~ read*ing/you read* the book in English.
7 If you ~~will~~ like science fiction, you'll probably like this book.
8 It is a good story ~~despite~~ *but* the main character is not very realistic.
9 The police are called in ~~for~~ *to* investigate the theft of a painting.
10 I didn't like the ending because ~~of~~ I thought it was disappointing.

3 1 Being – same time
2 Writing – same time
3 Having experienced – earlier
4 criticised – passive
5 having had – earlier
6 Having read – earlier
7 completely satisfied – past participle as adjective

4 2 It is about a young English woman who goes to India with her child because she wants to find out the true story of her grandmother.
3 Her English grandparents lived in India together, but her grandmother fell in love with an Indian man.
4 Having arrived there, she starts to follow the same life path as her grandmother when she falls in love with an Indian.
5 Being set in two periods and telling two women's similar stories, it shows that lifestyles and attitudes change a lot over two generations, but love and relationships never change.

Writing p.176

2 (a) a discursive composition
(b) an informal letter to a friend, containing a review

3a 2 (a) mainly plot; (b) mainly plot and characters

4a Possible answers:
Characters: lifelike P, weak N, passionate P, imaginative P, brave P, lovely P, successful P, interesting P, convincing P, funny P, clever P, attractive P, boring N, sensitive P/N
Events: lifelike P, weak N, unexpected P, predictable N, disappointing N, successful P, interesting P, convincing P, funny P, boring N, awful N
Setting (place): imaginative P, lovely P, interesting P, attractive P

5 Sample answer:

> *Dear Mohammed*
>
> *Thanks for your letter. Sorry I haven't replied before but I've been busy at work. You asked if I could think of a good book for your dad's birthday. I recommend the book that I have just read.*
>
> *It's called 'Animal Farm' and it was written by George Orwell. It is set on a farm where the animals get rid of the owner and take over, but it's really a story about communism.*
>
> *The story isn't exciting but it's clever. At first, after the revolution, the animals are equal but later the pigs become more powerful and start to change everything. By the end, the animals realise they have gone back to where they started.*
>
> *The characters are very convincing. Napoleon, the leader of the pigs, is strong and corrupt. Other animals are honest but weak. They all represent people or things in Russia in the 1920s and 30s.*
>
> *So if your father likes history and politics, I am sure he will like this book.*
>
> *Best wishes*
>
> *Fernando*

(170 words)

LANGUAGE SPOT: avoiding repetition

a does = writes stories
he = Mike
done so = written stories
ones = stories
them = the stories
so = you have read any of the stories
them = the stories
not = you haven't read any of the stories
some = some of the stories

b **1** so; **2** do so; **3** ones; **4** did; **5** not; **6** one;
7 some

Unit 24 The media

The unit continues the theme of 'Getting your message across' with topics such as journalism, advertising, paparazzi, and government special advisers.

Listening p.178

To set the ball rolling ...

If your students are from the same country, ask them if they think you can tell what type of person reads each type of paper, or if you can say what someone is like from the paper they read. If your students are from different countries, get them to talk about newspapers in their countries with questions such as *Are there different types of newspaper? Which types are most popular? Do people buy a lot of newspapers? What type of news stories do they mostly contain?* You might need to pre-teach words such as *national, local, domestic, international, tabloid, broadsheet.*

1a You could also ask *Which is the most important part of the paper for you?* or *Which part do you read first?*

1b Remind students of the importance of reading only the questions at first. The discussion questions here help focus students on that.

2 You could elicit the strategy before students listen.

3 **Possible further questions:** *Do you know any journalists? What qualities do they have?*

Speaking p.179

Here students practise a complete Paper 5, although they will have to rotate the role of examiner at each stage. If students know who their partner will be for the exam and they are in the class, it would obviously be sensible for them to work together. If possible, it would be useful to record some of the students at each stage and use the recording for whole class feedback.

1a Give the 'examiners' a moment to look at the questions first.

2a/b Remind students to keep an eye on the time while their partner is speaking, and stop them after approximately 1 minute.

3b Again, students need to watch the time. They should stop after approximately 3 minutes.

4 Remind students to expand their answers, e.g. in question 2 the answer *No* is not enough; if students don't drive they should say why, or what they do instead.

▶ **Student's Resource Book page 117**

Use of English 1 p.180

1 This exercise should serve as a reminder of the task. Get students to discuss it in pairs, and give reasons for their answers.

2a As always, students should skim the text first. Give them no more than 30 seconds.

2b Give the students no more than 15 minutes to do the task and then some time to compare their answers. Don't spend too long discussing the mistakes with *need* and *have something done* (questions 6, 7, 8, 15) as they are dealt with in Language development 2.

3 **Possible further question:** *Should advertising be aimed at children?*

Language development 2 p.181

LOOK With books closed, you could begin by writing on the board *The board/classroom is messy.* Elicit and write on the board *Someone needs to clean it.* Then move *it* to the start of a new sentence to elicit *It needs cleaning/It needs to be cleaned.* Then students read the grammar box and complete the task.

1a Get students to check their answers together.

1b You could elicit what needs doing just from the picture, before students look at the prompt sentences. After completing the exercise, they could talk about what needs doing in the room/building where they are studying.

2a It might be necessary to check some of the vocabulary – *install*, *blunt*, *sharpen* – before students begin the exercise.

2b When students have done this exercise, ask them to think of other examples of people/places we go to in order to have something done.

2c Introduce the expression *DIY* (do-it-yourself) and ask students if they are keen on it. Then get them to discuss the points, giving reasons for their answers and saying where they have something done/who they have it done by, and explaining.

3 Give students a few minutes' preparation time before they discuss the questions in groups. The discussion could be extended by asking what other things they would like to have done for them.

▶ **Student's Resource Book page 118**

Use of English 2 p.182

1 This is a reminder of the basic strategy for Paper 3 Part 5. Get students to discuss the questions in pairs first, giving reasons for their answers.

2a

Background

Paparazzi are photographers (and writers) that follow celebrities in the hope of getting a story. The word comes from a character called Paparazzo, a photographer in Fellini's 1960 Italian film *La Dolce Vita*, which is all about celebrities, rich people and their parties.

2b Remind students that, as well as making grammatical changes, they may need to alter the word to fit the meaning of the sentence.

3a When students have skimmed the text and answered the questions, you could ask them if they are aware of the role of special advisers in their country and if they think they have too much power/influence. In the UK, they are also known as 'spin doctors' as one of their roles is to put a positive spin (a positive/favourable appearance) on to news and information.

4 If students are interested in politics develop the first question. If not, focus more on the second question, introducing ideas such as privacy, security and sensitivity.

Photocopiable activity

Photocopiable activity 24 (pp. 172–173) could be used here or at the end of the unit. It is a grammar auction revising common mistakes at FCE level.

Language development 3 p.183

1a Complete the first part together. The noun *responsibility* was needed in Word formation (B) on page 182.

1b This exercise focuses on words that exist in all four forms. It might be useful to point out to students that not all words are so varied. When students have completed the table, get them to highlight the endings that are used to form the various words.

1c Remind students that Use of English word formation texts are likely to include a number of negative prefixes. When students have completed the exercise, get them to identify patterns, e.g. *il-* before adjectives starting with *l*, *ir-* before *r*, *im-* before *p*, *un-* for adjectives ending in *-ic*, *in-* for adjectives ending in *-ate*, but point out that there are always exceptions!

1d In each sentence, students first need to identify which word is needed, then the form. Do the first sentence together as an example.

2 Here again, students should think about both the word needed and the form. Start by checking that students know the form of the words given, e.g. *use* – noun and verb, *lonely* – adjective.

3a Get students to focus on the clues that tell them what type of word is needed in each case.

▶ **Module 12 Test: How much do you remember? TRB page 194**

▶ **Exam practice 6: Papers 1 and 3 CB pages 184–187; Papers 2 and 4 TRB pages 195–196**

Unit 24 Key

Listening p.178

2   **1** C (*It was my father who talked me into doing journalism.*)
2 B (*You had to follow a senior reporter around … He would … give you feedback.*)
3 A (*They were terribly suspicious of us at first …*)
4 C (*All the journalists sympathised with his situation and didn't want to spoil things for him.*)
5 A (*… this is not as important as having bags of energy and commitment.*)
6 B (*In my day, it was all going out and meeting people to get stories. Now it's much more office based.*)
7 B (*… as long as your family commitments aren't going to be a problem, given the long and unpredictable hours …*)

Use of English 1 p.180

1   **1** False. There will be many words in a text that can be removed, e.g. *that* (next to question 5) could be removed from the text, but it isn't a word that shouldn't be there.
2 True.
3 False. If the same word appears twice in one line, they should both be there, e.g. *that* (next to question 4).

2a **1** Likes: adverts that make him/her laugh. Dislikes: adverts that suggest that what he/she has isn't good enough.
2 It tells us the good things, but not some of the bad things.

2b **1** was – reduced relative clause
2 they – *all the rabbits* is the subject so the pronoun *they* is repetition
3 so – *think + (that)* + clause. *think so – so* replaces the clause
4 me – *suggest + that* + clause
5 ✓
6 to – *need(n't)* + infinitive without *to*
7 ✓
8 be – *have something done* (past participle)

9 out – *make something for someone* (not a phrasal verb)
10 have – *I know* (present simple)
11 for – *get someone to do something*
12 by – *given something by someone*
13 us – passive *we are told = someone told us*
14 ✓
15 the – no article before numbers, unless referring to a specific two years

Language development 2 p.181

Look   … ones that indicate that my house needs improving …
I'd have a conservatory added, a new shower installed and all my furniture specially made for me!
… it will have to have its bodywork repaired …

1a **1** It needs shortening/It needs to be shortened.
2 They need to be replaced/They need replacing.
1b **1** It needs tidying up.
2 It needs cutting.
3 They need watering.
4 It needs rebuilding.
5 They need cleaning.
6 They need repainting.
1c **1** First money needs to be raised.
2 Then the advert needs to be written.
3 A script needs to be prepared and brought to life.
4 A good production company needs to be found.
5 An experienced director needs to be hired.
6 Well-known actors need to be recruited.
7 The advert needs to be shot in a studio you can afford.

2a **2** 've had it stolen.
3 I'll/let's have/get it repaired.
4 I've had them checked/I'll have to get/have them checked.
5 we'll/let's have/get it installed.
6 I'll have/get them sharpened.
2b **Example answers:**
1 To have your teeth checked/a tooth removed.
2 To have your eyes tested/some glasses made.
3 To have your clothes cleaned.
4 To have your hair cut.
5 To have your nails done.
6 To have your photo taken.
7 To have a picture framed.
8 To have your shopping delivered.

Use of English 2 p.182

1   **1** Sentence by sentence, to get the complete sense of what is both before and after the gap.
2 Leave any you can't do and come back to them. When you have completed the text, you may have a better idea of what is needed.

2a 1 Hire a helicopter to get close to their subjects.
2 By saying the stars don't deserve privacy, as they court publicity when it suits them.

2b 1 growth – *a* + noun + *in*
2 glamorous – adjective + noun (*celebrities*)
3 embarrassing –pictures that embarrass them
4 frighteningly – *a* + adverb + adjective (*large*)
5 unbelievable – negative adjective + noun (*lengths*)
6 dangerously – verb (*fly*) + adverb + adjective (*close*)
7 annoyance – possessive adjective (*his or her*) + noun
8 privacy – noun
9 romantic – possessive (*their*) + adjective + noun (*weddings*)
10 extraordinary – possessive (*their*) + adjective + noun (*homes*)

3a 1 People who help politicians present news in a positive light.
2 They believe they reduce the freedom of the press.

3b 1 worrying – *a* + adjective + noun (*increase*)
2 responsibility – *whose* + noun
3 attention – possessive (*the public's*) + noun
4 reporters – *tell* + someone
5 powerful – *become very* + adjective
6 memorable – adjective + noun (*sentences*)
7 variety – *a* + noun + *of*
8 political – adjective + noun (*parties*)
9 arguments – *listen to* + (adjective) + noun
10 freedom – *the* + noun + *of* + *the* + noun (*press*)

Language development 3 p.183

1a Negative adjective: irresponsible
Noun: responsibility
Adverb: responsibly

ADJECTIVE	ADVERB	NOUN	VERB
believable	believably	belief	believe
worrying	worryingly	worry	worry
embarrassing	embarrassingly	embarrassment	embarrass
recognisable	recognisably	recognition	recognise
amazing	amazingly	amazement	amaze
decisive	decisively	decision	decide
thoughtful/ thoughtless	thoughtfully/ thoughtlessly	thought	think
legal	legally	legality/ law	legalise
satisfactory	satisfactorily	satisfaction	satisfy
astonishing/ astonished	astonishingly	astonishment	astonish

1c illegal; unsatisfactorily; unromantic; disappear; inaccurate; immoral; improbable; illogical; irregular; imperfectly

1d 1 irresponsible – negative adjective
2 embarrassment – noun
3 illogical – negative adjective
4 illegal – negative adjective
5 amazement/astonishment – noun
6 thoughtful – adjective
7 decisive – adjective
8 inaccurate – negative adjective

2 1 better relationship
2 absolutely useless
3 became fashionable
4 chance of survival
5 suffered from loneliness

3a 1 professionally – adverb to describe verb (*produced*)
2 entertaining – adjective after *quite* to describe something
unreadable – negative adjective – contrast after *but*.
3 generalise – verb after *had to*
stimulating – adjective to describe noun (*articles*)
4 admiration – noun after *have great*
creative – adjective after *so*
criticise – verb after *like to*
unreliable – adjective after *a bit*, negative after *however*
5 intelligence – noun after *my*
relationships – noun after *the*, plural = in general
boring – adjective after *be*, negative as linked with *offensive*
offensive – adjective after *find them*

Teacher's Resource Book
Module 12 Test: How much do
you remember? p.194

1   1 D; 2 B; 3 B; 4 C; 5 D

2   1 whether; 2 Having; 3 of; 4 so (therefore);
5 had

3   1 The chickens *need to/have to be fed* every day.
2 These instructions *are totally illogical, aren't*
they?
3 I'm *having some new curtains made* for the
bedroom.
4 I bought the book *in order to* give it to Kathy
for her birthday.
5 Read *the book before seeing* the film.

4   1 too; 2 ✓; 3 ✓; 4 no; 5 it

5   1 historical; 2 sympathise; 3 journalism;
4 insecurity; 5 improbable

Coursebook
Exam practice 6 p. 184

Paper 1 Reading
Part 3 1 F; 2 B; 3 G; 4 C; 5 A; 6 E

Paper 3 Use of English
Part 1 1 C; 2 A; 3 B; 4 B; 5 D; 6 A; 7 C; 8 B;
9 A; 10 D; 11 B; 12 D; 13 A; 14 C; 15 D

Part 2 1 so; 2 up; 3 soon; 4 which; 5 are;
6 get; 7 who; 8 does; 9 such; 10 What;
11 though; 12 there; 13 because/as/since;
14 of; 15 on

Part 3 1 Tom was *so ill that he could* not get out of
bed.
2 Sue failed to win the race *despite the fact that
she* did her best.
3 I've *never seen such a strange* game before!
4 I'm going to *have my knee examined by* a
specialist next week.
5 Hilary earned *such a good salary that* she
could afford a new car.
6 Anna has decided to *cut down on* the number
of phone calls she makes.
7 By the way, *neither Tania nor Tom likes* eating
meat.
8 The open-air concert *was cancelled owing to*
the bad weather.
9 In the tennis team, *Pietro is being replaced by*
Adrian.
10 Does *this jumper need washing* before I
wear it?

Part 4 1 some; 2 to; 3 been; 4 ✓; 5 as; 6 for;
7 too; 8 ✓; 9 that; 10 ✓; 11 of; 12 up; 13 the;
14 ✓; 15 it

Teacher's Resource Book
Exam practice 6 pp.195–196

Paper 2 Writing
Style:
Informal.
Content:
Tell your friend about the good points (food,
swimming pool, etc.) of the hotel.
Warn your friend about the things which were not so
good.

Paper 4 Listening
Part 2 1 Seabird; 2 motor racing; 3 reliability;
4 autopilot; 5 weather; 6 tiredness;
7 93/ninety-three days; 8 relax; 9 jogging;
10 Across the Ocean

UNIVERSITY *of* CAMBRIDGE
Local Examinations Syndicate

SAMPLE

Candidate Name
If not already printed, write name in CAPITALS and complete the Candidate No. grid (in pencil).

Candidate's signature

Examination Title

Centre

Supervisor:

[X] If the candidate is ABSENT or has WITHDRAWN shade here ▭

Centre No.

Candidate No.

Examination Details

0	0	0	0
1	1	1	1
2	2	2	2
3	3	3	3
4	4	4	4
5	5	5	5
6	6	6	6
7	7	7	7
8	8	8	8
9	9	9	9

Candidate Answer Sheet: FCE paper 1 Reading

Use a pencil

Mark ONE letter for each question.

For example, if you think **B** is the right answer to the question, mark your answer sheet like this:

0 | A B C D

Change your answer like this:

0 | A B C D

1	A B C D E F G H I
2	A B C D E F G H I
3	A B C D E F G H I
4	A B C D E F G H I
5	A B C D E F G H I

6	A B C D E F G H I
7	A B C D E F G H I
8	A B C D E F G H I
9	A B C D E F G H I
10	A B C D E F G H I
11	A B C D E F G H I
12	A B C D E F G H I
13	A B C D E F G H I
14	A B C D E F G H I
15	A B C D E F G H I
16	A B C D E F G H I
17	A B C D E F G H I
18	A B C D E F G H I
19	A B C D E F G H I
20	A B C D E F G H I

21	A B C D E F G H I
22	A B C D E F G H I
23	A B C D E F G H I
24	A B C D E F G H I
25	A B C D E F G H I
26	A B C D E F G H I
27	A B C D E F G H I
28	A B C D E F G H I
29	A B C D E F G H I
30	A B C D E F G H I
31	A B C D E F G H I
32	A B C D E F G H I
33	A B C D E F G H I
34	A B C D E F G H I
35	A B C D E F G H I

FCE-1

DP318/92

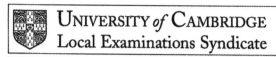

UNIVERSITY *of* CAMBRIDGE
Local Examinations Syndicate

SAMPLE

Candidate Name
If not already printed, write name
in CAPITALS and complete the
Candidate No. grid (in pencil).

Candidate's signature

Examination Title

Centre

Supervisor:

☒ If the candidate is ABSENT or has WITHDRAWN shade here ▭

Centre No.

Candidate No.

Examination Details

0	0	0	0
1	1	1	1
2	2	2	2
3	3	3	3
4	4	4	4
5	5	5	5
6	6	6	6
7	7	7	7
8	8	8	8
9	9	9	9

Candidate Answer Sheet: FCE paper 3 Use of English

Use a pencil

For **Part 1**: Mark ONE letter for each question.

For example, if you think **C** is the right answer to the question, mark your answer sheet like this:

0	A B C D

For **Parts 2, 3, 4** and **5**: Write your answers in the spaces next to the numbers like this:

0	

Part 1				
1	A	B	C	D
2	A	B	C	D
3	A	B	C	D
4	A	B	C	D
5	A	B	C	D
6	A	B	C	D
7	A	B	C	D
8	A	B	C	D
9	A	B	C	D
10	A	B	C	D
11	A	B	C	D
12	A	B	C	D
13	A	B	C	D
14	A	B	C	D
15	A	B	C	D

Part 2	Do not write here
16	▭ 16 ▭
17	▭ 17 ▭
18	▭ 18 ▭
19	▭ 19 ▭
20	▭ 20 ▭
21	▭ 21 ▭
22	▭ 22 ▭
23	▭ 23 ▭
24	▭ 24 ▭
25	▭ 25 ▭
26	▭ 26 ▭
27	▭ 27 ▭
28	▭ 28 ▭
29	▭ 29 ▭
30	▭ 30 ▭

Turn over for Parts 3 - 5 →

FCE-3

DP319/93

© UCLES

SAMPLE

Part 3		Do not write here
31		31 0 ▭ 1 ▭ 2 ▭
32		32 0 ▭ 1 ▭ 2 ▭
33		33 0 ▭ 1 ▭ 2 ▭
34		34 0 ▭ 1 ▭ 2 ▭
35		35 0 ▭ 1 ▭ 2 ▭
36		36 0 ▭ 1 ▭ 2 ▭
37		37 0 ▭ 1 ▭ 2 ▭
38		38 0 ▭ 1 ▭ 2 ▭
39		39 0 ▭ 1 ▭ 2 ▭
40		40 0 ▭ 1 ▭ 2 ▭

Part 4		Do not write here
41		▭ 41 ▭
42		▭ 42 ▭
43		▭ 43 ▭
44		▭ 44 ▭
45		▭ 45 ▭
46		▭ 46 ▭
47		▭ 47 ▭
48		▭ 48 ▭
49		▭ 49 ▭
50		▭ 50 ▭
51		▭ 51 ▭
52		▭ 52 ▭
53		▭ 53 ▭
54		▭ 54 ▭
55		▭ 55 ▭

Part 5		Do not write here
56		▭ 56 ▭
57		▭ 57 ▭
58		▭ 58 ▭
59		▭ 59 ▭
60		▭ 60 ▭
61		▭ 61 ▭
62		▭ 62 ▭
63		▭ 63 ▭
64		▭ 64 ▭
65		▭ 65 ▭

UNIVERSITY *of* CAMBRIDGE
Local Examinations Syndicate

SAMPLE

Candidate Name
If not already printed, write name
in CAPITALS and complete the
Candidate No. grid (in pencil).

Candidate's signature

Examination Title

Centre

Supervisor:

☒ If the candidate is ABSENT or has WITHDRAWN shade here ▭

Centre No.

Candidate No.

**Examination
Details**

0	0	0	0
1	1	1	1
2	2	2	2
3	3	3	3
4	4	4	4
5	5	5	5
6	6	6	6
7	7	7	7
8	8	8	8
9	9	9	9

Candidate Answer Sheet: FCE paper 4 Listening

Mark test version below

A B C D E

Special arrangements S H

Use a pencil

For **Parts 1** and **3**:
Mark ONE letter for
each question.

For example, if you
think **B** is the right
answer to the
question, mark your
answer sheet like this:

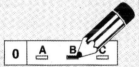

0	A	B	C

For **Parts 2** and **4**:
Write your answers in
the spaces next to the
numbers like this:

0	EXAMPLE

Part 1

1	A	B	C
2	A	B	C
3	A	B	C
4	A	B	C
5	A	B	C
6	A	B	C
7	A	B	C
8	A	B	C

Part 2

		Do not write here
9		9
10		10
11		11
12		12
13		13
14		14
15		15
16		16
17		17
18		18

Part 3

19	A	B	C	D	E	F
20	A	B	C	D	E	F
21	A	B	C	D	E	F
22	A	B	C	D	E	F
23	A	B	C	D	E	F

Part 4

		Do not write here
24		24
25		25
26		26
27		27
28		28
29		29
30		30

FCE-4

DP320/94

Photocopiable activities teacher's notes

Pre-course: FCE exam quiz

- Use at the start of the course, before Unit 1.

Aim:	To raise awareness of various aspects of the FCE exam and to answer some common questions.
Time:	15–20 minutes
Activity type:	Pairwork/Groupwork. Students find out how much they know about the exam by doing a quiz.
Preparation:	Make one copy of the quiz (p. 125) per student.

Procedure

1 Ask students what FCE stands for. Is it: **A** First Certificate Exam or **B** First Certificate in English? (Answer – **B**.) Tell the students that they are going to do a quick quiz to learn more about the exam.

2 Give out a copy of the quiz to each student and set a time limit (5 minutes) to complete it. Students should first have a go on their own and then compare with a partner or in groups.

3 Refer students to the Exam overview on page 6 of the Coursebook and the Top 20 Questions printed on the inside front cover and get them to check their answers.

4 Discuss answers with the class and answer any other questions about the exam that the students have.

1 B; **2** A; **3** C (you can't pass/fail individual papers); **4** C; **5** B (both questions have equal marks); **6** A; **7** C; **8** B (in Parts 1, 2 and 4 you speak to the examiner, in Part 3 just to your partner); **9** B (in Paper 2 poor spelling and handwriting can affect the overall impression mark); **10** C; **11** T (each paper is rounded up/down to 40 marks); **12** F (the word count is a guide but if you write too little you can't answer the question, if you write too much the examiner might not read it); **13** F (*isn't* counts as two words; *is* + *not*); **14** T (as long as the examiner can recognise the word. Words spelt out loud must be correct.); **15** F (in pairs or a group of three where there is an odd number)

Follow-up

Show students where they can find the Exam reference in the Coursebook (p. 188) and explain that they can find more detailed information about the exam there.

1A Lifestyle and families

- Use this activity after Reading (CB pp. 8–9) or as an introduction to Unit 1.

Aim:	To practise giving and exchanging personal information.
Time:	20–25 minutes
Activity type:	Pairwork/Groupwork. Students play a board game answering questions about themselves and their families.
Exam focus:	The questions are similar to possible questions in Paper 5 Parts 1 and 4.
Preparation:	Make one copy of the board game (p. 126) per group of four students enlarged to A3 size if possible. One dice per group and counters of different colours (students can make their own).

Procedure

1 Divide the class into groups of four (or three) and give each group a copy of the board game and counters. Quickly demonstrate how to play the game.

2 Tell students to expand on their answers if they wish.

3 Each student starts from a different corner of the board. They take it in turns to roll the dice and move around the board. When they land on a square they read out the question (or another student reads it out to them), and answer it. The other students can ask a follow-up question. The next student then has a turn.

4 If anyone lands on a square with a question that they have already answered they move forward to the next square. In squares with a slash (e.g. *house/flat*) students should choose the most appropriate word for their situation when reading out the question.

5 As the students are discussing the answers make a note of typical/common mistakes. As there is no 'start' or 'finish' there are no winners and the game can be played for as long or short a time as is available.

Follow-up

Spend 5–10 minutes giving students feedback on their performance, both positive and negative, and correct any common mistakes noted. (You could write students' incorrect sentences on the board and, in pairs, get students to correct them.)

1B Habits

> • Use after Language development 1 (CB pp. 10–11).
> **Aim:** To practise using language to describe present and past habits.
> **Time:** 25–30 minutes
> **Activity type:** Pairwork. Students compare a house and its inhabitants in the 1930s with the same house today.
> **Preparation:** Make one copy of the pictures (pp. 127–128) for each pair of students.

Procedure

1 Elicit a few examples of how students spend time at home, e.g. *I eat dinner with my parents, then I ...* .

2 Divide the class into pairs. In each pair, give one student picture A and one picture B and tell them their picture is of a family spending time at home. Tell them not to show their pictures to each other at this stage.

3 Students describe what is happening in their picture to find out if they have pictures of the same house or different houses. Remind students that we usually use the present continuous when describing a scene in a picture, e.g. *a boy is playing.*

4 Establish that it is the same house but a different time. Picture A is in the 1930s and picture B is the same house now. Students look at both pictures to compare modern-day and 1930s lifestyles. Remind students to use the target structures *would* and *used to* by eliciting/giving a model, e.g. *Families used to be much larger. People didn't have bathrooms so they would wash in the kitchen.*

5 Compare ideas with the whole class.

Follow-up

Students discuss if changes are for the better or not. They could also discuss how their lifestyle is different from their parents' when they were the same age.

2 Collocations: adjectives and nouns

> • Use after completing Language development 3 (CB p. 19).
> **Aim:** To practise some common adjective + noun collocations from Unit 2, and introduce some new ones.
> **Time:** 25–30 minutes
> **Activity type:** Groupwork. Students match adjectives to nouns and then use the collocations to complete a text.
> **Exam focus:** Collocations are tested in Paper 3 Part 1.
> **Preparation:** Copy and cut up one set of adjective cards (grey) and one set of noun cards (white) per group of 3–4 students, and one copy of the text per student (pp. 129–130).

Procedure

Part 1

1 Write the following nouns on the board and ask students if they can remember which of them collocate with *sour: milk, tea, look, sound, banana, grapes.*

2 Divide the class into groups of 3–4. Give each group a set of adjective cards (grey) and noun cards (white).

3 Tell students to work together to match them. Check the answers with the class before they go on to do Part 2 of the activity. Answers are the same collocations as for Part 2 of the activity, but in no particular order.

Part 2

1 Give each student a copy of the text and ask them to work individually to complete it, using the adjective + noun combinations from the first part of the activity.

2 Check answers with the class.

> 1 guided tour; 2 unique opportunity; 3 domestic life; 4 high speed; 5 slight change; 6 exact date; 7 wide gap; 8 hard work; 9 quick breakfast; 10 central heating; 11 strong influence; 12 memorable experience; 13 natural light; 14 valuable paintings; 15 final destination

Follow-up

Ask students to think of the opposites of some of the collocations, e.g. *high speed – low speed, wide gap – narrow gap, strong influence – weak influence*, etc.

3A Work

> • This activity can be used after Reading
> (CB pp. 22–23). (See also Alternative below.)
>
> **Aim:** To practise giving and exchanging opinions and reaching a consensus. To revise and extend jobs vocabulary.
>
> **Time:** 30 minutes
>
> **Activity type:** Groupwork. Students discuss a number of jobs in different categories and reach a consensus.
>
> **Exam focus:** Paper 5 Part 3
>
> **Preparation:** Make one copy of the cards (p. 131) per group of 3–4 students.

Procedure

1 Pre-teach some of the more difficult vocabulary, e.g. *miner, surgeon, chef, midwife, traffic warden, bouncer, civil servant* and *undertaker* by putting the words on the board and getting students in groups to discuss meanings and/or refer to dictionaries. Check pronunciation of difficult words, e.g. *chef, architect, pilot*.

2 Divide the class into groups of 3–4. Explain that students should discuss each question giving reasons to support their opinions.

3 Students choose a card at random from the set and discuss the question. When/If they reach a consensus they choose another card. Set a time limit (5–10 minutes per card) and signal when time is up.

4 While students are discussing the questions check that they are supporting their opinions with reasons and encouraging turn-taking. Stop after the first round and give feedback on their use of functional language.

5 Conduct feedback with the class, correcting common mistakes. Compare answers between the groups.

Follow-up

In their groups, students think of a job in each category that beats those listed.

Alternative

Use the cards one at a time for 5-minute speaking activities at different times during the unit.

Suggested answers:
1 Some surveys suggest being a miner is the most stressful because of the physical dangers, others say that being a prison officer is.
2 Although some company directors and musicians are very highly paid, on average the answer is more likely to be a lawyer or a surgeon.
3 In the UK the answer is a judge because, in addition to formal legal training, you need many years courtroom experience as a lawyer before becoming a judge.
4, 5 and 6 are a matter of opinion.

3B Experience

> • Use after Language development 1 (CB pp. 24–25) and before the Writing section.
>
> **Aim:** To practise asking and speaking about past experiences using the past simple and present perfect (simple and continuous) tenses.
>
> **Time:** 25–30 minutes
>
> **Activity type:** Students roleplay interviewing candidates for a job.
>
> **Preparation:** Make one set of rolecards (p. 132) per group of four students.

Procedure

1 Elicit the meaning of *au pair* (a young person, who lives with a family in a foreign country to look after the children, in order to learn the language). Ask what skills or qualities are needed to be an au pair.

2 Divide the class into groups of four. In each group students A and B are a couple looking for an au pair, students C and D are applicants for the job.

3 Students read rolecards and have a few minutes to prepare their questions/answers. Applicants should think about questions they could ask (hours of work/own room/time off, etc.) at the end of the interview.

4 First A interviews C, while B interviews D, giving the applicants a chance to ask questions at the end. For any information not on the card applicants should answer as themselves. Employers can invent any details of the job not given.

5 A interviews D while B interviews C.

6 The two employers discuss and choose who they prefer for the job while the applicants discuss who seems nicer to work for.

7 A and B announce who gets the job.

Follow-up

Discuss whether students like the idea of being an au pair in the UK or elsewhere.

4 Articles

> • Use after Language development 2 (CB p. 31).
>
> **Aim:** To practise use of articles *a/an, the* and zero article.
>
> **Time:** 25–30 minutes
>
> **Activity type:** Pairwork. Students complete a story by adding articles where necessary and then retell it to a partner.
>
> **Exam focus:** Paper 3 Parts 2 and 4.
>
> **Preparation:** Prepare enough copies (pp. 133–134) so that half the students have story A, and half B, with the answer keys removed.

Procedure

Explain that some stories have a 'moral' and elicit what that means (a practical lesson about what to do or how to behave which you learn from the story). Tell the students that they are going to read and tell two stories with a moral.

Part 1

1 Divide the class in two. Give the students in one half a copy of story A and students in the other half story B.

2 Give them 5 minutes to read the story and fill in the gaps with either *a, the* or ø (when no article is required).

3 Get them to compare their answers in pairs or small groups explaining choices.

4 Give out the answer keys to each group and help with any problems or questions.

Part 2

1 Form the students into pairs with an A and a B in each.

2 They tell each other their story. Stronger students should retell the story from memory, paying attention to the use of articles, weaker students can read the text. Their partner has to try to guess what the moral of the story is.

3 Ask students which story they prefer and why.

5A Tourism

<table>
<tr><td colspan="2">• Use after Reading (CB pp. 38–39).</td></tr>
<tr><td>Aim:</td><td>To practise language associated with tourism and language used for discussion.</td></tr>
<tr><td>Time:</td><td>30–40 minutes (+ Follow-up)</td></tr>
<tr><td>Activity type:</td><td>Whole class. Students debate the pros and cons of tourism.</td></tr>
<tr><td>Exam focus:</td><td>The organisation of ideas and much of the functional language is relevant to Paper 2 Part 2 (discursive composition).</td></tr>
<tr><td>Preparation:</td><td>Make one copy of either A or B (pp. 135–136) for each student.</td></tr>
</table>

Procedure

1 Ask students where they have been as tourists. Elicit a variety of destination types, e.g. cities, places of natural beauty, historic towns, coasts, mountains, developed and developing countries.

2 Ask the students if they think their visits were generally good or bad for the places they visited. Divide the class into two groups according to their answers to the question (one group = good effect, other group = bad effect).

3 Explain that the class is going to debate the motion '*Tourism should be encouraged: it is good for a country.*' One group must present the argument in favour and the other group present the argument against.

4 Write the motion on the board and give the two groups a few minutes to think of ideas to support their side of the argument. When their ideas dry up give each side their cue card and let them continue discussing it.

5 Ask each group to elect a proposer and a seconder and decide which points each will present. Ask students to try to use the 'useful language' on the cards when presenting their argument.

6 The four speakers present their arguments (A, B, A, B) with the rest of the class listening. Allow a few questions or points from the rest of the class.

7 Take a vote on those who support the motion and those who oppose it.

Follow-up

Ask students if they have heard of the motto from ecotourism '*Take nothing but photos, leave nothing but footprints*' and consider what it means. In pairs or groups, ask students to think of other dos/don'ts for good tourism and report them back to the class.

5B Adjectives and adverbs

<table>
<tr><td colspan="2">• Use after Language development 1 (CB pp. 40–41).</td></tr>
<tr><td>Aim:</td><td>To practise using adverbs of degree and adjectives studied in Unit 5.</td></tr>
<tr><td>Time:</td><td>25–30 minutes</td></tr>
<tr><td>Activity type:</td><td>Groupwork. Students play a game of pelmanism, matching adjectives and adverbs to gapped sentences.</td></tr>
<tr><td>Preparation:</td><td>Make a copy of both sets of cards (pp. 137–138) per group of 4–5 students, copied onto card if possible and cut up into individual cards.</td></tr>
</table>

Procedure

1 Put students into groups of 4–5. Demonstrate how to play the game.

2 Place the cards face down on the table, in their two sets (grey and white). Students take it in turns to turn over a card from each set – one sentence card and one adjective/adverb card. If they match the student keeps the pair and has another turn. If they don't match the student should turn them face down again in the same place.

3 Groups can discuss whether a pair matches or not and ask for help where necessary. As the students play go round the groups monitoring the pairs of cards collected. If any are wrong explain why and return the cards to the game. Some words can be used in more than one sentence.

4 The winner is the student with the most pairs.

1 surprisingly/remarkably; **2** hardly; **3** bleak; **4** lively; **5** well; **6** hard; **7** friendly; **8** fast; **9** rather/pretty; **10** extremely; **11** practically; **12** absolutely; **13** a bit; **14** pretty/rather/quite; **15** quite a; **16** actually; **17** as well; **18** seriously; **19** remarkably/surprisingly; **20** rather/pretty

6 *-ing* forms and infinitives

> • Use after Language development 2 (CB p. 47).
>
> **Aim:** To practise using words/phrases that need to be followed by verbs in either the infinitive (with or without *to*) or *-ing* form.
>
> **Time:** 20–25 minutes
>
> **Activity type:** Groupwork. A game, combining A cards and B cards to make correct sentences.
>
> **Exam focus:** Paper 3 Parts 1, 3 and 4.
>
> **Preparation:** Make one copy of both sets of cards (pp. 139–140) for each group of four students.

Procedure

1 Explain that the items on the A cards are followed either by the *-ing* form or the infinitive (with or without *to*). In some cases both are possible.

2 Tell the students that, in the game, they will need to combine A and B cards, making a logical sentence, either positive or negative, in any tense. Demonstrate with two cards, e.g.

(*think of + learn = I'm thinking of learning Spanish next year.*)

3 Shuffle the A cards and deal out three to each player, and place the remaining cards face down on the table. Turn the top card over and place it next to the pile. Do the same with the B cards.

4 Students take turns to combine an A card or a B card in their hand to make a sentence, placing the cards on the table in front of them as they do so. After making a sentence they replace the two cards by taking one from each of the face-down piles.

5 If students cannot make a sentence, they can use their turn to change one of their cards, taking either the face-up card or the next face-down card from the corresponding pile. The card they put down goes on the face-up pile. Players should always have six cards (three from each set) in their hand.

6 Other players in the group accept or contest sentences. As students play, monitor their use of the structures, if necessary checking by asking students to repeat the pairs in front of them, returning the cards to the pile if they are not correct.

7 The student with the most pairs is the winner.

7A Raising money

> • Use after Reading (CB pp. 52–53).
>
> **Aim:** To practise giving and exchanging opinions and reaching a consensus.
>
> **Time:** 20–30 minutes
>
> **Activity type:** Groupwork. Students discuss possible ways of raising money for a club that they belong to and reach a consensus on the best way of raising the money.
>
> **Exam focus:** Paper 5 Part 3. Paper 5 Part 4 in the Follow-up activity.
>
> **Preparation:** Make one copy of the activity (p. 141) per group of 3–4 students (or one per pair if you use the Variation.)

Procedure

1 Check that students are familiar with the concept of a *charity*. Ask students to name some charities that they have heard of and how charities raise money. Tell them that in some countries individuals often raise money for charities and elicit possible ways of doing so.

2 Pre-teach: *bungee jump, busking, raffle*.

3 Divide the class into groups of 3–4 students and explain that for this activity they are all members of a club or society that needs to buy some new equipment.

4 Give each group a copy of the activity and tell them that they must work together to decide on the best method to raise some money.

5 Model the activity using *run a marathon* as an example, using the language in the speech bubbles and referring to the four prompt questions.

6 Give students a time limit (10 minutes) to discuss and agree on the best method.

7 Different groups should report back to the class and explain their choice.

Variation

Doing the activity in larger groups will encourage more discussion, but for more authentic exam-type practice do the activity in pairs.

Follow-up

Ask students if any of them have ever done anything like this before for charity. Ask if they ever give money to buskers, beggars or street collectors and why/why not.

7B Narrative tenses

• Use after Language development 1 (CB pp. 54–55) and before the Writing section.

Aim:	To practise narrative tenses.
Time:	20–25 minutes
Activity type:	Groupwork. Students work out a scenario from clues and devise a story.
Exam focus:	In Paper 2 Part 2 (narrative composition/short story) narrative tenses are particularly relevant.
Preparation:	Make one copy of the picture (p. 142) per group of 2–4 students.

Procedure

1 Find out if students read detective stories or watch such programmes on TV. Tell students that for this activity, they will be detectives.

2 Set the scene. It is 9 May, a man called Peter disappeared a few days ago and they are looking for him. In his flat they find various items which are clues to what has happened.

3 Divide the class into groups of 2–4 and give each group a copy of the picture.

4 Students have 5–10 minutes to discuss what the picture tells them about Peter and the time before he disappeared. Elicit an example, e.g. the coke bottle – *He had been drinking coke/He had drunk a bottle of coke* or *He was writing/had been writing a letter*.

5 Compare ideas with the whole class, paying attention to use of tenses.

6 Students have 5 minutes to put the clues together to make a story to say what happened.

7 The class compare their different stories.

Suggestions for items:
He was/had been writing a letter. He had been to/visited Moscow. He had been smoking/He had smoked nearly a whole packet … . He had been eating a pizza/He hadn't finished his pizza. He had been sent a letter by someone called Natasha, etc.
Possible solution:
Peter had been going out with a Russian girl called Natasha and had been to Moscow to visit her and had a great holiday. After he had left she wrote to him to say it was all over, so he booked another flight and went back to see her … .

8 Confusing adjectives

• This is an extension to Language development 3 (CB p. 63).

Aim:	To extend work on comparing and contrasting commonly confused adjectives.
Time:	30–45 minutes. Note that this activity is in two parts, which can be done on separate occasions.
Activity type:	Part 1: whole class. Students mingle, teaching each other the difference between confusing adjectives. Part 2: groupwork. A board game asking and answering questions using the adjectives.
Exam focus:	Paper 3 Part 1
Preparation:	Part 1: one set of the vocabulary cards (p. 143) per class, cut up; dictionaries. Part 2: one copy of the board game (p. 144), enlarged to A3 if possible, per group of 4–5 students; dice and counters.

Procedure

Part 1 (10–15 minutes)

1 Distribute the Part 1 vocabulary cards. If there are more students than cards, some can share.

2 Students check the difference between the words in a dictionary and think of or look up examples to explain the meanings.

3 Students mingle and, each time they meet another student, they ask them to explain the difference between the words on their card (without showing it to them). Students help/teach each other where necessary.

Part 2 (15–25 minutes)

1 Divide the class into groups of 4–5 students and give each group a copy of the board game.

2 Students take it in turns to roll dice and move around the board.

3 At each square they read the question and decide who in the group to ask, choosing the correct word from the alternatives each time.

4 Monitor the whole class, noting errors for feedback at the end.

9A The human body

> • Use as an introduction to Unit 9 and Reading (CB pp. 68–69).
>
> **Aim:** To generate interest in the topic of the human body and to pre-teach some important vocabulary for the Reading section in Unit 9. To practise giving and exchanging opinions.
>
> **Time:** 20–25 minutes
>
> **Activity type:** Individual and pairwork. Students complete a general knowledge quiz on the subject of the human body and compare answers.
>
> **Preparation:** Make one copy of the quiz (p. 145) per student.

Procedure

1 Tell the class that they are going to do a general knowledge quiz on the subject of the human body. Ask the students how much they know about the subject and if they study/studied biology at school.

2 If there are any doctors or medical students in the class sit them together.

3 Give each student a copy of the quiz and a time limit of 5–6 minutes to complete the quiz.

4 Students then compare their answers in pairs.

5 Check the answers with the whole class.

> **1** C; **2** A; **3** B (in an adult, and the male brain is slightly heavier than the female!); **4** B (it's in the centre but the left side is bigger so it leans that way); **5** B (in a reasonably fit young adult); **6** C; **7** A (the study of mental illness is psychiatry); **8** C; **9** B (DNA stands for 'deoxyribonucleic acid'); **10** A (the liver is about 1.5 kgs); **11** B; **12** C (in Europe)

Follow-up

Ask students what surprised them most in the quiz.

9B The future

> • Use after Language development 1 (CB pp. 70–71).
>
> **Aim:** To practise using a variety of future forms.
>
> **Time:** 20–25 minutes
>
> **Activity type:** Pairwork. Students complete a timeline of their future and discuss it with a partner.
>
> **Preparation:** Make one copy of the activity (p. 146) per student.

Procedure

1 Ask students how they feel about the future. Do they worry about it? Or do they enjoy making plans?

2 Draw a rough copy of the path (see activity) on the board and explain that it is a map of the future. Demonstrate with your own examples, e.g. *I'm visiting some friends this week.*

3 Using the exam as an example, demonstrate/elicit how many different tenses might be possible for talking about a future event.

- *The exam takes place every (March).*
- *I am taking the exam in (March).*
- *My mum thinks I will pass!*
- *I am going to study hard before the exam.*
- *We will be taking the exam in mid (March).*
- *I will have taken the exam by the summer.*

4 Give each student a copy of the activity.

5 Students mark points on the path and label them according to their plans, hopes and predictions. Point out that, if students need to, they can use the verbs in the box for ideas.

6 Students should think about which tense they will use to talk about each point but should not write out the sentences in full. They tick the boxes in the table as they think of an example for each tense.

7 After a suitable time limit (7–8 minutes) the students form pairs and explain their diagram to their partner. Their partner can ask follow-up questions about their plans if they wish.

10 Forming nouns

> • Use after Language development 3 (CB p. 79).
> **Aim:** To consolidate and extend forming nouns from verbs.
> **Time:** 15–20 minutes
> **Activity type:** Groupwork. Students play a game of dominoes, joining suffixes to verbs to make nouns.
> **Exam focus:** Paper 3 Part 5
> **Preparation:** Make one copy of the dominoes (p. 147) per group of 4–5 students, cut up into individual dominoes.

Procedure

1 Review the concept of forming nouns from verbs by adding a suffix. Use the following verbs and elicit the nouns: *develop-ment, accept-ance, discuss-ion*.

2 Divide the class into groups of 4–5, giving each group a set of dominoes. Demonstrate how the final -*e* that is dropped is shown in brackets, e.g. *combin(e) + -ation = combination*.

3 One student deals four dominoes to each player, the rest of the dominoes remain face down on the desk in a pile.

4 Students take turns to place a domino, building a chain, (using either end). As they place each domino they should say the word they have formed.

5 After placing a domino students take another from the pile. If they are unable to place a domino to make a word, they take one from the pile and the next student has a turn.

6 As the students are playing, monitor that they have placed the dominoes correctly (especially with the difficult -*ance* and -*ence* endings).

7 The winner is the first to get rid of all their dominoes.

Follow-up

Point out how pronunciation changes in some words as the noun is formed, either in sounds, e.g. *please* /iː/ *pleasure* /e/) or stress, e.g. *prefer – preference, hesitate – hesitation* and ask students to find other examples.

11A Ambition

> • Use at the start of Unit 11 before Reading (CB pp. 82–83).
> **Aim:** To raise interest in the topic of ambition.
> **Time:** 20–25 minutes
> **Activity type:** Individual and whole class. Students complete a questionnaire to see how ambitious they are.
> **Preparation:** Make one copy of the questionnaire (p. 148) per student.

Procedure

1 Write the word *goal* on the board and ask students what they think of. Elicit its meaning of *ambition* as well as *football*. Elicit other words of similar meaning (*target, aims, dream*). Elicit the adjective of *ambition* (*ambitious*).

2 Pre-teach the following words/phrases: *community, put off, to mix with someone*.

3 Give each student a copy of the questionnaire. Students have 5 minutes to answer the questions working individually.

4 Explain the scoring system – odd questions: 2 points for *yes* and 1 point for *maybe*, even questions: 2 points for *no* and 1 for *maybe*.

5 Check totals: the higher the score the more ambitious the person is. 12 is the average. Compare scores within the class and see who is the most/least ambitious person in the class.

6 Elicit different types of ambition (work, money, family, spiritual, health, etc.)

Follow-up

Students ask a partner what their ambitions are and report back to the class.

11B The arts (relative clauses)

- Use after Language development 1 (CB pp. 84–85).

Aim: To practise relative clauses and arts vocabulary.

Time: 15–20 minutes

Activity type: Groupwork. Students play a game defining words for their team members to guess.

Exam focus: Paper 3 Part 2

Preparation: Make one copy of the cards (p. 149) per group of 4–5 students and cut them up.

Procedure

1 Ask if students are interested in the arts (music, dance, theatre, etc.). Ask how often they go to performances and if they have ever performed in public.

2 Divide the class into groups of 4–5 students. Give each group a set of cards and get them to sort them into words they know and words they don't. Get students to explain the words they know to the class. Teach the meaning of any that no one knows.

3 Each group collects up all their cards and shuffles them well.

4 Students play a game defining the words on the cards, using phrases such as *a person who … / a place where … / a thing which …* Demonstrate with a couple of cards. Give each group a copy of the useful language in speech bubbles at the foot of the photocopiable page.

5 The first player in the team takes a card from the pile and without showing it to their team, defines the word. When the team guess it, the player puts it down on the table and defines the next word. If the player can't define the word or the team can't guess it the player puts it to the bottom of the pile and continues.

6 After every minute or so shout 'Change!' and the player passes the pile to the next person in the team who has a go at defining words.

7 After 5–10 minutes stop the game. The winning team is the one with the most cards on the table.

12 Adjectives and nouns + preposition

- Use after Language development 2 (CB p. 91).

Aim: To practise dependent prepositions with adjectives and nouns from Unit 12.

Time: 20–25 minutes

Activity type: Pairwork. Students play a version of the game 'battleships'.

Exam focus: Paper 3 Parts 2 and 4

Preparation: Make one copy of worksheets A and B (pp. 150–151) for each pair of students.

Procedure

1 Tell students that they are going to play a version of a game called 'battleships' and ask if anyone knows how to play it.

2 Divide the class into pairs and give each student a worksheet for Student A or B, telling them not to show each other their worksheets.

3 Each student has a shaded complete side (on the left) and an unshaded, incomplete side (on the right).

4 Demonstrate how, on the shaded side, students pick six squares for their partner to find. They select three blocks of two squares together (vertically or horizontally) and mark them. These are the areas the partner will be looking for.

5 When they are ready to begin Student A chooses a word on the unshaded side and adds the preposition, putting it into a sentence, e.g. *I have a good relationship with my brother*. If the preposition is correct and the square is a selected one B says 'hit' and A writes in the preposition and marks it with an *X*. If it is not a selected one B says 'miss' and A can write in the answer. If the preposition is incorrect B says 'wrong' but does not say if the square is a hit or miss. It is then B's turn.

6 Students take it in turn to hunt for the hidden squares. If more than one preposition is possible students only need give one.

7 The game is over when one player has identified which six squares their partner selected.

13A Global food and drink

• Use before Reading (CB pp. 98–99).	
Aim:	To practise giving and exchanging opinions and to generate interest in the reading topic.
Time:	20–25 minutes
Activity type:	Pairwork/Groupwork. Students complete a quiz on the subject of global food/drink.
Exam focus:	Paper 5 Part 3
Preparation:	Make one copy of the quiz (p. 152) per student.

Procedure

1 Ask students to work in pairs to name five global food/drink companies, e.g. McDonald's, KFC (Kentucky Fried Chicken), Coca-Cola, Starbucks, Mars, Nestlé, Cadburys, Ferrero, etc.

2 Put students into pairs or groups of three. Tell them that it is a competition to see which pair is the most knowledgeable about the global food market. They are not expected to know the answers but will have to guess them. Show them the speech bubbles containing useful language for discussion.

3 Give each pair/group a copy of the questionnaire and a suitable time limit (10 minutes) to discuss the questions.

4 Check answers with the whole class. Find out which pair is the winner. Ask which answers surprised them most.

> **1** C; **2** C; **3** B (in the 'Happy Meals'); **4** C (in 10,800 outlets); **5** D (but 34% of sales are in North America); **6** A; **7** B (with sales of $2 billion a year); **8** A; **9** B (8.7kg/person/year, then – USA, France and Italy); **10** D (3.6kg/person/year, then – UK, Turkey and Egypt)

Follow-up

Ask students to think of three positive and three negative aspects of globalisation and then discuss them with the whole class.

13B Cultural guide

• Use after Language development 1 (CB pp. 100–101).	
Aim:	To practise expressions of permission, necessity, advice and recommendation.
Time:	15–20 minutes
Activity type:	Pairwork. Students complete a cultural guide.
Exam focus:	Paper 3 Part 3
Preparation:	Make one copy of the activity (p. 153) per student.

Procedure

1 Ask students when they give flowers, e.g. birthdays, anniversaries, to people in hospital and if there are any 'rules' that they follow.

2 On the board put the table:

You	should(n't)/ought to are(n't) supposed to are(n't) allowed to must(n't)/have to	give	an even number. an odd number. white flowers. a single flower.

Get students to make sentences that show various ways of saying the same thing, e.g. *In some countries you are supposed to give an odd number/you aren't supposed to give an even number.*

3 Pre-teach: *earlobe, escalators, edible, sole.*

4 Divide the class into pairs and give each student a copy of the activity. Students work together to make 12 sentences that they think are true. Check answers with the whole class.

> 1 not supposed to, red (red is only used for names of the dead)
> 2 aren't supposed to, teacher's (use the title 'Teacher')
> 3 must, before (the bath is for soaking/relaxing)
> 4 shouldn't, earlobe (it is a rude gesture)
> 5 mustn't, your left (the left hand is unclean)
> 6 mustn't, coin (it shows disrespect to the king whose head is on the coins)
> 7 are supposed to, on the right
> 8 must, to an older person (it shows respect)
> 9 ought to, lift
> 10 shouldn't, gifts
> 11 mustn't, the soles of your feet (it shows disrespect)
> 12 are supposed to, hands

Follow-up

Students write more sentences for their own country and share them with the class.

14 Modals of deduction

• Use after Language development 2
(CB p. 106).

Aim:	To practise using modals of deduction (past and present).
Time:	15–20 minutes
Activity type:	Whole class mingle. Students respond to or correct remarks made by other students.
Exam focus:	Paper 3 Part 3
Preparation:	Prepare one copy of the activity (p. 154) per class, cut up into individual cards. Prepare two sets if there are more than 16 students.

Procedure

1 Write a sentence on the board, containing a factual mistake such as: *I'm 20 years old, I was born in 1980* (where the age and date don't add up) and ask students what is wrong with it.

2 Elicit possible corrections: *You can't be 20/ You must be ??, if you were born in 1980.* or: *You can't have been born in 1980/you must have been born in 19??.*

3 Give each student a card. They read it and decide on the answer or spot what is wrong with it. At this stage if students don't know what the correction should be they could check with the teacher.

4 Students stand up and mingle, telling people the information on their card.

5 Each student they meet listens and responds or 'corrects' it. If they don't know what the correction should be they can ask the other student to explain. If students can give the correct response they score a point, before moving on to speak to another student.

6 The winner could be the first one to win a set number of points or the one with the most points after a set time.

Notes: (some examples)
• Penguins live in the Antarctic not the Arctic.
• Brazilians speak Portuguese.
• The first moon landing was in 1969.
• The Euro was introduced in 2002.
• In Japan people drive on the left.
• The Berlin Wall came down in 1989.
• People didn't watch TV in the 1920s.
• There are no snakes in New Zealand.

15A Relationships (prepositions)

• Use as an introduction to Unit 15 before Reading
(CB pp. 112–113).

Aim:	To activate students' knowledge of phrases that refer to relationships (most of which are used in the unit).
Time:	15–20 minutes
Activity type:	Individual and pairwork. Students complete expressions about relationships by adding missing prepositions and then order them.
Exam focus:	Paper 3 Part 1
Preparation:	Make one copy of the activity (p. 155) per student. Dictionaries would be useful.

Procedure

1 Ask students to define *relationship*. Establish that there are many different types of relationships (parent/child, family, teacher/student, client/server, etc.) and that this activity is about boyfriend/girlfriend relationships.

2 Give each student a copy of the activity and a suitable time limit (5 minutes) to work individually to complete the gaps. Point out that, in some, no preposition is required.

3 Students compare their answers with a partner.

4 Give students the answers, checking meaning.

5 In pairs, students discuss a logical order for them. Point out that there is no correct answer, it's a matter of opinion and that some expressions are very similar. Compare answers with the whole class.

be attracted *to* someone; fall *in* love (with someone); to split *up* (with someone); to get engaged *to* someone; to go *out* (with someone); to propose *to* someone; to finish *with* someone; to separate *from* someone; to be *in* love *with* someone; to chat someone *up*; to fancy φ someone; to get *on* well (with someone); to ask someone *out*; to get married *to* someone; to catch φ someone's eye; to fall *out* (with someone); to take someone *out*; to have a crush *on* someone; to flirt *with* someone; to move *in* (with someone)

15B Reported speech

> • Use after Language development 1 (CB pp. 114–115).
>
> **Aim:** To practise reporting what someone said and use reporting verbs.
>
> **Time:** 20–25 minutes
>
> **Activity type:** Pairwork. Students put film quotes into reported speech and guess which film they came from.
>
> **Exam focus:** Paper 3 Part 3
>
> **Preparation:** Make one copy of A and B (p. 156–157) for each pair of students.

Procedure

1 Put the quote '*Play it again, Sam*' on the board. Ask students if they know which film it is from (*Casablanca*). Ask 'Who told Sam to play it again?' (Answer: No one says it! It is a famous misquote!)

2 Do the same with '*I hate snakes*' ('Who said that he hated snakes?' Indiana Jones in '*Raiders of the Lost Ark*'). Or use another well-known film quote.

3 Divide students into pairs and give each student either copy A or B.

4 Students have a few minutes to think about how they will put the quotes into reported speech. Before they start, point out the example on their sheets from *The Godfather*.

5 Write some of the reporting verbs from Unit 15 on the board, e.g. *warn, advise, promise, suggest* and remind students to try to use them in the activity.

6 Students take it in turn to ask. If their partner doesn't know the answer they can guess from the choices at the bottom of their sheet.

Follow-up

In pairs, students think of their own favourite quotes to ask the rest of the class.

16 Leisure activities

> • Use after Listening (CB p. 118).
>
> **Aim:** To discuss leisure interests and to practise giving and exchanging opinions and reaching a consensus.
>
> **Time:** 25–30 minutes
>
> **Activity type:** Groupwork. Students choose a leisure activity to do together.
>
> **Exam focus:** Paper 5 part 3
>
> **Preparation:** Make one copy of the activity (p. 158) per group of 3–4 students.

Procedure

1 Ask students how they usually spend their weekends. What influences their choice (hobbies/interests, money, time available, friends)?

2 Introduce the activity – students work in a group to choose a way to spend a weekend together doing something special (maybe before one goes off to study/join the army/get married, etc.).

3 Divide students into groups, mixing students up from usual partners if possible, and give each group a copy of the activity.

4 Remind students that they will need to discuss, suggest, agree, disagree, and reach a consensus. Elicit some functional language they could use and if necessary refer them to the Functions reference (CB p. 224).

5 Students have 10 minutes to discuss and choose a trip.

6 Groups feed back to class on which trip they chose and why.

Follow-up

Find out if any of the students have ever done any of the activities given and if they enjoyed them.

17A Money

> • Use either at the start of Unit 17 to activate the vocabulary or as a review after Reading (CB pp. 128–129).
>
> | | |
> |---|---|
> | **Aim:** | To practise vocabulary around the topic of money and to generate interest in the topic of the unit. |
> | **Time:** | 25–35 minutes |
> | **Activity type:** | Groupwork. Students play a board game where they gain or lose money each turn. |
> | **Exam focus:** | Paper 3 Part 1 |
> | **Preparation:** | Make one copy of the game (p. 159) per group of 3–4 students (enlarged to A3 if possible). One dice per group and counters of different colours. |

Procedure

1 Students brainstorm first ways to gain money, e.g. *earn, win, inherit* then ways to lose money, e.g. *spend, pay, go bust*, then adjectives that describe having or not having money, e.g. *well off, wealthy, broke, bankrupt*. Build up three lists of the words on the board.

2 Divide the class into groups of 3–4. Each group has a copy of the game.

3 Students place counters on square 1. One player in each group is also chosen to be the banker.

4 For a quicker game use dice, for a longer game use a coin, moving one square for heads and three for tails.

5 Each player starts with £1,000. At each turn players throw the dice and move around the board. The banker keeps a running total of how much they have and if they invest in a business or shares.

6 While students are playing, monitor and help with vocabulary. Continue until everyone has finished.

7 At the finish, anyone who started a business (in square 5 or 7) who hasn't lost it (21) or sold it (22) has double what they put in. Anyone who invested in the stock market (square 6) has double what they invested.

8 The winner is the one with the most money!

Follow-up

Discuss whether students are savers or spenders, cautious or risk-taking with their money.

17B Conditionals

> • Use after Language development 1 (CB pp. 130–131).
>
> | | |
> |---|---|
> | **Aim:** | To practise making conditional sentences and recognising which is required in a given situation. |
> | **Time:** | 20–40 minutes (or see Variations below). |
> | **Activity type:** | Groupwork. Students make, ask and answer questions on real and hypothetical issues. |
> | **Exam focus:** | Paper 3 Part 3 |
> | **Preparation:** | Make one copy of the activity (p. 160) per group of 3–4 students. Cut up into individual cards. |

Procedure

1 Write on the board: *If you (stop be) a teacher, what you (do)?* Ask students to make questions from it and elicit three conditional forms are possible (*If you stop/ stopped/had stopped being a teacher, what will you do/ would you do/would you have done?*). Demonstrate how time expressions (*next year, last year*) would affect your choice of conditional.

2 Divide the class into groups of 3–4 students.

3 Shuffle the cards and place face down on the table.

4 Students take it in turns to take a card from the pile and make a question in an appropriate form and choose which of the people in the group they would like to answer it. Demonstrate with one of the cards. Point out that the conditional form they choose depends on either how likely they see the event or which time phrase they choose.

5 Students ask each other the questions and discuss answers, refusing to answer if they don't think the question is formed correctly.

6 Monitor closely and check that students are forming the questions correctly.

Follow-up

Discuss any interesting or amusing answers given.

Variations

1 For a quicker game select fewer cards.

2 Use the cards a few at a time as 5-minute fillers over the next few lessons.

18 Money vocabulary

• Use after Language development 3 (CB p. 139).	
Aim:	To revise money vocabulary from Units 17 and 18 and practise word formation.
Time:	15–20 minutes
Activity type:	Pairwork. Students work together to complete a crossword.
Exam focus:	Paper 3 Part 5
Preparation:	Make one copy of crosswords A and B (p. 161) for each pair of students.

Procedure

1 Give students the word *tax* and get them to think of all the words formed from it (*taxes, taxable, untaxable, taxation*).

2 Explain that they will work together to complete a crossword which contains nouns and adjectives related to money. They will have to form clues using the roots of the words, so they will need to think what type of word it is and what the root is.

3 Demonstrate with examples 'It's the noun of the verb *to tax*' (= *taxation*) or 'It's the adjective of the noun *price*' (= *priceless*).

4 Divide the class into pairs and give students in each pair either Part A or Part B of the crossword.

5 Students check the form and meaning of the words on their half of the crossword.

6 Students take it in turns to ask for clues, e.g. *What's 3 across?* with their partner giving a word formation clue: *It's the noun of … .* or *It's the (negative) adjective of… .*

7 When they have finished students check answers by showing each other their completed crosswords, which should be identical.

19A Travel

• Use at the start of Unit 19 before Reading (CB pp. 142–143).	
Aim:	To pre-teach some vocabulary and generate interest in the topic of travel.
Time:	20–30 minutes
Activity type:	Individual, then whole class. Students complete a travel survey and find a travelling companion.
Preparation:	Make one copy of the questionnaire (p. 162) per student.

Procedure

1 In pairs, students have a minute to tell a partner about their most recent holiday.

2 Discuss the difference between going on holiday and travelling. Explain the purpose of the activity: to find the most suitable travelling partner in the class.

3 Pre-teach difficult vocabulary, e.g. *exotic, basics, souvenirs, racy novel.*

4 Students spend 5 minutes choosing their answers individually.

5 Students mingle and ask questions in order to find out who in the class has the most similar answers to them.

6 Students select a travelling companion with similar likes and interests to themselves.

Follow-up

Companions plan a trip together and report their plans back to the class.

19B Passives

> • Use after Language development 1 (CB pp. 144–145).
>
> **Aim:** To review passive structures.
>
> **Time:** 15–20 minutes
>
> **Activity type:** Groupwork. Students prepare extracts of travel news.
>
> **Exam focus:** Paper 3 Part 3
>
> **Preparation:** Make one copy of the activity (pp. 163–164) and cut up into individual cards.

Procedure

1 Ask students what type of news might be included in a section of 'Travel News', e.g. strikes, delays, new ideas/companies, special offers.

2 Tell students that the class is going to prepare a travel news feature.

3 Divide the class into six groups (fewer with a small class). Give each group one card.

4 Each group uses the information on the card to write the news story, adding more information if they wish. Remind students to use passive structures where they would be more appropriate.

5 Groups take it in turn to read out their stories to the class.

6 Give feedback on their use (or not) of passive structures and give alternative ways of expressing points if necessary.

Variation

In Procedure, step 3, the six stories could be neatly written out and compiled into a class newspaper.

20 Wishes and regrets

> • Use after Language development 2 (CB p. 150).
>
> **Aim:** To practise making sentences with *wish* and *if only, it's about time* and *I'd rather*.
>
> **Time:** 20–30 minutes (or see Variation below)
>
> **Activity type:** Groupwork. Students use picture cues to imagine what wishes people are making in different leisure situations.
>
> **Exam focus:** Paper 3 Part 3
>
> **Preparation:** Make one copy of the activity (pp. 165–166) per group of three students and cut the cards up.

Procedure

1 Introduce the activity by asking students about the leisure facilities in their town. What does it need? What needs improving? What was better in the past?

2 Write on the board *I wish, If only, It's about time* and *I'd rather*. Get students to use them to express their ideas, e.g. *I wish/It's about time we had a sports centre.*

3 Divide the class into groups of three and give each group a set of cards face down on the table.

4 One student should take a card from the top of the pile and place it face up on the table. Each student should, in turn, think of at least one wish/regret per card. For every correct sentence, accepted by the others in the group, a student scores 1 point.

5 Remind students to use the structures on the board. Wishes could be about the speaker/thinker, other people in the picture or the situation as a whole. Wishes could be about the present or the past.

6 Demonstrate activity with one of the cards, e.g. the first card: *I wish he would let me in/If only I hadn't worn trainers.*

7 Set a time limit (10 minutes). The winner in each group is the student with the highest score.

Variation

Use cards a few at a time as 5-minute fillers over the next few lessons.

21A Happiness

• Use at the start of Unit 21, before Reading (CB pp. 158–159).

Aim:	To generate interest in the topic of happiness. To practise discussing and trying to reach a consensus.
Time:	15–20 minutes
Activity type:	Pairwork. Students rank factors that create happiness.
Exam focus:	Paper 5 Part 3 (collaborative task)
Preparation:	Make one copy of the activity (p. 167) for each pair of students.

Procedure

1 Ask students if they feel happy today or not. At this stage try to focus students on superficial things, e.g. *It's raining, It's Friday,* etc. Tell them that in this activity you want them to think about true happiness and contentment.

2 Divide the class into pairs and give each pair a copy of the activity.

3 Check quickly for any unknown vocabulary. If you feel it's necessary, refer students to the Functions reference on (CB p. 224).

4 Set a time limit of 5–10 minutes. (**Note:** in the exam they would have about 3 minutes).

5 Students work together to decide which points are more or less important and agree on the three which are the most important.

6 Hold class feedback to compare opinions.

Follow-up

Discuss which of the points in the list are easier or harder to obtain.

21B Clauses of reason, purpose and contrast

• Use after Language development 1 (CB pp. 160–161).

Aim:	To practise using linking words to make clauses of reason, purpose and contrast.
Time:	20–25 minutes (+ Follow-up)
Activity type:	Groupwork. Students make sentences from prompts to win points.
Preparation:	Make one copy of the activity (p. 168) per group of 3–4 students and cut up into individual cards.

Procedure

1 Divide the class into groups of 3–4 students. Each group has a pile of linking word cards (grey) and topic cards (white).

2 Explain that the object of the activity is for students to make sentences using the linking words and the topic words, e.g. *although + music: Although I like classical music, I don't often go to concerts.*

3 Students shuffle the linking words (grey) and place in a pile face down, then do the same with the topic cards (white).

4 Students take one card from each pile and use them to make a true sentence about themselves. They can use the word on the topic card or any related to the topic. If students are stuck they can change one of the two cards by putting it to the bottom of the pile and taking the next one from the top.

5 Other students in the group listen and judge if the sentence is grammatically correct or not (referring any disputes to the teacher).

6 If correct, the student keeps the cards and gains a point. If incorrect, the cards go back to the bottom of the pile. At the end the student with the most cards/points is the winner.

7 Teacher gives feedback on students' performance, eliciting more examples of any clause types that are causing problems.

Follow-up

Students choose three linking words from the grey cards and write three sentences about themselves, two of which are true and one false. They then read them out to their group, who guess which one is false.

22 Health

> • Use at the start of Unit 22 before Listening (CB p. 164).
> **Aim:** To introduce the unit topic of health and to pre-teach some vocabulary.
> **Time:** 20–30 minutes
> **Activity type:** Individual and pairwork. Students do a light-hearted questionnaire to find out how healthy they are.
> **Preparation:** Make one copy of the questionnaire (p. 169) per student, with the answer key removed.

Procedure

1 In pairs students discuss who they think is the healthiest person in the class and why, or they tell a partner about the healthiest person they know.

2 Give each student a copy of the questionnaire and 5–10 minutes to complete it.

3 Give students the key. Students check their answers and work out their score. (Question 6: note that although too much sunshine can be harmful, a little sunshine is better for you than none at all.)

4 Dictate the analysis below.

5 Find out who is the healthiest in the class (the person/people with the highest score).

6 In pairs, students compare the answers they gave.

> **Analysis:**
> 0–10 I am surprised that you made it this far! The clock is ticking. You need to make some drastic changes to your life and quickly.
> 11–20 Not too bad, but you still have a long way to go. There are signs of hope for you so don't give up.
> 21–30 You are doing well but don't get complacent, you can still do a lot more. With a bit of effort you could soon make the top group.
> 31–40 Are you an athlete? Or just a liar? You seem to be doing almost everything right, perhaps you should relax and let your hair down a bit.

Follow-up

In groups students think of other factors or tips for a healthy life.

23A Stories

> • Use after Reading (CB pp. 172–173).
> **Aim:** To revise storytelling and to look at how extracts can be taken from a story.
> **Time:** 25–30 minutes
> **Activity type:** Groupwork. Students put together a story from picture prompts and write an extract.
> **Preparation:** Make six copies of the picture story (p. 170) and cut up (fewer if the class is too small for six groups of 2–3 students).

Procedure

1 Ask students if they enjoy reading fiction, how many novels they read a year and how it compares to watching movies.

2 Divide the class into six groups, (or groups of 2–3 students in classes of fewer than 12 students).

3 Give each group a set of cut-up pictures and 5 minutes to put them in order, discussing what is happening in each picture, and summarising the whole story.

4 With the whole class elicit a group version of the story, establishing names for the characters, time and locations.

5 Collect one set of pictures, shuffle and give one to each group, pointing out that they now each have an extract from the story.

6 Each group has 10 minutes, working together, to write their extract. Encourage them to think about what has happened previously and about each character's feelings and motivation. Monitor, helping with tenses and encouraging them to use richer vocabulary.

7 Students read out their extracts in order. Alternatively collect them in and give students a copy to read.

> **Story: possible Synopsis**
> The young woman got married and had a baby, but her husband had to go away to fight in a war. She received a letter saying he was dead, so she decided to emigrate to another country to start a new life. After some time she met someone and remarried. Then, one day her first husband appeared at the door – he had not been killed, but had been a prisoner of war, and when he was released he came to look for her.

Follow-up

Ask students if they think it would make a good movie and, if so, who they would cast in the various roles.

23B Conjunctions and connectors

> • Use after Language development 1 (CB pp. 174–175).
> **Aim:** To practise using connecting words and participle clauses while telling a story.
> **Time:** 20–25 minutes
> **Activity type:** Groupwork. Students play a game, taking turns to tell parts of the same story, but working towards different endings.
> **Exam focus:** Paper 2 Part 2, Paper 3 Parts 2 and 3
> **Preparation:** Make one copy of the activity (p. 171) per group of 3–4, cut up into the four cards.

Procedure

1 Divide the class into groups of 3–4 and give each student a card.

2 Explain the object of the game: to finish a joint story with the words on their card. Students tell the same story taking it in turns to tell a part.

3 Select one student to begin the story. Turns then rotate around the group.

4 At each turn students must follow on logically from what came before but try to turn the story in the direction of their ending by introducing characters, objects or incidents as necessary.

5 Each turn, a student must try to use one of the structures listed on the card which is then ticked off. Each student can use each structure once only.

6 Other students can challenge if they think the link is not logical or the use of the structure is incorrect. If they cannot think of a sentence using one of the target structures, they can make up another sentence, just to continue the story.

7 When someone has ticked off five structures from their card they can finish the story (with the ending on their card) and win the game.

8 As students are playing, monitor by helping with use of target structures and noting errors to correct at the end of the activity.

24 Media mistakes

> • Use after Language development 3 (CB p. 183).
> **Aim:** To practise word-building and focus on common student errors.
> **Time:** 25–30 minutes
> **Activity type:** Pairwork and whole class. Students gamble for points on whether sentences are correct or not.
> **Exam focus:** Paper 3 Parts 1 and 5
> **Preparation:** Make one copy of each page (pp. 172–173) per pair of students.

Procedure

1 Write on the board: *I don't know how Sarah was yesterday but she looked happily.* Ask students, in pairs, to decide if it is correct or not. If incorrect, they should say why and be able to correct it.

2 Explain the object of the game; to win as many points as possible by gambling on whether sentences are correct or incorrect.

3 Give each pair of students a copy of the worksheet (Common mistakes) and 10–15 minutes to look at the sentences and decide if each one is correct and if they are sure. Students can gamble 1, 2, 5 or 10 points for each sentence depending on how sure they are.

4 Hand out cut-up game cards, students put *correct* and *incorrect* cards on the desk in front of them. Check answers one by one. For every question each pair puts 1, 2, 5 or 10 points on either the *correct* or *incorrect* card in front of them.

5 For each sentence select a pair to say why they made their choice and to correct the sentence if necessary. If a pair is wrong they lose the number of points they have put down, if they are right then they win that number.

6 Pairs write down their own points adding + or – to their score each time, e.g. they might write *+5* or *10* in the points column, depending how much they gamble and if they are correct or not.

7 At the end students add up the total. Any pairs with more than 60 pass, the pair with the highest score wins.

> **1 ✗** (*as* a journalist); **2 ✓**; **3 ✗** (*now/at the moment I'm working*); **4 ✓**; **5 ✗** (*it* was boring/I was *bored*); **6 ✗** (*one another/each other*); **7 ✓**; **8 ✗** (*illegal*); **9 ✗** (*such an* interesting story); **10 ✓**; **11 ✓**; **12 ✗** (that had *robbed* a bank); **13 ✗** (a bit *depressing*); **14 ✗** (on a *two-year* contract); **15 ✗** (an *inconvenient* time)

How much do you know about the FCE exam?

Answer the following questions by choosing the correct answer A, B or C.

1 **How many papers are there in the exam?**
A 4
B 5
C 6

2 **What's the pass mark?**
A about 60%
B about 65%
C about 70%

3 **Do you need to pass all the papers?**
A Yes, of course!
B No, passing most of them is enough.
C No, it's the total mark that is important.

4 **In Paper 1 (Reading) which part is the most important?**
A Part 1, because the questions are worth more marks.
B Part 4, because there are more questions.
C All four parts are equally important and have the same number of marks.

5 **In Paper 2 (Writing) do you have to answer all the questions?**
A Yes, so write quickly.
B You must answer question 1 and one other from Part 2.
C You can answer any two questions.

6 **In Paper 3 (Use of English) do you lose marks if the answer is wrong?**
A No, so take a chance if you don't know, you might be lucky.
B Yes, so only write an answer if you are really sure.
C Sometimes, it depends on how the examiner is feeling.

7 **In Paper 4 (Listening) how many times do you hear each part?**
A Only once, so listen carefully.
B Twice (or more if you ask the examiner nicely).
C You will hear each part twice before going on to the next part.

8 **In Paper 5 (Speaking) do you speak to the examiner or your partner?**
A You only discuss things with your partner.
B Sometimes to the examiner and sometimes to your partner.
C You say everything to the examiner.

9 **Is correct spelling essential?**
A Yes – all words must be spelt correctly in all papers.
B It's essential in Papers 2 and 3.
C No – everyone knows English spelling is difficult!

10 **Which of the following can you take into the exam: a dictionary, a bottle of water, a lucky rabbit's foot?**
A all of them
B none of them
C just the water and lucky rabbit's foot

Decide if the following statements are *True* (T) or *False* (F).

11 **All papers are worth the same number of marks.**
True ☐   False ☐

12 **In Paper 2 (Writing) you should keep a careful count of the words.**
True ☐   False ☐

13 **Contractions count as one word in Paper 3 (Use of English).**
True ☐   False ☐

14 **Spelling is not so important in Paper 4 (Listening).**
True ☐   False ☐

15 **You can take Paper 5 (Speaking) on your own if you are shy.**
True ☐   False ☐

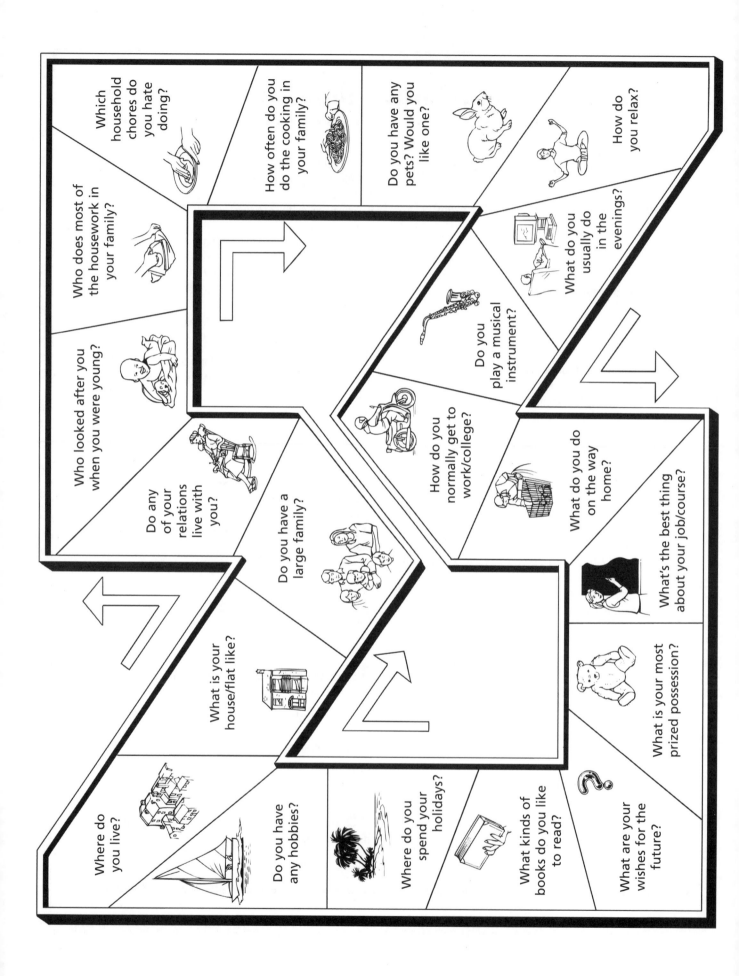

Picture A

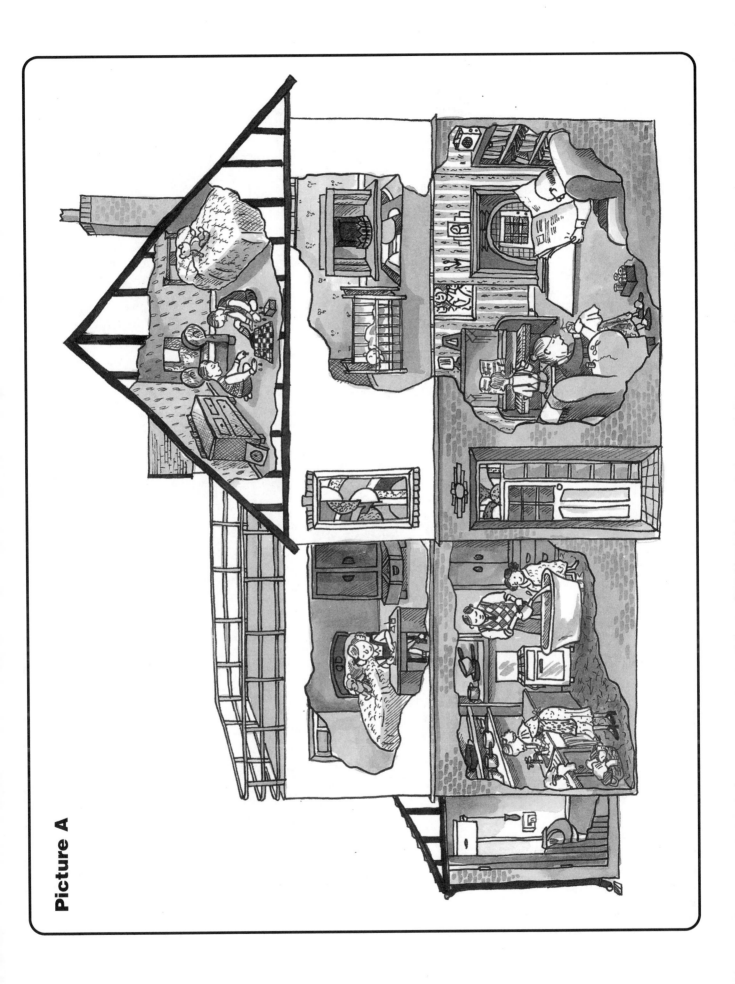

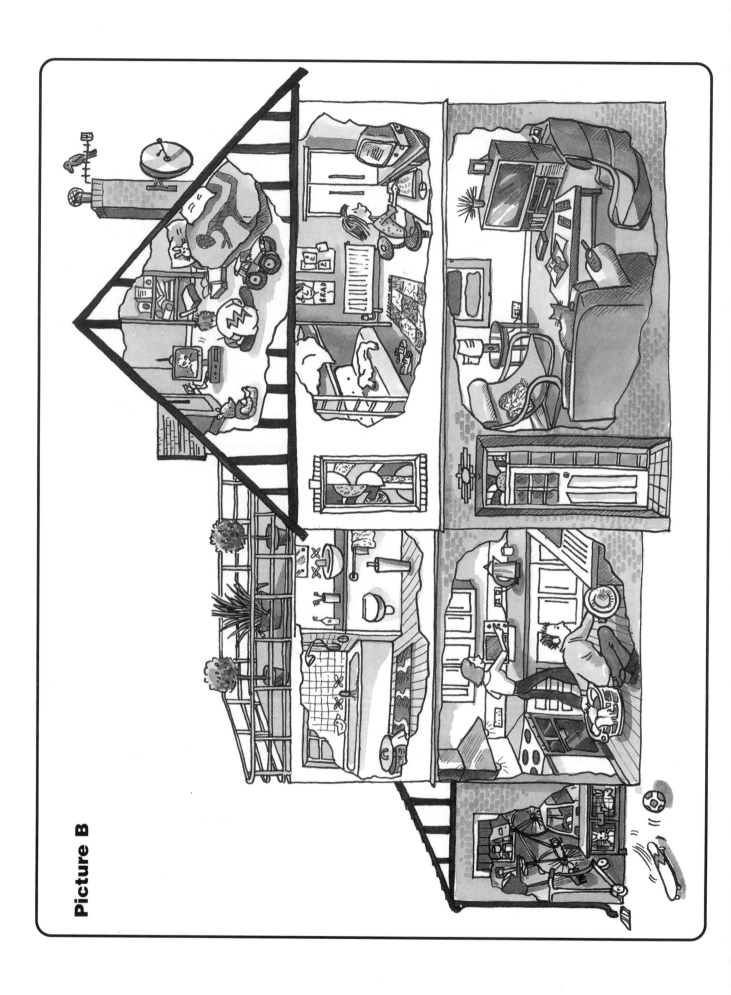

Picture B

Part 1

unique	final	quick
high	memorable	valuable
strong	natural	domestic
wide	central	exact
hard	guided	slight

opportunity	destination	breakfast
speed	experience	paintings
influence	light	life
gap	heating	date
work	tour	change

Part 2

Complete the text with the correct collocation.

Streatham Palace

Come for a day out at Streatham Palace. Join our knowledgeable staff on a **(1)**................. of this magnificent home. There is nothing else like this in London so this is a **(2)**................. to learn about **(3)**................. in the eighteenth century before the modern era of electricity and **(4)**................. communication. There has only been a **(5)**................. to the appearance of the house since it was built sometime between 1760 and 1780, the **(6)**................. is not known.

See the **(7)**................. in lifestyles between the rich house owner and the life of the staff. Staff at the time were used to **(8)**................. ; they worked twelve hours a day, six days a week. Actors in period costume play the parts of the people who lived there, telling you about their lifestyles.

After a **(9)**................. in the kitchen, the staff would start work. One of the first jobs was making up the fires in every room each morning. (These were the days before **(10)**................. !).

In the main part of the house you can see the **(11)**................. of French design, shown in the choice of furniture and fabrics. Visit the fantastic dining room where an invitation to dinner would have been a truly **(12)**................. . In the living room the large windows fill the room with **(13)**................. . The house contains many **(14)**................. by famous British artists of the time.

In the main bedroom see the huge bed that was made in 1825 as a present for an Indian Prince but never reached its **(15)**................. .

The tour continues to the area where the staff lived in the attic and finishes in our tearoom and gift shop.

This is a chance to make history come alive!

1 Which of these jobs do you think is the most stressful?

- fire fighter
- prison officer
- football referee
- miner
- actor
- soldier

2 Which of these jobs is the best paid? Which one should be the best paid?

- company director
- surgeon
- lawyer
- politician
- accountant
- musician

3 Which of these jobs requires the longest training?

- judge
- dentist
- vet
- ballet dancer
- architect
- chef

4 Which of these jobs would you find the most satisfying?

- midwife
- teacher
- farmer
- pilot
- photographer
- builder

5 Which of these jobs do you think is the easiest to do?

- librarian
- fashion model
- DJ
- traffic warden
- lifeguard
- bouncer

6 Which of these jobs do you think is the most useful for society?

- lorry driver
- dustman
- civil servant
- undertaker
- shop assistant
- TV/radio newsreader

Employer A

You and **B** are a couple. You have three children (8, 5 and 18 months). You have had two au pairs before.

You want an au pair who:

- **is artistic/musical**
  study?   what?   how long?

- **is experienced at looking after children**
  experienced?   how long?   who?   when?

- **speaks good English**
  study?   how long?

- **has lived/worked abroad**
  yes/no?   where/when?

- **can cook for a large family**
  experience of cooking?
  how long?   how often?

Employer B

You and **A** are a couple. You have three children (8, 5 and 18 months). You have had two au pairs before.

You want an au pair who:

- **is into sports**
  which sports?   how long?
  played cricket/hockey?   been skiing?

- **is fit/energetic**
  exercise?   played games with kids?

- **is a good driver**
  drive?   how long?
  any accidents?   driven on the left?

- **is good with pets**
  experience?
  what animals looked after?
  experience of fish or snakes?

- **is good with computers**
  studied computing?
  used Internet for homework?

Applicant C

In the future you want to be a dancer or an actor.
Now, you want to be an au pair in the UK because you need to learn English.

You:

- **can cook quite well**
- **can drive**
- **hate computers**
(For everything else answer as is true for you.)

You want to work for a family that:

- **has had an au pair before**
  yes/no?   how many?   how long?   when?

- **knows the local area well**
  lived there – how long?

Applicant D

In the future you want to run your own business.
Now, you want to be an au pair in the UK because you need to learn English.

You:

- **are a great cook**
- **passed your driving test recently**
- **don't like animals**
(For everything else answer as is true for you.)

You want to work for a family that:

- **knows about your country and traditions**
  visited?   when?

- **has lots of holidays (and trips to places)**
  how many this year?

Story A

Complete the gaps with *a/an*, *the* or *ø* (if no article is required).

The Girl and the Wolf

One afternoon .... wolf waited in .... dark forest for ....
girl to come by. He was very hungry because it had been ....
long time since he had eaten anything. Finally, ... little girl did
come along .... path and she was carrying .... basket of
food.

.... girl was happy, ... weather was good, ... sun was
shining and .... birds were singing. She loved .... nature and
being with .... animals. 'What .... beautiful day!' she
thought. She was happy that it was .... holiday and that she
wasn't at .... school.

.... wolf asked her if she was going to visit her grandmother and
she said that she was. So .... wolf asked her where her
grandmother lived and .... little girl told him. Then he ran off.
When .... little girl opened .... door of .... Granny's house
she saw that there was somebody in .... bed listening to ....
radio, wearing .... nightcap and nightdress. When she was no
nearer than ten metres from .... bed she saw that it was not her
grandmother but .... wolf, because everybody knows that
.... wolf in .... nightcap looks nothing like your granny. So
she took .... gun from her basket and shot .... wolf dead.

Moral: It is not so easy to fool .... little girls nowadays as it used to be.

Key (story A):

One afternoon *a* wolf waited in *a* dark forest for *a* girl to come by. He was very hungry because it had been *a* long time since he had eaten anything. Finally, *a* little girl did come along *the* path and she was carrying *a* basket of food.

The girl was happy, *the* weather was good, *the* sun was shining and *the* birds were singing. She loved *x* nature and being with *x* animals. 'What *a* beautiful day!' she thought. She was happy that it was *a* holiday and that she wasn't at *x* school.

The wolf asked her if she was going to visit her grandmother and she said that she was. So *the* wolf asked her where her grandmother lived and *the* little girl told him. Then he ran off.

When *the* little girl opened *the* door of *x* Granny's house she saw that there was somebody in *x* bed listening to *the* radio, wearing *a* nightcap and nightdress. When she was no nearer than ten metres from *the* bed she saw that it was not her grandmother but *the* wolf, because everybody knows that *a* wolf in *a* nightcap looks nothing like your granny. So she took *a* gun from her basket and shot *the* wolf dead.

Moral: It is not so easy to fool x little girls nowadays as it used to be.

Story B

Complete the gaps with *a/an, the* or *ø* (if no article is required).

The Girl and the Shoe

There was once .... poor young girl who was very unhappy. She had to spend all .... day cleaning .... house. She had two big ugly sisters who were unkind to her.

One day all .... girls were invited to .... party. .... beautiful young girl couldn't go because her big ugly sisters said she had to stay at .... home and do some housework. Anyway, although she loved .... music and dancing, she didn't have anything to wear.

Suddenly .... fairy godmother appeared. 'What .... pity!' said .... fairy godmother, 'Let me help you.' and gave her everything she needed: .... clothes, shoes and .... golden carriage. .... girl went to .... party and had .... great time. She met .... rich young man and danced with him all .... night.

At .... midnight she had to leave and was in such .... hurry that she left one of her shoes behind. .... young man kept it and spent .... next few days looking for .... girl who had lost it. Finally, he came to her house and asked her to try it on. .... shoe fitted perfectly. He asked her to marry him. She refused and said that first she wanted to go to .... university and get .... job, then when .... time was right she would consider getting married.

Moral: These days .... *marriage is less important than* .... *career.*

Key (story B):

There was once *a* poor young girl who was very unhappy. She had to spend all *x* day cleaning *the* house. She had two big ugly sisters who were unkind to her.

One day all *the* girls were invited to *a* party. *The* beautiful young girl couldn't go because her big ugly sisters said she had to stay at *x* home and do some housework. Anyway, although she loved *x* music and dancing, she didn't have anything to wear.

Suddenly *a* fairy godmother appeared. 'What *a* pity!' said *the* fairy godmother, 'Let me help you.' and gave her everything she needed: *x* clothes, shoes and *a* golden carriage. *The* girl went to *the* party and had *a* great time. She met *a* rich young man and danced with him all *x* night.

At *x* midnight she had to leave and was in such *a* hurry that she left one of her shoes behind. *The* young man kept it and spent *the* next few days looking for *the* girl who had lost it. Finally, he came to her house and asked her to try it on. *The* shoe fitted perfectly. He asked her to marry him. She refused and said that first she wanted to go to *x* university and get *a* job, then when *the* time was right she would consider getting married.

Moral: These days *x* marriage is less important than *a* career.

Group A – For

'Tourism should be encouraged: it is good for a country.'

- Creates work – many jobs are needed in tourist industry.
- Good for local economy – tourists spend money and for the country it brings in foreign exchange.
- Educational – people learn about other places, languages, etc.
- Helps to preserve and protect monuments, traditions and cultures – that's what tourists like to see.
- Transport is improved – tourists need better roads, trains, etc.
- Cultural exchange – visitors and tourists learn about each other's cultures.

Useful language – presenting

Sequencing: *Expressing opinions:*

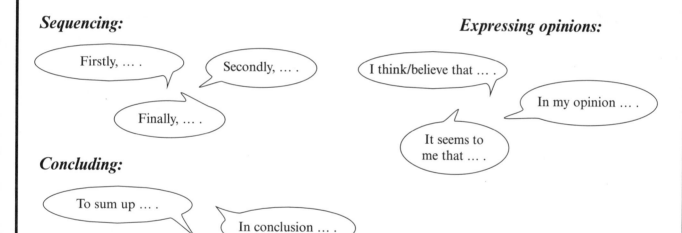

Useful language – discussing

Responding: *Suggesting:*

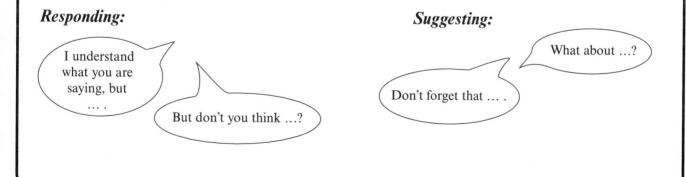

Group B – Against

'Tourism should be encouraged: it is good for a country.'

- Increases local prices – tourists will pay more than locals, so prices go up.
- Tourists use valuable resources – water, land, food, etc. go to tourists not locals.
- Creates pollution, disturbs wildlife.
- Destroys local culture – everywhere becomes the same.
- Jobs are seasonal and low-skilled – shop, restaurant and hotel work.
- Tourists don't respect places and people they visit – tourists can be rude and offend against local religions and customs.

Useful language – presenting

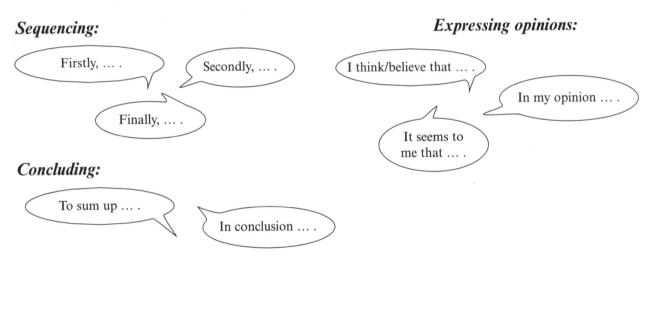

Sequencing:

Firstly, … .

Secondly, … .

Finally, … .

Expressing opinions:

I think/believe that … .

In my opinion … .

It seems to me that … .

Concluding:

To sum up … .

In conclusion … .

Useful language – discussing

Responding:

I understand what you are saying, but … .

But don't you think …?

Suggesting:

What about …?

Don't forget that … .

Set A: sentence cards

1 I had thought it would be really difficult to find, but it was .... easy.

11 It is .... impossible to find a parking space in the town centre, but occasionally you are lucky.

2 The tour had .... started when it started to rain.

12 We were .... starving when we got home as we hadn't eaten all day.

3 The situation is difficult and the future of the island looks ....

13 The castle is worth visiting, but the climb up to it is .... tough.

4 The town centre is very .... on a Saturday evening when all the bars and clubs are busy.

14 Why don't you come in autumn? The weather is usually .... good then.

5 The food is good so it's .... worth visiting this restaurant.

15 Famous residents include Fleming, who is .... well-known writer.

6 They try really .... to attract more tourists each year.

16 I tried sailing, which was .... very easy after the first few minutes.

7 We received a .... welcome from the smiling staff when we arrived at the hotel.

17 The CD was faulty and the case was damaged ....

8 Plans for the future need to be made now as the population is rising ....

18 If you don't improve safety someone could be .... injured.

9 Unfortunately, it is .... far from the city centre.

19 I was amazed – booking the holiday on line was .... simple and only took a few minutes.

10 The restaurant at the top of the mountain is .... expensive, so few people can afford it.

20 The service in the restaurant was .... slow and when the food did come it was cold.

Set B: adjective/adverb cards

surprisingly	pretty
hardly	quite a
bleak	as well
well	seriously
hard	remarkably
friendly	lively
quite	fast
extremely	absolutely
practically	actually
a bit	rather

Set A

think of	eager	keen on	regret
agree	enjoy	let	remember
apologise for	finish	look forward to	stop
can't help	hard	make	teach
decision	have trouble	opportunity	try
dream of	interested in	refuse	unable

Set B

wear	make	go	learn
watch	build	take	get
play	study	write	buy
feel	work	clean	spend
live	read	tidy up	predict
change	walk	turn down	ignore

Your club/society wants to raise money to buy some new equipment. Look at the options below and decide what the best method to raise the money would be. Discuss them and agree on the best way. For each method think about:

• **how much money you would need to start with**
• **how long it would take**
• **how easy it would be for you**
• **how successful it would be.**

write letters asking for money

busking

sponsored parachute/bungee jump

making and selling something

organise a raffle

street collection

washing cars

organising a concert or party

Where shall we start?

That's a good point.

Don't you think …?

Tell me what you think about this one.

I'm not sure I agree with you there.

So, have we decided?

Missing person

It's 9 May and Peter Brown is missing. Where is he? Why? What happened?
Look at his room – what can you say about him before he disappeared?

Part 1

alone – with no one else (physical) **lonely** – unhappy, missing friends (a feeling)	**shy** – not confident speaking to unknown people **nervous** – worried/frightened about something that may happen
imaginative – creative, with a good imagination **imaginary** – not real, fictitious **fantastic** – very good	**slim** – opposite of fat (positive) **thin** – opposite of fat (negative)
childish – behaviour like a child (negative) **childlike** – appearance, quality	**priceless** – worth a lot of money **worthless** – worth nothing **invaluable** – very useful, essential
economic – trade and industry **economical** – good value, using money/time well	**terrific** – very good **terrifying** – very frightening **terrible** – very bad
similar – almost the same (before noun) **alike** – the same (not before noun) **familiar** – easy to recognise, known	**convenient** – not causing problems **useful** – helping you get what you want
classic – well known, typical, influential **classical** – traditional	**high** – distance from ground **tall** – for people, and narrow things **long** – horizontal measure
foreign – from another country **strange** – unusual, different	**old-fashioned** – not modern, not usual any more **out of date** – no longer useful/correct
fun – enjoyable **funny** – amusing, makes you laugh	**injured** – hurt physically by accident **wounded** – hurt with a weapon (in a fight/war)

Part 2

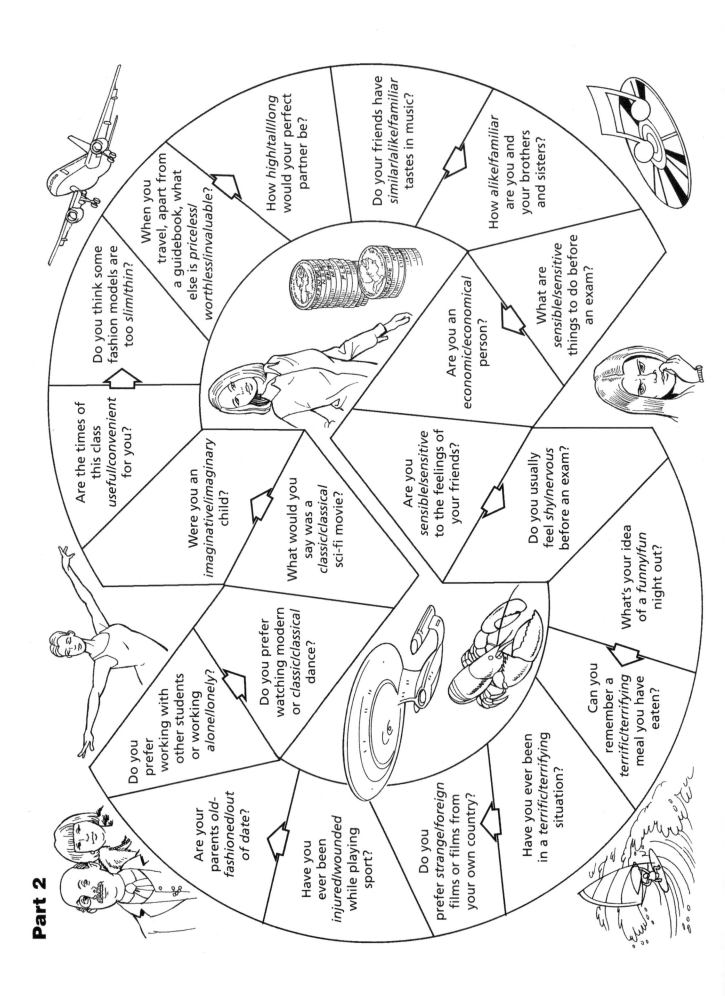

How *high/tall/long* would your perfect partner be?

Do your friends have *similar/alike/familiar* tastes in music?

How *alike/familiar* are you and your brothers and sisters?

When you travel, apart from a guidebook, what else is *priceless/ worthless/invaluable*?

Do you think some fashion models are too *slim/thin*?

Are you an *economic/economical* person?

What are *sensible/sensitive* things to do before an exam?

Are the times of this class *useful/convenient* for you?

Were you an *imaginative/imaginary* child?

What would you say was a *classic/classical* sci-fi movie?

Are you *sensible/sensitive* to the feelings of your friends?

Do you usually feel *shy/nervous* before an exam?

What's your idea of a *funny/fun* night out?

Do you prefer working with other students or working *alone/lonely*?

Do you prefer watching modern or *classic/classical* dance?

Can you remember a *terrific/terrifying* meal you have eaten?

Are your parents *old-fashioned/out of date*?

Have you ever been *injured/wounded* while playing sport?

Do you prefer *strange/foreign* films or films from your own country?

Have you ever been in a *terrific/terrifying* situation?

The **human body** quiz

How much do you know about the human body? Can you answer these questions by choosing A, B or C?

If you're not sure, have a guess!

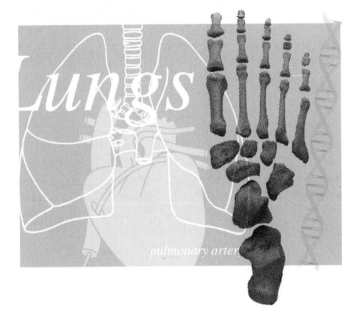

pulmonary arter

1 How many bones are there in the human body?
A 68
B 149
C 213

2 How much blood does an average adult have?
A 5 litres
B 6.5 litres
C 8 litres

3 How heavy is your brain?
A 0.6 kg
B 1.4 kg
C 3.2 kg

4 Is your heart
A on the left?
B in the centre?
C on the right?

5 What is a typical heartbeat for someone resting?
A 40–60 beats a minute
B 60–80 beats a minute
C 80–100 beats a minute

6 The study of how characteristics are passed from one generation to another is called
A genealogy.
B jeanetics.
C genetics.

7 Psychology is the study of
A mental processes.
B mental illness.
C mental intelligence.

8 Information in your body is stored in genes. How many are there in each cell of your body?
A 10,000
B 25,000
C 50,000

9 Genes are made up of a chemical called
A ADN.
B DNA.
C NAD.

10 The largest organ in your body is
A the liver.
B the heart.
C the lungs.

11 How many muscles are there in the human body?
A about 300
B about 600
C about 900

12 How much does a new-born baby weigh on average?
A 2.4 kgs
B 2.9 kgs
C 3.4 kgs

Your future

Look at this diagram of the future. Mark plans or predictions about <u>your</u> future on the diagram. You can use the words in the box or your own ideas.

go	meet	get	buy	change school/job
give up	find	become	take up	start work/a business
travel	move house	get married	have a baby	retire

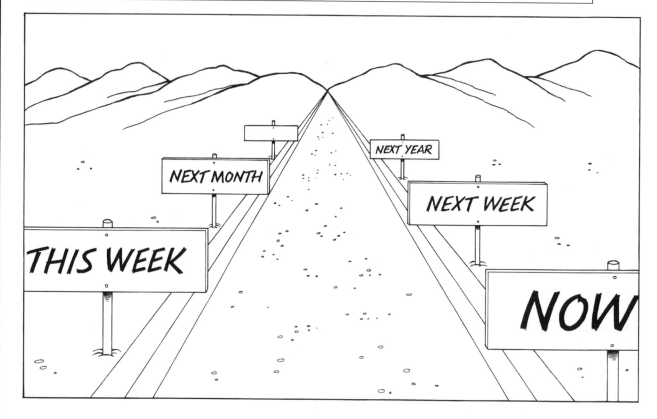

Think about which tense you will use to talk about each point that you have marked on the diagram. Tick (✔) the *Can you use it?* column in the table each time you use one of the forms.

Form	Example	Can you use it?
Present simple	The exam takes place every … .	
Present continuous	I am taking the exam in … .	
Will/Shall	I hope I will pass!	
Going to	I'm going to study hard.	
Future continuous	We will be taking the exam at that time.	
Future perfect	We will have taken the exam by… .	

ure	excite	ion	encourage
ment	combin(e)	ment	exist
ation	perform	ence	surviv(e)
ance	correspond	al	assist
ence	fail	ance	contribut(e)
ure	hesitat(e)	ion	embarrass
ion	approv(e)	ment	press
al	achieve	ure	organis(e)
ment	appear	ation	protect
ance	clos(e)	ion	attend
ure	refus(e)	ance	propos(e)
al	confirm	al	prefer
ation	depend	ence	imagin(e)
ence	restrict	ation	pleas(e)

HOW **AMBITIOUS** ARE YOU?

Answer the following questions by choosing *Yes*, *No* or *Maybe* each time.

1 Do you want to be an important person in your community?

Yes ☐   Maybe ☐   No ☐

2 Do you tend to be lazy?

Yes ☐   Maybe ☐   No ☐

3 Do you compare your ability and performance with that of other people?

Yes ☐   Maybe ☐   No ☐

4 Do you set your targets low in order to avoid disappointments?

Yes ☐   Maybe ☐   No ☐

5 Do you try to do things immediately rather than put them off until later?

Yes ☐   Maybe ☐   No ☐

6 Are you satisfied with your current achievements?

Yes ☐   Maybe ☐   No ☐

7 When you play a game is it important that you do well?

Yes ☐   Maybe ☐   No ☐

8 Would you prefer to laze on a beach rather than work/study?

Yes ☐   Maybe ☐   No ☐

'One day, Mr Blond, all this will be mine …'

9 Do you prefer to mix with ambitious and successful people?

Yes ☐   Maybe ☐   No ☐

10 Do you sometimes have days when you haven't done a thing?

Yes ☐   Maybe ☐   No ☐

11 Are you embarrassed if you are caught being lazy?

Yes ☐   Maybe ☐   No ☐

12 On an escalator, do you let it carry you along rather than walking up it yourself?

Yes ☐   Maybe ☐   No ☐

audience	standing ovation	director
choreographer	curtain	interval
rehearsals	stalls	first night
stage	review	front row
conductor	role	composer
ballet	costume	performance
box office	orchestra	programme
encore	critic	principal dancer
actors	spotlight	backstage
a play	concert	theatregoer

It's a place where ... .

They're people who ... .

It's a thing which ... .

It's a time when ... .

He/She's a person who ... .

It's an occasion when ... .

Student A

similar *to*	tired *of*	enthusiastic *about*	responsible *for*	right *about* something/ *for* someone	involved *in* something/ *with* someone
congratulations *on*	attitude *to/towards*	interested *in*	no hope *of*	linked *to*	suspicious *of/about*
full *of*	respect *for*	solution *to*	difference *between/in*	satisfied *with*	ready *for*
annoyed	excited	relevant	unusual	result (n.)	worried ....
relationship	capable	advantage	invitation	included	keen ....
famous	comparison	fed up	proud	suitable	jealous ....

at   of   in   for   with   on   about   to   between

Student B

annoyed *with* someone/*about* something	relationship *with/between*	famous *for*	similar	congratulations	full ....
excited *about/at*	capable *of*	comparison *with/to*	tired	attitude	respect ....
relevant *to*	advantage *of*	fed up *with*	enthusiastic	interested	solution ....
unusual *for*	invitation *to* something/*for* someone	proud *of*	responsible	no hope	difference ....
result (n.) *of*	included *in*	suitable *for*	right	linked	satisfied ....
worried *about*	keen *on*	jealous *of*	involved	suspicious	ready ....

towards   of   in   for   with   on   about   to   between

The global food and drink quiz

Can you answer these questions by choosing A, B, C or D? If you're not sure, have a guess!

1 How many branches of McDonald's are there in the world?

A 5,000
B 15,000
C 30,000
D 50,000

2 How many countries does McDonald's operate in?

A 48
B 99
C 121
D 187

3 McDonald's is the world's largest distributor of what?

A orange juice
B toys
C spoons
D forks

4 How many people work for KFC worldwide?

A 50,000
B 100,000
C 300,000
D 500,000

5 How many countries is Coca-Cola sold in?

A 140–160
B 160–180
C 180–200
D more than 200

6 How long does it take the Coca-Cola corporation to sell 1 billion (1,000,000,000) cokes?

A 2 days
B 6 days
C 10 days
D 14 days

7 What is the best selling confectionery brand in the world?

A Kit Kat
B M&M's
C Snickers
D Hershey Bar

8 Brazil is the world's largest producer of coffee. Which country is the second largest?

A Vietnam
B Kenya
C Guatemala
D Colombia

9 Which country drinks more coffee per person than any other?

A USA
B Switzerland
C Italy
D France

10 Which country drinks more tea per person than any other?

A Egypt
B UK
C Turkey
D Ireland

I'm not sure.

Personally, I think/reckon it's … .

I think it could/might be … .

Which one shall we go for?

CULTURAL DOS AND DON'TS

Work together to make 12 statements that you believe to be true.

1 In Korea you are (supposed to / not supposed to / not allowed to) write someone's name in (pink / green / red.)

2 In China you (mustn't / aren't allowed to / aren't supposed to) use your (teacher's / partner's / neighbour's) name when talking to him or her.

3 In Japan you (don't need to / are allowed to / must) wash (before / while / after) you have a bath.

4 In Greece you (shouldn't / ought to / are allowed to) touch your (earlobe / nose / chin) while you are talking to someone.

5 In Muslim countries you (don't have to / mustn't / don't need to) pass or receive things with (your left / your right / both) hand(s).

6 In Thailand you (mustn't / ought to / have to) put your foot on a (cigarette / coin / apple) if you drop it and it is rolling away.

7 In the UK you (don't have to / are supposed to / aren't allowed to) stand (on the left / on the right / at the bottom) on escalators on the Underground.

8 In Japan and Korea you (must / mustn't / shouldn't) use both hands when giving something (valuable / to an older person / edible.)

9 In Spain you (aren't supposed to / ought to / are allowed to) say 'hello' to everyone when you enter a (bar / lift / bus.)

10 In Arabic countries you (must / shouldn't / don't need to) open (gifts / letters / umbrellas) in front of the person who gives them to you.

11 In Buddhist countries you (can't / mustn't / don't need to) point (the soles of your feet / a finger / an umbrella) at people or religious images.

12 In Germany you (are supposed to / aren't supposed to / oughtn't to) keep your (hands / knife and fork / phone) on or above the table during a meal.

I've got a great photo of my grandad standing on the ice with lots of penguins. It was taken on a trip to the Arctic.

I remember going to Berlin about ten years ago and seeing the famous wall and wondering how much longer it would last.

My friend Jorge speaks Spanish as he comes from South America, but I can't remember if he's from Brazil or Colombia.

My brother is working in Italy now. I can't remember where exactly, but it is a town with a famous leaning tower.

My house used to be a railway station on a line that disappeared in the 1950s. It was built about 200 years ago.

I've been driving for years and have never had an accident. I think I was 15 when I passed my test.

My father got his first mobile phone in the 1970s. It was expensive, but very useful.

The first time I used some Euro banknotes in 2000 I thought that they were ugly, but now I quite like them.

My favourite painting by the artist Monet is his picture of the airport at Giverny.

Yesterday I was reading about the type of television programmes people watched in the 1920s – they were very different from now.

My cousin recently returned from a holiday in South Africa. He told me all about the strange animals he saw there, such as kangaroos.

My favourite picture of my friend Lucy is one of her sitting with a surfboard on a beach in Switzerland.

I think my parents got married in 1971, but I'm not sure. I know it was on the same day that people first landed on the moon.

I usually go on holiday with my friend John who arranges everything. This year I think we are going skiing in Holland.

My friend had a car accident in Asia. I can't remember if it was Japan or Korea, but it was a place where people drive on the left.

My friend in New Zealand is always having problems. Recently she was bitten by a snake when she was hill walking.

Relationships

Add the missing prepositions: *in, out, to, from, up, on, with,* **or** *ø*
(if no preposition is required) to the expressions below.

♥ to be attracted .... someone

♥ to fall .... love (with someone)

♥ to split .... (with someone)

♥ to get engaged .... someone

♥ to go .... (with someone)

♥ to propose .... someone

♥ to finish .... someone

♥ to separate .... someone

♥ to be .... love .... someone

♥ to chat someone ....

♥ to fancy .... someone

♥ to get .... well (with someone)

♥ to ask someone ....

♥ to get married .... someone

♥ to catch .... someone's eye

♥ to fall .... (with someone)

♥ to take someone ....

♥ to have a crush .... someone

♥ to flirt .... someone

♥ to move .... (with someone)

**Now put them in the order they might happen in a relationship, by numbering
them 1–20.**

Student A

Put these quotes from well-known films into reported speech and report them to your partner. Don't say who said them. Your partner will guess. Use reporting verbs (Who said/told/promised/explained/warned, etc.).

EXAMPLE: Don Corleone in *The Godfather*
'We'll make him an offer he can't refuse.'
Who said they would make someone an offer he couldn't refuse?

> Wait here.
> I'll be back.

Terminator in *Terminator*

> Life's a box of chocolates, son. You never know what you're going to get.

Forrest's Mother in *Forrest Gump*

> Look Jessie, ... I have to go back. I'm still Andy's toy. If you knew Andy, you'd understand.

Woody in *Toy Story 2*

> We've never lost an American in space, we're not going to lose one on my shift. Failure is not an option.

Gene Kranz in *Apollo 13*

> The force is what gives a Jedi his power. It's an energy field.

Obi-wan Kenobi in *Star Wars*

> With great power comes great responsibility. That is my gift, my curse.

Peter Parker in *Spider-Man*

> It is not a comedy I'm writing now.

William Shakespeare in *Shakespeare in Love*

Listen to your partner's quotes and choose the answers from here.

1 Jim Lovell in *Apollo 13*
2 William Wallace in *Braveheart*
3 Forrest in *Forrest Gump*
4 Rose in *Titanic*
5 Billy in *Billy Elliot*
6 Dr Hannibal Lecter in *Silence of the Lambs*
7 Dr Frankenstein in *Frankenstein*

Student B

Put these quotes from well-known films into reported speech and report them to your partner. Don't say who said them. Your partner will guess. Use reporting verbs (Who said/told/promised/explained/warned, etc.).

EXAMPLE: Don Corleone in *The Godfather*
'We'll make him an offer he can't refuse.'
Who said they would make someone an offer he couldn't refuse?

I'll never let go, Jack.

Rose in *Titanic*

I don't want a childhood, I want to be a ballet dancer.

Billy in *Billy Elliot*

The neck's broken, the brain is useless, we must find another brain.

Dr Frankenstein in *Frankenstein*

I came home to raise crops and a family. If I can live in peace I will.

William Wallace in *Braveheart*

I'm not a smart man, but I know what love is.

Forrest in *Forrest Gump*

I do wish we could chat longer, but I'm having an old friend for dinner.

Dr Hannibal Lecter in *Silence of the Lambs*

Houston, we have a problem.

Jim Lovell in *Apollo 13*

Listen to your partner's quotes and choose the answers from here.

1 William Shakespeare in *Shakespeare in Love*
2 Woody in *Toy Story 2*
3 Gene Kranz in *Apollo 13*
4 Peter Parker in *Spider-Man*
5 Terminator in *Terminator*
6 Obi-wan Kenobi in *Star Wars*
7 Forrest's Mother in *Forrest Gump*

A weekend away

You and your friends have decided to spend a weekend together doing something interesting. Look at the activities in the pictures and choose the one that would be most interesting for you, as a group.

A meditation course

A golfing trip

A trip to a grand prix race

Working on a conservation project

A trip to a health farm/beauty spa

A music festival

Camping in a local forest

Horse-riding in the mountains

Start

1. You have £1,000 in the bank.

2. Win £5,000 on the lottery.

3. You get a grant of £2,000 to spend on your house.

4. Inherit £6,000 from your aunt.

5. Start a business. Put in all your money.

6. Invest half your money in the stock market. Put in 50% of what you have.

7. Invest in a friend's new business. Put in 25% of what you have.

8. Get a new job and a pay rise. Save £500.

9. See a bargain in the sales. Spend £200.

10. Get into debt. Pay £200 in interest.

11. Splash out on a new DVD player. Spend £500.

12. You are careful with your money. Save £400.

13. You are caught speeding. Pay a fine of £200.

14. Buy and sell shares in a quick trade. Make £700.

15. Interest rates go up. Earn an extra £300.

16. You are extravagant with your money – use £400 of savings.

17. Lend a friend £200 – never see him again! Lose £200.

18. At work your company does well. Get a bonus of £1,200.

19. Lose money on a gamble investing in property. Lose £4,000.

20. The stock market crashes. Lose £3,000.

21. Your business, if you have one, (5,7) goes bust, bankrupting you. Lose everything!

22. Your business, if you have one, (5,7) is valued at £30,000. Sell it!

23. **Finish**

How much are you worth?

Shares £x2
Business £x2

What you (do), if you (go) into the red last/next month?

If you (win) a lot of money, what you (do) with it?

If you (start) a business one day, what it (be)?

What you (say), if I (ask) you to lend me some money yesterday/tomorrow?

What you (do), if you (find) some money in the street?

When/If a shop assistant (give) you too much change, what you (do)?

What you (do), when this course (finish)?

If you (not do) this course, what you (do) now?

If you (not start) this course, what you (do) now?

What you (do), if you (cannot) do the homework this week?

If I (have) a party at the weekend, you (come)?

If you (visit) anywhere in the world, where you (go)?

If you (change) one law, what it (be)?

If you (feel) ill this/tomorrow morning, what you (do)?

If you (watch) TV tonight, what you (watch)?

If/When you (make) your favourite meal, what you (cook)?

If you (go) to a party, what you usually (wear)?

If/When you (have) a cold, what you (do)?

Where you (go), if you (have) another holiday this/last year?

What you (say), if I (say) I love you?

If/When you (get) a headache, what you (do)?

Student A

Student B

Find the perfect (travelling) partner.

Look at the sentences below and choose the answers that are most true for you.

1 When I am on holiday I prefer

A to stay at home and relax. ☐
B to stay in my country. ☐
C to visit a country I know. ☐
D to visit a new country. ☐

2 For holiday accommodation I prefer

A camping. ☐
B youth hostels. ☐
C cheap hotels. ☐
D luxury hotels. ☐

3 I prefer to go on holiday

A on my own. ☐
B with one close friend. ☐
C with a big group of friends. ☐
D with my parents. ☐

4 For the arrangements, I prefer to

A do it all myself in advance. ☐
B let a travel agent do it all. ☐
C make them as I go along. ☐
D just see what happens. ☐

5 My ideal holiday would be

A a safari. ☐
B a tropical beach holiday. ☐
C in an interesting city. ☐
D in the mountains. ☐

6 I like to take

A just a few basics. ☐
B a small backpack. ☐
C a suitcase. ☐
D as much as possible. ☐

7 On holiday, what I like to see most is

A exotic animals. ☐
B famous works of art. ☐
C fantastic sunsets. ☐
D good-looking locals. ☐

8 When I travel I usually read

A a local phrase book. ☐
B a guidebook. ☐
C a racy novel. ☐
D a timetable. ☐

9 The thing I enjoy most on holiday is

A doing nothing. ☐
B visiting museums. ☐
C physical exercise. ☐
D learning about local customs. ☐

10 I think travel should be about

A history and culture. ☐
B food and drink. ☐
C falling in love. ☐
D looking for adventure. ☐

11 My photos are mainly of

A me. ☐
B historical buildings. ☐
C local people. ☐
D wild parties. ☐

12 I like to bring back

A lots of photos. ☐
B a few souvenirs. ☐
C traditional local crafts. ☐
D a new partner. ☐

Record Climb

Keiko Fujita, a 65-year-old Japanese woman, has climbed Everest by the North Face – the oldest person to do so. A team of local climbers helped her.

Everest facts

- Highest mountain in the world.
- First successful climb to the top was in 1953 by Tenzing and Hillary.
- Situated on the border of Nepal and Tibet.
- People consider the North Face to be the hardest route to the top.

New Car Rental Company

Some people have started a new Internet-based car rental company. They call it Simple Cars. You can find them at www.simplecars.com.

Simple Cars facts

- You must reserve and pay for cars online.
- You can collect a car from 22 airports around Europe.
- They charge customers per hour.
- People say they are the cheapest rental cars in Europe.

Record Balloon Flight

Diane May has flown a balloon solo non-stop around the world – the first woman to do so.

Flight facts

- A team of experts helped her.
- The wind blew her off course twice.
- A storm almost forced her to crash.
- She equipped her balloon with the latest technology.
- Her friends expect her to try to break another record next year.

New Hotel

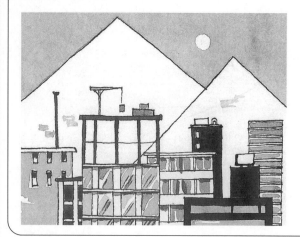

A company has announced that they are going to build a new hotel in Cairo next to the pyramids. A famous architect is going to design it and a local company will build it. Tour groups will use it, mainly.

Pyramid facts

- Someone built them 4,500 years ago.

- The government has protected them for many years.

- We think that conservation groups are opposing the plans.

Discount Card

Some organisations in London have launched a 'Tourist discount card'. They will also give cardholders a chance to book things more easily.

Card facts

- Hotels and train stations sell the card.

- You can use it to get up to 25% discount at many places.

- It costs £100.

- Many hotels, travel companies and restaurants in London accept it.

- We think it is the first discount card just for tourists.

Holiday Company in Trouble

Zoom Holidays has announced big discounts on their holidays after losing many customers. They have reduced some prices by 30–40%. They will give a free flight to all customers that book this month.

Company facts

- Two men started the company five years ago.

- The company employs 1,700 people.

- Analysts do not expect the company to survive.

PHOTOCOPIABLE

Happiness

Here are some things that might offer 'the secret of true happiness'.

Talk to each other about how important each one is and then choose the <u>three</u> that are most important.

✶ Excellent health and fitness

✶ Being in a stable relationship with a loving partner

✶ Having an interesting and worthwhile job

✶ Material wealth and a high standard of living

✶ Being good-looking and having a great figure

✶ A wide circle of supportive friends and family

✶ Being content spiritually

✶ Achieving promotion and/or respect at work

owing to	due to	because of
since	as	so as to
so that	in order to	in spite of
even though	despite	to
whereas	in case	although

money	clothes	friends
happiness	music	parents
work/job	holidays	children
food/drink	lifestyle	school
health	family	weekends

How healthy are you?

For each question choose the best answer for you.

1 How many glasses of water do you drink each day?

A 5
B 3
C 1
D none

2 How much alcohol do you drink?

A 3–4 beers or 1/2 bottle of wine per day
B 1 beer or glass of wine per day
C 2–3 beers or glasses of wine per week
D none

3 How much do you smoke?

A I don't smoke.
B the odd cigar or cigarette
C a few cigarettes a day
D like a chimney

4 Is your sleep disturbed?

A often
B sometimes
C occasionally
D never

5 How often do you have physical workouts of 30 minutes or more?

A 3 or more times a week
B 2–3 times most weeks
C once a week if I'm lucky
D never

6 Sunbathing – which is true for you?

A I sunbathe whenever and wherever I can.
B I sunbathe using sunblock.
C I hardly ever lie in the sun.
D I hide from the sun.

7 Do you eat breakfast?

A every day
B most days
C some days
D Who has time for breakfast?

8 Does your occupation use all of your talents?

A never
B rarely
C sometimes
D always

9 Can you freely express emotions such as anger, fear and sadness?

A always
B usually
C occasionally
D never

10 Do you feel physically attractive?

A Absolutely!
B I'm fairly attractive, I suppose.
C Well, better than I used to!
D Oh dear. Ask my mirror.

Answer key:

1 A 4, B 3, C 1, D 0	**4** A 0, B 1, C 3, D 4	**8** A 0, B 1, C 2, D 4
2 A 0, B 4, C 2, D 1	**5** A 4, B 2, C 1, D 0	**9** A 4, B 3, C 1, D 0
3 A 4, B 2, C 1, D 0	**6** A 0, B 1, C 4, D 3	**10** A 4, B 2, C 1, D 0
	7 A 4, B 3, C 2, D 0	

A

'And that's why he never went to the city again.'

	✔
Conjunction + clause (*when/while* …)	☐
Conjunction + *-ing* (*after/before -ing* …)	☐
Modifier (… *so/such a … that* …)	☐
Clause of purpose (… *to/in order to* …)	☐
Clause of reason (*as/since* …)	☐

Participle clauses:

Present (*-ing … he/she/they* …)	☐
(*Not -ing … he/she/they* …)	☐
Perfect (*Having + past participle … he/she/they* …)	☐

B

'And she never mentioned the incident from that day onwards.'

	✔
Conjunction + clause (*when/while* …)	☐
Conjunction + *-ing* (*after/before -ing* …)	☐
Modifier (… *so/such a … that* …)	☐
Clause of purpose (… *to/in order to* …)	☐
Clause of reason (*as/since* …)	☐

Participle clauses:

Present (*-ing … he/she/they* …)	☐
(*Not -ing … he/she/they* …)	☐
Perfect (*Having + past participle … he/she/they* …)	☐

C

'It was almost midnight by the time they had cleared up all the mess.'

	✔
Conjunction + clause (*when/while* …)	☐
Conjunction + *-ing* (*after/before -ing* …)	☐
Modifier (… *so/such a … that* …)	☐
Clause of purpose (… *to/in order to* …)	☐
Clause of reason (*as/since* …)	☐

Participle clauses:

Present (*-ing … he/she/they* …)	☐
(*Not -ing … he/she/they* …)	☐
Perfect (*Having + past participle … he/she/they* …)	☐

D

'When she got home she realised it had been in her bag all along.'

	✔
Conjunction + clause (*when/while* …)	☐
Conjunction + *-ing* (*after/before -ing* …)	☐
Modifier (… *so/such a … that* …)	☐
Clause of purpose (… *to/in order to* …)	☐
Clause of reason (*as/since* …)	☐

Participle clauses:

Present (*-ing … he/she/they* …)	☐
(*Not -ing … he/she/they* …)	☐
Perfect (*Having + past participle … he/she/they* …)	☐

Common mistakes

1　First decide if the following sentences are *correct* or *incorrect*. Put a tick (✔) or a cross (✖) in the first column.

2　Then decide how many points you want to gamble on each sentence – 1, 2, 5 or 10 – and write this in the second column. The more sure you are, the more you should gamble. You have 20 points to start with.

3　Gamble with the rest of the class. If you are right, you win the number of points you gambled. If you are wrong, you lose them. The team with the most points at the end are the winners!

20

		✓ OR ✖	POINTS
1	When I left university I worked like a journalist for a local paper for a few years.		
2	He has hardly worked since becoming a freelance journalist.		
3	**I used to work on radio but actually I'm working for a TV company.**		
4	There was a very low attendance at yesterday's news conference.		
5	I tried to read the article but I couldn't finish it because I was really boring.		
6	My sisters and I usually give each others books for Christmas.		
7	**She's a good journalist because she writes well.**		
8	Journalists must be careful that they don't do anything unlegal.		
9	It was a so interesting story that I read it twice.		
10	The problem with some reports is that they are inaccurate.		
11	**She had lots of frightening experiences when she was a war correspondent.**		
12	The front-page story was about a gang that had stolen a bank.		
13	I didn't read the story about the economy; it looked a bit depressed.		
14	They employed the reporter on a two years contract.		
15	**I don't watch the TV news as it is always on at an unconvenient time.**		
		TOTAL	

Game cards

correct

incorrect

1 point

2 points

5 points

10 points

Module 1 Test: How much do you remember?

Part 1 Lexical cloze

Choose which answer A, B, C or D best fits each space.

1 I prefer theatre to cinema because I like .... performances.

   A alive **B** direct **C** live **D** personal

2 Sam and Linda both .... to be quite well off.

   A believe **B** seem **C** see **D** think

3 New Year is one of the most .... celebrated festivals in the world.

   A fully **B** widely **C** largely **D** completely

4 We didn't know he was a police officer as he was in .... clothes.

   A plain **B** simple **C** uniform **D** secret

5 I'm not lazy but I hate doing .... chores.

   A house **B** housework **C** household **D** housewife

Part 2 Structural cloze

Think of the word which best fits into each space.

1 Clare didn't .... to like cheese but now she loves it.

2 Pete looks .... his brother but his personality is very different.

3 As a child, my brother loved fishing; he .... do it for hours.

4 Can you tell the difference .... British and American English?

5 .... anyone living in that house now or did they all move out?

Part 3 Key word transformation

Complete the second sentence so that it has a similar meaning to the first sentence, using the word given. Do not change the word given. You must use between two and five words, including the word given.

1 He never remembered to lock the back door.

   always

   He .... the back door.

2 John's cooking is much better than Jane's.

   nearly

   Jane's cooking .... as John's.

3 Would you like me to collect you at 8.00p.m.?

   up

   Shall .... at 8.00p.m.?

4 He has a few more books than I do.

   many

   I don't have .... he does.

5 Every time I try to speak my boss interrupts me.

   is

   My boss .... when I speak.

Part 4 Error correction

Some of these sentences are correct and some have a word which should not be there. Cross out the extra words.

1 My family were used to go to France every summer.

2 I would rather to work at home than travel into an office every day.

3 I think she is more happier than she was yesterday.

4 This hotel is a little bit more expensive but it's much better.

5 They've put a lot of new houses up to in the last few years.

Part 5 Word formation

Use the word given in capitals at the end of each sentence to form a word that fits in the space.

1 The village has only 250 ....   INHABIT

2 I like Maggie because she has a great ....   PERSON

3 Ten countries took part in the .... competition.   NATION

4 Mike lives on the .... of the town.   SKIRT

5 The problem with Jack is that he is very ....   TALK

Module 2 Test: How much do you remember?

Part 1 Lexical cloze

Choose which answer A, B, C or D best fits each space.

1 Sorry I'm late. I was .... in traffic for two hours.

   A standing **B** stopping **C** sitting **D** starting

2 It's important to do your homework if you want to keep .... the class.

   A on with **B** up with **C** up to **D** down on

3 In his latest film, Lacey plays a .... who likes living dangerously.

   A role **B** part **C** character **D** protagonist

4 Our postman .... our mail at about 8.00a.m.

   A delivers **B** gives **C** sends **D** gets

5 Nigel's only got a part time .... but he's looking for a full time one.

   A career **B** work **C** profession **D** job

Part 2 Structural cloze

Think of the word which best fits into each space.

1 I look forward to .... from you soon.

2 Carol likes studying science, and so .... Eve.

3 How long .... this been going on?

4 Can you play .... guitar or any other instrument?

5 It was .... days later that Norma found her glasses.

Part 3 Key word transformation

Complete the second sentence so that it has a similar meaning to the first sentence, using the word given. Do not change the word given. You must use between two and five words, including the word given.

1 Paul took up tennis three years ago.

   playing

   Paul .... three years.

2 Susan started to like jazz when she was a teenager.

   has

   Susan .... she was a teenager.

3 There's very little to do at the weekends.

   hardly

   There .... at the weekends.

4 Nina's looking for a job that suits her better.

   more

   Nina's looking for a .... job.

5 I can attend an interview at any time.

   available

   I .... an interview at any time.

Part 4 Error correction

Some of these sentences are correct and some have a word which should not be there. Cross out the extra words.

1 Vince has been worked for a bank since 2001.

2 I am agree that a good education is the most important thing.

3 Clare regrets that she hasn't had any experience of this type of work.

4 We have been studying the physics for two years.

5 Last year my friends and I have decided to go on holiday together.

Part 5 Word formation

Use the word given in capitals at the end of each sentence to form a word that fits in the space.

1 It was .... of Mark to leave the children on their own. RESPONSIBILITY

2 Linda can't drive a normal car because of her .... ABLE

3 It's horrible! It's the .... kitchen I have ever seen. DIRT

4 The company are .... about when I go on holiday. FLEX

5 Florence was given the job on the .... of her qualifications. STRONG

Exam practice 1: Writing and Listening

Paper 2 Part 2

Write an answer to **one** of the Questions **1–2** in this part. Write your answer in **120–180** words in an appropriate style.

1   This is part of a letter you received from an English pen friend.

> *In your last letter, you said you were going on a picnic in the country with some friends. Where did you go? What was the food like? I'd love to know whether you enjoyed yourselves.*

Write your **letter**, answering your friend's questions and giving relevant details. Do not write any addresses.

2   You have seen this advertisement in an international magazine. You are interested in applying for the job.

> We are looking for someone to write travel articles about cities round the world. If you are interested in this job, please write explaining why and outline the aspects of city life you would be able to write articles about.

Write your **letter** of application.

Paper 4 Part 4

You will hear an interview with Anita Perry and her son Darren, who is training to be a clown in the circus. For questions **1–7**, decide if the statements are **true** or **false**.

1   Anita used to like clowns when she was a child.

2   Anita was surprised when her husband lost his job.

3   Darren persuaded his father to apply for work in a circus.

4   Darren was confident that all three of them would get work in a circus.

5   Anita remembers how much she enjoyed their first summer in the circus.

6   Darren now finds his normal school lessons frustrating.

7   Anita remains unsure whether joining the circus was the right decision.

Module 3 Test: How much do you remember?

Part 1 Lexical cloze

Choose which answer A, B, C or D best fits each space.

1 It's .... a long way; I think we should go by car.

   A fairly **B** pretty **C** very **D** rather

2 That new exhibition of Mexican art is very ....

   A wonderful **B** marvellous **C** impressive
   D incredible

3 Only one of these cars was ever made so it's totally
   ....

   A unique **B** rare **C** unusual **D** strange

4 The critics love Newman's art but he hasn't had much
   .... success.

   A economic **B** economical **C** commercial

   D businesslike

5 We were just going out when there was a sudden
   heavy ....

   A rain **B** downpour **C** drizzle **D** hail

Part 2 Structural cloze

Think of the word which best fits into each space.

1 The capital is about two hours .... by train.

2 How do you .... coming round for a meal
   this weekend?

3 I haven't decided .... to go for my holiday this
   year.

4 Tom wants to be a vet because he's very interested
   .... animals.

5 I began .... read this book last week.

Part 3 Key word transformation

**Complete the second sentence so that it has a similar
meaning to the first sentence, using the word given. Do
not change the word given. You must use between two and
five words, including the word given.**

1 I smoked until my 26th birthday.

   stopped

   I .... 26.

2 Did you pay that bill, do you know?

   remember

   Do .... that bill?

3 Dan doesn't live very far from his office.

   fairly

   Dan's office .... his house.

4 Five years ago very few tourists went to the city.

   any

   There .... the city five
   years ago.

5 The children had wanted to go to the zoo for ages.

   forward

   They had been .... the zoo
   for ages.

Part 4 Error correction

**Some of these sentences are correct and some have a
word which should not be there. Cross out the extra
words.**

1 I was excited to hear the news that you're
   getting married.

2 It's usually worth asking at him for a lift home.

3 It was my decision for to hand in my notice.

4 He's not here, I saw him to leave about ten minutes
   ago.

5 What about getting a pizza before we see the film?

Part 5 Word formation

**Use the word given in capitals at the end of each sentence
to form a word that fits in the space.**

1 The survival of many animals is
   .... by humans.   THREAT

2 There are some .... between the
   two animals.   SIMILAR

3 Can the difference in the results be
   explained ....?   SCIENCE

4 Terry's probably the .... person
   I know.   FRIEND

5 .... is good for the economy but
   bad for wildlife.   TOUR

Module 4 Test: How much do you remember?

Part 1 Lexical cloze

Choose which answer A, B, C or D best fits each space.

1 It was .... of Steve to arrive late.

   A normal **B** usual **C** typical **D** general

2 Liz .... a company selling sports equipment on the Internet.

   A set off **B** set up **C** set out **D** set on

3 When I took up sailing, I loved it from the word ....

   A go **B** start **C** begin **D** do

4 If you've never tried windsurfing, you should .... it a go.

   A get **B** give **C** have **D** try

5 Greg has .... for the yoga course that starts next week.

   A written up **B** taken up **C** drawn up **D** signed up

Part 2 Structural cloze

Think of the word which best fits into each space.

1 Let's start .... talking about why it went wrong.

2 Kevin couldn't find his watch, so .... the end he bought a new one.

3 We .... been waiting 30 minutes when the bus finally came.

4 I don't get .... opportunity to speak French nowadays.

5 Sorry .... interrupt, but can I ask a question?

Part 3 Key word transformation

Complete the second sentence so that it has a similar meaning to the first sentence, using the word given. Do not change the word given. You must use between two and five words, including the word given.

1 The course was cancelled because there weren't many people.

   lack

   The course was cancelled because .... people.

2 That day Nick started work at 6.00a.m.

   been

   Nick .... 6.00a.m that day.

3 Ann watched TV from 8.00a.m to 10.00p.m.

   at

   Ann .... 9.00p.m.

4 He left, then later I arrived at his house.

   time

   He .... I arrived at his house.

5 She left university, then got married immediately.

   soon

   She got married .... left university.

Part 4 Error correction

Some of these sentences are correct and some have a word which should not be there. Cross out the extra words.

1 When I was studying, my friend he was working in a hotel.

2 Rob is interested in objects from ancient cultures.

3 If we want to do the job well we need two more equipment.

4 Jade gave to her sister a watch for her birthday.

5 Shall we make us a decision about which one to buy?

Part 5 Word formation

Use the word given in capitals at the end of each sentence to form a word that fits in the space.

1 There is nothing we can do; doctors say the illness is ....   TREAT

2 It would be more .... to take a taxi than to walk home.   SENSE

3 I don't want to sit next to Jack; he's so ....   BORE

4 I found the tourist office very .... about the city.   INFORM

5 I couldn't live without my personal organiser; it's ....   VALUE

Exam practice 2: Writing

Paper 2 Part 1

1   You are planning to do an evening class with a friend who has sent you a letter and a leaflet advertising a music school. Read the letter and the leaflet together with your friend's notes. Then write to the school asking for the information which your friend has suggested, adding any relevant questions of your own.

> *I think this is the type of course we're looking for. Could you write to the school to get more details?*
> *I've made some notes and maybe you can think of any other questions we need to ask.*

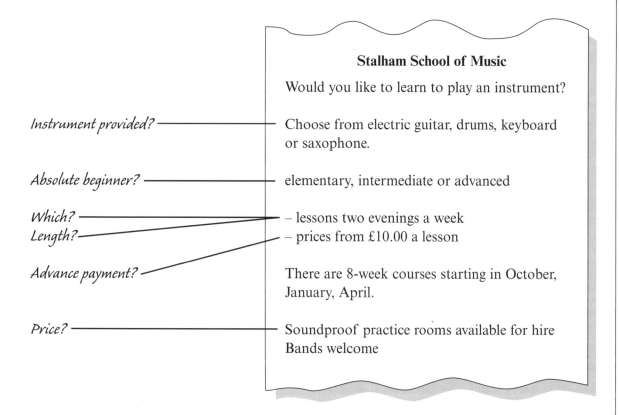

Instrument provided? ——————— Choose from electric guitar, drums, keyboard or saxophone.

Absolute beginner? ——————— elementary, intermediate or advanced

Which? ———————
Length? ———————
– lessons two evenings a week
– prices from £10.00 a lesson

Advance payment? ———————

There are 8-week courses starting in October, January, April.

Price? ——————— Soundproof practice rooms available for hire
Bands welcome

Stalham School of Music

Would you like to learn to play an instrument?

Write a **letter** of between **120** and **180** words in an appropriate style. Do not write any addresses.

Exam practice 2: Listening

Paper 4 Part 3

You will hear five people talking about newspapers. For questions **1–5**, choose from the list **A–F** the reason each person gives for choosing the particular newspaper they buy. Use the letters only once. There is one extra letter which you do not need to use.

A   good articles and photography

Speaker 1   [ ] 1

B   useful advertisements

Speaker 2   [ ] 2

C   interesting fashion pages

Speaker 3   [ ] 3

D   relevant sports coverage

Speaker 4   [ ] 4

E   informative reviews

Speaker 5   [ ] 5

F   reliable gossip columns

Module 5 Test: How much do you remember?

Part 1 Lexical cloze

Choose which answer A, B, C or D best fits each space.

1 I think it's quite .... that oil prices will
    rise soon.

    A probably   B likely   C surely   D definitely

2 You will .... a lot of opposition if you try to
    change things quickly.

    A come in for   B come up with   C come out with
    D come up against

3 We gave the job to Gordon because we know he is
    .... of doing it.

    A qualified   B able   C capable   D experienced

4 Cook was the first European to .... Australia.

    A reach   B arrive   C travel   D go

5 Alan hopes to get a good job in the .... future.

    A close   B near   C soon   D next

Part 2 Structural cloze

Think of the word which best fits into each space.

1 Ken fell and hurt .... when he was mending the
    fence.

2 Please come with me. I don't want to go on my
    ....

3 When Rachel heard the news, she didn't know ....
    to do.

4 I would be grateful .... you could inform me as
    soon as possible.

5 Could you tell me .... the nearest book shop is?

Part 3 Key word transformation

**Complete the second sentence so that it has a similar
meaning to the first sentence, using the word given. Do
not change the word given. You must use between two and
five words, including the word given.**

1 Jackie wanted someone to help her cook.

    cooking

    Jackie didn't want to do all
    .... own.

2 We did the work without help from anyone so it
    would be cheaper.

    keep

    We did all the .... costs down.

3 Will you have a room available next month?

    know

    Could you .... you will have a
    room available next month?

4 I am going to move house before the end of the year.

    moved

    I .... the end of the year.

5 A cure for cancer will be discovered soon.

    someone

    It won't be .... a cure for
    cancer.

Part 4 Error correction

**Some of these sentences are correct and some have a
word which should not be there. Cross out the extra
words.**

1 This time next week I'll be lying on a beach
    in Thailand.

2 While Sam was cooking he cut his finger badly
    himself.

3 Let's get a good seat before the other people will
    arrive.

4 The trains are every hour and the next one leaves at
    six o'clock.

5 Ron had a problem and he didn't know what to do it.

Part 5 Word formation

**Use the word given in capitals at the end of each sentence
to form a word that fits in the space.**

1 Marie always talks about her children
    with ....   PROUD

2 The results are worthless because the
    experiment was ....   SCIENCE

3 You should see Dr Jones as she is a
    .... in that area.   SPECIAL

4 Sexual .... is still a long way off
    in many companies.   EQUAL

5 *Lord of the Rings* is one of the ....
    films I've ever seen.   LENGTH

Module 6 Test: How much do you remember?

Part 1 Lexical cloze

Choose which answer A, B, C or D best fits each space.

1 The courts are very tough on young people who .... crimes.

   A make B do C commit D perform

2 Ted watches the World Cup but generally he's not .... on football.

   A interested B keen C enthusiastic D excited

3 We should use bright colours to make the words ....

   A stand out B stand up C stand off D stand in

4 They were too far away so I couldn't .... what they were talking about.

   A oversee B overtake C overlook D overhear

5 I think you should be honest and .... your mind.

   A say B speak C tell D talk

Part 2 Structural cloze

Think of the word which best fits into each space.

1 Sally was very upset and left the room .... tears.

2 Bill couldn't sleep because he isn't .... to so much noise.

3 It was very good .... you to help me last night.

4 I don't understand the relationship .... Chris and Alex.

5 That's the family .... house was damaged in the fire.

Part 3 Key word transformation

Complete the second sentence so that it has a similar meaning to the first sentence, using the word given. Do not change the word given. You must use between two and five words, including the word given.

1 Each month Sarah finds it a little easier to live alone.

   used

   Sarah is slowly .... her own.

2 My uncle owned the flat where I stayed.

   belonged

   I stayed in a .... my uncle.

3 This room is in a mess and I am certain it is Luke's fault.

   must

   Luke .... the mess in this room.

4 It seems to me that Pat can't drive.

   get

   I .... can't drive.

5 Brenda doesn't have enough experience for this office.

   too

   Brenda is .... work in this office.

Part 4 Error correction

Some of these sentences are correct and some have a word which should not be there. Cross out the extra words.

1 Determination is the quality that needed to be successful.

2 It's quite a good film but it's a bit slow in places.

3 We saw a man who carrying a large black bag.

4 Jean said she would be late but she didn't tell to me why.

5 Andy is used to hate working here but now he loves it.

Part 5 Word formation

Use the word given in capitals at the end of each sentence to form a word that fits in the space.

1 Ian's very ....; he hates waiting, even for a minute. PATIENCE

2 The story is slow because of the author's .... style. DESCRIBE

3 There's a very strong .... between the two girls. FRIEND

4 We could see the boss's .... with the poor quality of our work. SATISFY

5 That answer doesn't make sense; it's .... LOGIC

Exam practice 3: Writing

Paper 2 Part 2

Write an answer to **one** of the Questions **1–3** in this part. Write your answer in **120–180** words in an appropriate style.

1   You have decided to enter a short-story writing competition. The rules of the competition say that the story must begin with these words.

As Danny walked out on to the sports field, he suddenly felt nervous. Would he be able to do as well as everybody expected?

Write your **story**.

2   A tourist resort in your country would like to attract more young visitors. You have been asked to write an article for an international travel magazine describing the resort briefly and explaining why it is a good place for young people to go on holiday.

Write your **article**.

3   You have seen this advertisement in an English language newspaper.

HOLIDAY JOB

We need someone to help us look after our two children (12 and 13 years old) during their summer holidays. They are lively and only speak English. You will spend afternoons with them, organising fun activities and keeping them out of trouble.

If you think you're the right person for the job, please write telling us why and the dates when you'll be available.

Write to Mrs Catchpole.

Write a **letter of application** to Mrs Catchpole. Do not write any addresses.

Exam practice 3: Listening

You will hear an interview with a woman who runs her own company, providing training for businesspeople. For questions **1–10**, complete the sentences.

Fiona's company is called _____ **1**

Fiona originally trained as an _____ **2**

A friend of Fiona's who was talking at a _____ **3** asked for her help.

Fiona got financial help from her _____ **4**

Fiona's first client worked for a _____ **5**

The courses offered by Fiona's company cost at least £ _____ **6**

Businesspeople sometimes need training in how to use _____ **7** during talks.

At the end of each course, people give their talks in a _____ **8**

Fiona says that talks are most boring when speakers _____ **9**

Sometimes when speakers are nervous, they actually appear to be _____ **10**

Module 7 Test: How much do you remember?

Part 1 Lexical cloze

Choose which answer A, B, C or D best fits each space.

1 For the Oscar awards ceremony most actors wear a .... jacket.

   A tuxedo   **B** smoking   **C** dinner   **D** blazer

2 To be .... I have no idea what the solution is.

   A reliable   **B** honest   **C** trustworthy   **D** fair

3 Helen arrived wearing a beautiful yellow .... cotton shirt.

   A striped   **B** straight   **C** tight   **D** scruffy

4 If business doesn't improve we are in .... of losing everything.

   A risk   **B** chance   **C** uncertainty   **D** danger

5 The problem is that, ... from us, Matthew hasn't got any family.

   A apart   **B** besides   **C** also   **D** as well

Part 2 Structural cloze

Think of the word which best fits into each space.

1 If there's one thing Nicola loves it's shopping .... shoes.

2 We had a couple of bad days but .... the whole the weather was great.

3 We wanted to know .... there would be time to go shopping.

4 Your safety is important, so please pay attention at .... times.

5 I thought I would fail the exam, but to .... surprise I passed.

Part 3 Key word transformation

Complete the second sentence so that it has a similar meaning to the first sentence, using the word given. Do not change the word given. You must use between two and five words, including the word given.

1 I'm sure Gill hasn't left yet because her computer is still on.

   can't

   Gill .... because her computer is still on.

2 I partly agree with you, but you have forgotten one thing.

   extent

   I agree with you .... but you have forgotten one thing.

3 The club wouldn't let Jack buy a drink because he wasn't a member.

   allowed

   Jack .... a drink at the club because he wasn't a member.

4 Karen went to work but it wasn't necessary, as there was nothing to do.

   have

   Karen .... work as there was nothing to do.

5 You shouldn't eat in here.

   supposed

   You .... in here.

Part 4 Error correction

Some of these sentences are correct and some have a word which should not be there. Cross out the extra words.

1 Sometimes it's really hard to know what is in fashion.

2 It's important to look like smart if you want to do well at the interview.

3 You mustn't to tell anyone where I am going until tomorrow.

4 Willy ought to do relax more at the weekends.

5 After a while the situation went from bad to worse.

Part 5 Word formation

Use the word given in capitals at the end of each sentence to form a word that fits in the space.

1 The director's first film achieved .... success.   WORLD

2 I don't care if people think my clothes are ....   FASHION

3 It's hard to make a fair .... between different shops.   COMPARE

4 Lisa needs to eat more .... than she does at the moment.   HEALTH

5 What do you do for a ....?   LIFE

Module 8 Test: How much do you remember?

Part 1 Lexical cloze

Choose which answer A, B, C or D best fits each space.

1 Peter .... me to go to the party.

   A agreed   **B** persuaded   **C** offered   **D** refused

2 The contract said we couldn't do it but our lawyer found a way .... it.

   A round   **B** across   **C** off   **D** through

3 Many people dream that one day they will .... with someone very attractive.

   A chat up   **B** take out   **C** go out   **D** get married

4 I was very late but I had just enough time to quickly .... to the shops.

   A stroll   **B** dash   **C** creep   **D** wander

5 At first it was hard but in the end I .... to do it.

   A achieved   **B** succeeded   **C** knew   **D** managed

Part 2 Structural cloze

Think of the word which best fits into each space.

1 Don't cheat, you'll never get away .... it.

2 In the future you will .... able to watch any film when you want.

3 I'm too busy and I'm too tired. In .... words, I can't go out tonight.

4 Scientists haven't yet succeeded .... finding a cure for HIV.

5 I replied .... I had no idea what he was talking about.

Part 3 Key word transformation

Complete the second sentence so that it has a similar meaning to the first sentence, using the word given. Do not change the word given. You must use between two and five words, including the word given.

1 'I didn't break the window,' said the boy.

   breaking

   The boy .... window.

2 It is possible that we can do it for you tomorrow.

   might

   We .... it for you tomorrow.

3 'I must go this afternoon,' she said.

   that

   She said .... afternoon.

4 I can put petrol in my car but that's about it.

   know

   I .... petrol in my car but that's about it.

5 'Will you lend me some money?' she asked.

   I

   She asked me .... some money.

Part 4 Error correction

Some of these sentences are correct and some have a word which should not be there. Cross out the extra words.

1 He asked me what my name was it.

2 I like Jane because she has a good sense of humour.

3 Last but not the least, the trains are usually late.

4 To sum up, there are much arguments on both sides.

5 First of all, I'd like to say you that cars can be both useful and harmful.

Part 5 Word formation

Use the word given in capitals at the end of each sentence to form a word that fits in the space.

1 Try to make a good .... at the first meeting.   IMPRESS

2 I'd like to come but .... I'm busy that day.   FORTUNE

3 It is important that all .... look after their staff.   EMPLOY

4 This play should be good, it has a strong ....   RECOMMEND

5 We are quite different but we get on .... well.   INCREDIBLE

Exam practice 4: Writing

Paper 2 Part 2

Write an answer to one of the Questions **1–4** in this part. Write your answer in **120–180** words in an appropriate style.

1   Following a class discussion on the subject of clothes and fashion, your teacher has asked you to write a composition with this title:

Some people think you can tell a person's character by the clothes they wear. Do you agree?

Write your **composition**.

2   You have seen this announcement in an international magazine for young people.

> **What's your favourite family TV programme?**
>
> We're offering a prize of £200 for the best article recommending
> a good TV programme to our readers.
> The programme must be suitable for people of all ages.

Write your **article**.

3   You have decided to enter a short-story competition. The competition rules say that the story must **begin** with these words.

It all began with a mysterious text message.

Write your **story**.

4   This is part of a letter from an English-speaking friend.

> *In your last letter you said you were going to do a course in either photography or painting. Which did you choose in the end? What's the course like? Have you made any new friends there?*
>
> *Please write back soon with your news.*
>
> *Chris*

Write your **letter**. Do not write any addresses.

Exam practice 4: Listening

You will hear a radio interview with a woman who went on a special singing holiday in Spain. For questions **1–7**, choose the best answer **A, B** or **C**.

1 How did Janice first hear about the holiday?

    A from friends in Spain

    B from a travel agent

    C from a website

    `[ ] 1`

2 How did Janice react when her friend decided not to go on the holiday?

    A She tried to cancel her own booking.

    B She thought it was the right decision.

    C She blamed her friend for letting her down.

    `[ ] 2`

3 How does Janice feel now about going on holiday alone?

    A It's better because you can meet new people.

    B It's not how she'd prefer to travel in future.

    C It's an experience she wouldn't ever repeat.

    `[ ] 3`

4 What did Janice think of the singing classes?

    A Some knowledge of singing helped her to cope.

    B The elementary level classes were too hard for her.

    C She thought she should have been in a higher group.

    `[ ] 4`

5 What aspect of the holiday disappointed Janice?

    A the attitude of the singing tutors

    B the fact that the classes were in Spanish

    C the way some students slowed down the classes

    `[ ] 5`

6 What did Janice do in her free time?

    A She usually took the opportunity to relax.

    B She made friends at the local university.

    C She took advantage of the guided tours.

    `[ ] 6`

7 At the end of the interview, Janice says that

    A the holiday was good value for money.

    B she's looking forward to going to Spain again.

    C on her next holiday she'll do something less challenging.

    `[ ] 7`

Module 9 Test: How much do you remember?

Part 1 Lexical cloze

Choose which answer A, B, C or D best fits each space.

1 Would you like to be your own ………?

A boss   B manager   C employer   D chief

2 Val tries not to spend all her wages. She's saving for a ……… day.

A sunny   B wet   C rainy   D cloudy

3 I am writing to ……… about a report in yesterday's paper.

A object   B complain   C express   D disapprove

4 Chris has applied for a ……… so he's got an appointment at the bank.

A cash   B deposit   C debt   D loan

5 The ………, of the people I work with love football.

A all   B both   C majority   D most

Part 2 Structural cloze

Think of the word which best fits into each space.

1 I prefer to spend my money ……… going out.

2 Rose is very careful ……… her money.

3 Everyone ……… been very kind and helpful since my accident.

4 We have a few shops in my village but ……… isn't a post office.

5 If you don't have the cash you can pay ……… cheque.

Part 3 Key word transformation

Complete the second sentence so that it has a similar meaning to the first sentence, using the word given. Do not change the word given. You must use between two and five words, including the word given.

1 We must avoid anything that endangers the children at school.

puts

We must avoid anything that ……………………………… at school.

2 Keith said he would come at six if he hadn't heard from me before then.

hear

'I'll come at six unless ……………………………… before then,' Keith said.

3 Provided you're not a vegetarian, I'll cook for you.

long

I'll cook for you ……………………………… not a vegetarian.

4 Judith was late because her car didn't start.

started

If Judith's car ……………………………… been on time.

5 Very few people seem to be polite these days.

hardly

……………………………… to be polite these days.

Part 4 Error correction

Some of these sentences are correct and some have a word which should not be there. Cross out the extra words.

1 To make this model you need paper, some string and a scissors.

2 Having a party in our house on the New Year's Eve is a family tradition.

3 I'll be at work tomorrow unless I'm not sick.

4 When you stop complaining I'll do something about it.

5 More than one of Oliver's friends got into debt in last year.

Part 5 Word formation

Use the word given in capitals at the end of each sentence to form a word that fits in the space.

1 We are looking for people with talent and ……… .   CREATE

2 Sebastian is a ……… advisor in New York.   FINANCE

3 This new phone has a wonderful ……… design.   INNOVATE

4 I think there's too much ……… on TV.   ADVERTISE

5 There was a small cut in Ted's finger but it didn't ……… .   BLOOD

Module 10 Test: How much do you remember?

Part 1 Lexical cloze

Choose which answer A, B, C or D best fits each space.

1 The police went to Turner's house but, not ...., he had disappeared.

A amazingly   B incredibly   C surprisingly
D astonishingly

2 You must have insurance in case you .... an accident.

A endure   B receive   C undertake   D suffer

3 Sometimes finding the right place to stay can be a lot of ....

A hassle   B nuisance   C problem   D difficulty

4 Camping is very cheap after the .... investment in equipment.

A starting   B initial   C first   D primary

5 The number of people getting married each year is on the ....

A fall   B reduction   C decline   D drop

Part 2 Structural cloze

Think of the word which best fits into each space.

1 .... is expected that thousands of people will join the protest.

2 It's .... time we left; we don't want to be late.

3 Now we're lost! I wish we .... remembered to bring a map.

4 The aim .... the report is to highlight recent problems.

5 It's important to prepare everything well .... advance.

Part 3 Key word transformation

Complete the second sentence so that it has a similar meaning to the first sentence, using the word given. Do not change the word given. You must use between two and five words, including the word given.

1 The examiner will show you some pictures.

be

You will .... the examiner.

2 Nigel gets nervous when people ask questions.

make

People .... nervous.

3 I would have preferred you to tell me earlier.

rather

I .... me earlier.

4 We think someone has been rescued.

thought

Someone .... rescued.

5 I really want my girlfriend to call me tonight.

would

If .... me tonight.

Part 4 Error correction

Some of these sentences are correct and some have a word which should not be there. Cross out the extra words.

1 It appears that in the majority of people disagree with the company.

2 I spent a long time watching the birds in the garden.

3 The only one problem is that I can't remember where I put my wallet.

4 He looked at me as though I was crazy.

5 The tickets can be booked by phone and is collected at the airport.

Part 5 Word formation

Use the word given in capitals at the end of each sentence to form a word that fits in the space.

1 A few of us are going .... Do you want to come?   CLUB

2 I don't know what to say! The prize was completely ....   EXPECT

3 You're being .... to expect a good hotel at such a low price.   REAL

4 I have no .... in recommending this hotel.   HESITATE

5 Dan is .... to the fact that he might not get the job.   RESIGN

Exam practice 5: Writing

Paper 2 Part 2

Write an answer to **one** of the Questions **1–4** in this part. Write your answer in **120–180** words in an appropriate style.

1 This is part of a letter you have received from a friend in another country.

> *As part of my college course, I have to do an assignment about job opportunities for young people in different parts of the world. Please could you write me a short report about your country, saying how easy it is for young people to get a job and what opportunities are open to them. I can then include the information in my project.*

Write your **report**.

2 In class, you have been discussing attitudes towards means of transport in your country. Now your teacher has asked you to write a composition on the following subject.

Public transport is only for people who can't afford their own car. Do you agree?

Write your **composition**.

3 This is part of a letter you have received from an English-speaking pen friend.

> Thanks very much for the invitation to stay with you this summer. I'd love to come! Will it be hot? What clothes and sports equipment do I need to bring? Also, I'd like to bring a gift to thank your family — what sort of thing would be appropriate?

Write your **letter**, answering your friend's questions and giving relevant details. Do not write any addresses.

4 You decide to enter a competition which is being organised by an international wildlife magazine. Readers have been invited to send in articles on the following topic:

Should wild animals be kept in city centre zoos?

Write your **article**.

Exam practice 5: Listening

You will hear five people talking about adventurous activities they once took part in. For questions **1–5**, choose from the list **A–F** how each person says they felt about the activity. Use the letters only once. There is one extra letter which you do not need to use.

A   satisfied with a personal achievement

Speaker 1 | 1

B   put off by the attitude of others

Speaker 2 | 2

C   impressed by the way people behaved

Speaker 3 | 3

D   disappointed not to get value for money

Speaker 4 | 4

E   determined to seek financial compensation

Speaker 5 | 5

F   relieved not to feel out of place

Module 11 Test: How much do you remember?

Part 1 Lexical cloze

Choose which answer A, B, C or D best fits each space.

1 As far as I'm .... , the accident should never have happened.

  A worried **B** concerned **C** disturbed **D** distressed

2 Everyone is aware of the .... between pollution and global warming.

  A join **B** line **C** relation **D** link

3 Angela's going home early; she's feeling a bit .... the weather.

  A under **B** below **C** on top of **D** out of

4 Gary's had his car for ten years and it's still going ....

  A long **B** far **C** strong **D** fast

5 The doctor told Jenny to .... red meat completely.

  A cut out **B** put on **C** take up **D** get over

Part 2 Structural cloze

Think of the word which best fits into each space.

1 I am writing .... response to an advertisement in yesterday's paper.

2 George is worried about his cat; it's .... its food again.

3 Beckham has been described .... England's greatest footballer.

4 Take your mobile in .... I need to contact you.

5 Fiona has been to a number of European countries, ... as Italy and France.

Part 3 Key word transformation

Complete the second sentence so that it has a similar meaning to the first sentence, using the word given. Do not change the word given. You must use between two and five words, including the word given.

1 My feet are too big for these shoes.

  not

  These shoes .... for my feet.

2 There were so many people there that Ellen couldn't get in.

  lot

  There were .... people there that Ellen couldn't get in.

3 It looks like a win for England; they're 3–0 up.

  going

  It looks .... to win; they're 3–0 up.

4 Neil did well at university, but he still can't get a job.

  spite

  Neil can't get a job .... that he did well at university.

5 That's a lovely smell; it probably means it's time for lunch.

  if

  It .... ready.

Part 4 Error correction

Some of these sentences are correct and some have a word which should not be there. Cross out the extra words.

1 Tanya finds that yoga and massage give in her a sense of well-being.

2 You shouldn't take Annette's loyalty for granted.

3 Phil can't play tomorrow because of he has a bad leg.

4 We set off early in case the traffic was heavy.

5 The doctor gave Walt a clean bill of my health.

Part 5 Word formation

Use the word given in capitals at the end of each sentence to form a word that fits in the space.

1 There was great .... in the class before the exam.   ANXIOUS

2 The director's last film was very successful ....   FINANCE

3 The sound of .... filled the room.   LAUGH

4 Next year I want to have a .... lifestyle than this year.   HEALTH

5 He resigned because of worry and ....   FRUSTRATE

Module 12 Test: How much do you remember?

Part 1 Lexical cloze

Choose which answer A, B, C or D best fits each space.

1 The characters were good but the plot was ....

   A lifelike   **B** interesting   **C** convincing   **D** predictable

2 You can't drive through here; it's .... the law.

   A opposed   **B** against   **C** outside   **D** opposite

3 The events happen in the .... between the two World Wars.

   A history   **B** period   **C** date   **D** space

4 When you have read it I'd like some .... on what you thought of it.

   A report   **B** reaction   **C** feedback   **D** opinion

5 Science fiction is Maskell's least favourite .... of books.

   A group   **B** make   **C** writer   **D** genre

Part 2 Structural cloze

Think of the word which best fits into each space.

1 Clive has asked me to help him and I'm unsure .... to agree or not.

2 .... written the letter, Maria decided not to post it.

3 I'll go instead .... you, if you want me to.

4 I haven't met him .... I can't tell you what he's like.

5 We .... our bags searched but they didn't find anything.

Part 3 Key word transformation

Complete the second sentence so that it has a similar meaning to the first sentence, using the word given. Do not change the word given. You must use between two and five words, including the word given.

1 Someone has to feed the chickens every day.

   be

   The chickens .... every day.

2 These instructions don't have any logic at all, do they?

   totally

   These instructions .... they?

3 Someone is making me some new curtains for the bedroom.

   made

   I'm .... for the bedroom.

4 I bought the book because I wanted to give it to Kathy for her birthday.

   order

   I bought the book .... give it to Kathy for her birthday.

5 Don't see the film until you have read the book.

   seeing

   Read .... the film.

Part 4 Error correction

Some of these sentences are correct and some have a word which should not be there. Cross out the extra words.

1 This is a great story; it's too full of exciting events and interesting characters.

2 The editor gave Becky's story to a more experienced colleague.

3 I got a nice skirt in the sales, but it needs shortening.

4 I'm not interested in reading about the private lives of no celebrities.

5 If you haven't read any of Marple's books I'll lend it you one.

Part 5 Word formation

Use the word given in capitals at the end of each sentence to form a word that fits in the space.

1 It's a long .... drama set in China.   HISTORY

2 Having been in the same situation I can .... with you.   SYMPATHY

3 Alex is hoping to have a career in ....   JOURNAL

4 People are worried because of the financial .... at present.   SECURE

5 Ben's explanation was highly ....; I didn't believe a word of it.   PROBABLE

Exam practice 6: Writing

Your friend has seen this advertisement for a holiday hotel and is planning to make a booking. You went on holiday at the same place last year. Using the information in the advertisement and the notes you have made on it, tell your friend what the hotel was really like and give him or her any advice necessary.

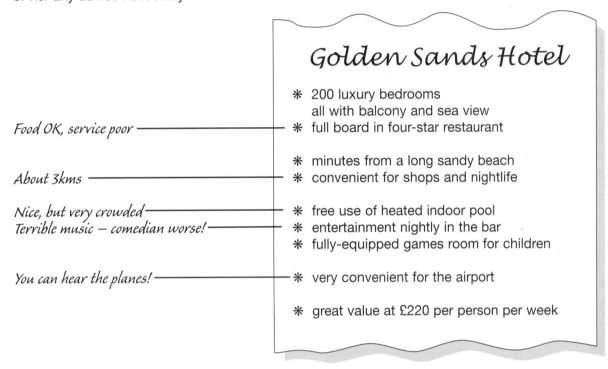

Golden Sands Hotel

* 200 luxury bedrooms
  all with balcony and sea view

Food OK, service poor ——————————— * full board in four-star restaurant

* minutes from a long sandy beach
About 3kms ——————————— * convenient for shops and nightlife

Nice, but very crowded ——————— * free use of heated indoor pool
Terrible music – comedian worse! —— * entertainment nightly in the bar
  * fully-equipped games room for children

You can hear the planes! —————— * very convenient for the airport

* great value at £220 per person per week

Write a **letter** of between **120** and **180** words in an appropriate style. Do not write any postal addresses.

Exam practice 6: Listening

Tapescripts

Unit 2

Listening. Page 14. Exercises 2a and 3a.

Speaker 1

Hindus all over the world – not just in India – celebrate this festival. It's called Diwali, which means the Festival of Lights, because people decorate their homes and temples with little lamps called diwas, which are really pretty. People also buy new things to wear, and sometimes put on necklaces made with flowers. There's also a big emphasis on eating, but everyone makes their own favourite dishes and Indian sweets, there is no set menu. Outside, people learn old Hindu dances, watch plays based on ancient Diwali legends handed down over the generations, and let off fireworks. It's a really exciting time. At this festival, people also worship the goddess of wealth, because everyone hopes to be well-off and successful.

Speaker 2

Songkran is the most important festival held in Thailand and it means the new solar year. On the night before, Thai people clean their houses from top to bottom and get rid of any rubbish. Some people buy birds and fish from the market and then set them free from their cages and bowls – all of this, they hope, will mean they have good fortune in the year ahead. Statues and images of Buddha are bathed in water and young people pour scented water into the hands of their elders and parents as a mark of respect. There are also boat races and pageants on rivers and lakes; people throw water at each other and get absolutely soaked. It's great fun!

Speaker 3

On this day in the United States, people remember the Pilgrim Fathers who settled in North America in the seventeenth century and the Native Americans who helped them make a home in the New World. The food that people always eat on this day reminds them of those simple lives and it all comes from North America – turkey, mashed potatoes and pumpkin pie. There are also some public parades and pageants where children enjoy dressing up in Pilgrim costumes from the seventeenth century – tall hats, dark clothes and so on. But more importantly, Thanksgiving is a celebration of domestic life and almost all Americans, rich and poor, wherever they are, meet together with family or friends, have a traditional holiday feast and watch football together on TV.

Speaking. Page 15. Exercise 2b.

Both of these celebrations are obviously very proud family occasions, and they both seem to be for one of the younger people in the family; in this one it's this girl's birthday – perhaps it's a special one – it could be her eighteenth – and this one clearly shows the girl's graduation ceremony.

The main difference between the birthday and the graduation is that this one is very informal – everybody's wearing casual clothes and laughing, whereas the graduation ceremony is a much more formal celebration.

I would like to be at the birthday party; it looks a lot of fun, but it might be quite noisy! And although the graduation ceremony looks more formal, I'd like to be there if this was my family, because it's a very important moment in the girl's life. Of the two, I think I'd prefer the birthday party, though, as it's more relaxed and probably more fun than the graduation ceremony.

Unit 4

Listening. Page 28. Exercises 2 and 3b.

P = Presenter, C = Caroline; T = Tim

P: Welcome to this week's edition of *Issues in Education*. A report published today shows that girls have overtaken boys in public examination results in the UK. They now pass more exams, and get better grades. I don't think it comes as a surprise to educationalists; and to discuss the report, I have with me Dr Caroline Riches from Cambridge University and Tim Rice, head teacher at Broadoaks School in Bristol, a typical state secondary school. Caroline, can I start with you? Are boys these days less intelligent than girls or just not as hard-working?

C: I don't think we should make too many generalisations from just one report. There's no evidence at all to show that girls are brighter than boys.

P: So why are boys not doing so well, Caroline? Is it something to do with maturity? Or is it linked in some way with behaviour?

C: I think a key issue is peer pressure – pressure from other boys. Boys are generally not as mature as girls of the same age, and are therefore more easily influenced. They tend to get teased and laughed at by other boys if they work hard; it's not seen as masculine, it's not 'cool' to take schoolwork too seriously.

P: Tim Rice, do you agree with that?

T: Yes, absolutely, and it doesn't help matters that only 17 per cent of primary and nursery teachers are men. But in my opinion, learning styles are the biggest factor. In the past, we had an assessment system that depended completely on end-of-year exams, and this system was good for boys, because they tended to leave studying to the last minute, revising like mad and hoping to get through. Girls, on the other hand, tend to work more consistently, with more concentration throughout the whole course. Therefore, the system presently in operation in this country, which involves the assessment of year-round course work as well as exams, suits girls better.

C: Plus the fact that girls have more reason to work hard than they used to. They're aware that university and top jobs are more achievable for them nowadays than in the past, and there are lots of role models around for them to follow. This must be more motivating for them.

P: So what is being done to help the boys, Tim?

T: Well, quite a few schools – like ours – are experimenting with splitting boys and girls up and teaching certain subjects in single-sex classes. This seems to work quite well.

C: Well, I'm sorry Tim, but that seems a shame to me. What we've found is that just separating groups of boys within the class and having a boy–girl seating plan works just as well because it helps to change attitudes. Boys and girls are often good at different things – girls can help boys to communicate more effectively and boys can often show girls a more analytical way of approaching tasks. So they have valuable skills to learn from one another.

T: In any case, the important thing is to have a culture where boys feel it's OK to study hard. This is not just up to the teachers, I might add, but parents as well. A positive attitude in the home is actually by far the most important influence.

C: Yes, that's true. I must add, too, that this is an international problem – it's not just in this country that the gap between sexes at school is widening.

P: Interestingly, boys are still getting better degrees at university though. Girls tend not to follow through this early promise in later life and don't end up with the best-paid jobs. What do you think could be the reasons for this? Caroline …

Speaking. Page 29. Exercise 2b.

A: Well, for me, one of the most important things is how <u>small the classes are.</u>

B: I agree absolutely, it's important for children to have a lot of <u>individual attention</u>.

A: Good exam results are also a big factor, too.

B: Do you think so? Exam results aren't that important to me, not for children that young. Actually, I think it's more important for them to go to a school near their home at this age. It means they have <u>lots of friends who live nearby.</u>

A: That's true. And they can walk there instead of spending ages on a bus, so they have more free time.

B: Yes. And then there's <u>uniform. It's important that they all wear the same clothes.</u>

A: I agree up to a point, although it's not as important as for older children.

B: <u>The least important factor for me is equipment. I just don't think it matters at this age.</u>

A: I couldn't agree more.

Exam practice 1: Teacher's Book

Listening. Page 176. (Paper 4 Part 4).

P = Presenter; A = Anita; D = Darren

P: Today I'm talking to Anita Perry, and her son Darren, who's 14. Now lots of children dream of running away to join the circus, but this is the story of a whole family that did just that. Anita, first of all tell me, do either you or your husband come from a circus family?

A: Not at all. I was a housewife and Terry, my husband, had a good job as an electrical engineer. What happened was, when Darren was three, we took him to see a travelling circus and, for some reason, he just couldn't keep his eyes off the clowns – he was fascinated by them. <u>It's strange because, as a child, I always found them rather frightening.</u> Anyway, after that, Darren became a real circus fan.

P: Right. And so how did this lead to the family actually joining a circus?

A: Well, when Darren was nine, my husband was suddenly made redundant. <u>Although we live in an area of high unemployment, it still came as quite a shock to us.</u> We didn't know what to do, because Darren's two older brothers were just going through university, which was expensive, and there wasn't much work going in the area, so we were pretty desperate.

P: So Darren, what happened next?

D: Well, I said that <u>my dad should try and get work in the circus</u>. We had a car and a caravan, and they always need electricians, so he had the right skills already. At first he thought I was joking, but <u>when I explained that circuses often employ whole families, he began to take me more seriously.</u> I'd read about circuses, and I'd seen some TV documentaries too.

P: So you knew what you were talking about?

D: Not really, but I convinced Dad that he should write away to all the circuses asking if they'd got any work for the three of us. <u>I didn't hold out much hope actually, because I had no idea how easy or difficult it was to get in as a family.</u> But within a week, we'd got an offer from one of the large travelling circuses. Dad was taken on as a spotlight operator, Mum would be selling tickets, and I was accepted as a trainee clown.

P: As easy as that Anita?

A: Well, it wasn't an easy decision to make, and then there was a great deal to organise. I mean, Darren says we had a caravan, but it was only one of those little ones that people take on holiday with them. So it was tough at first, deciding what we needed to take and how it could all be fitted in. <u>We only go away for the summer months, but that first year it seemed to go on forever. At times I wanted to give it all up, I can tell you.</u> It was a great relief to get home and sort things out.

P: And Darren?

D: Well, I'm not old enough yet to perform in front of an audience, but I've learnt a great deal about clowning just watching the real professionals night after night. People ask about my education, but I only miss the summer term. I follow the same books with a private teacher and I have my laptop computer. It's actually better because on your own it doesn't take long. <u>At school, the teacher wastes a lot of time trying to get everyone to listen and do what they're told, which annoys me.</u> I have to fit in my clowning lessons as well, so I want to get the schoolwork done as quickly as possible.

P: And the future, Anita?

A: <u>Well it was a risk to take, but it's working out, so I guess it was worth it, and we're enjoying it too.</u> We've made lots of friends and, of course, we now have a proper van and a big caravan, so it's quite comfortable. I mean we could've sat at home and got depressed about Terry losing his job, and I'm glad we didn't do that. In a way, I suppose, we had nothing to lose.

Unit 6

Listening. Page 44. Part 1. Exercise 1b.

P = Presenter; N = Nick

P: When you first went into the rainforest what did you think – what was your reaction?

N: Oh, that was that. I just completely fell in love with it – <u>the heat, the humidity, the snakes, the insects, the animals, the people.</u> I was Rainforest Man.

P: But it can't have been easy to live in that kind of environment.

N: No, it's difficult. It's <u>lonely. You pour sweat, you smell. The insects are like flying motorbikes and you're bitten all the time. And people don't realise how claustrophobic it is – no real daylight gets through the forest canopy.</u>

P: So why did you stay out there so long?

N: Well, the reason <u>I was sent out to the Amazon in the first place was to make a TV documentary about monkeys and birds</u>. But the reason I stayed out there for another ten years was that I decided I had to make one about jaguars.

Listening. Page 44. Part 2. Exercise 2b.

P: Tell us about your first meeting with a jaguar.

N: Well, I'd been out since before four o'clock that morning – trying to photograph a group of black vultures – ugly birds – but it was <u>half past five</u> when she appeared. I'd just looked at my watch because I had to report back to camp at 5:45. Anyway, suddenly there was a change in atmosphere – every hair on my body stood on end. Then I caught sight of her.

P: What did she do?

N: This absolutely magnificent creature – she emerged from the forest greenery about 60 metres away and started walking towards me. The jaguar's coat is really impressive and she had beautiful <u>black</u> markings all over her deep <u>yellow</u> fur. I could even see the whites of her eyes.

P: Then what happened?

N: Time seemed to stand still for a while. I hardly breathed. I don't think she actually saw me – she showed no sign of it if she did – and she had a drink from a river a few metres away, and then disappeared into the forest again.

P: Did you take a <u>photograph</u> of her? <u>I couldn't,</u> because I'd used all my film on the vultures. <u>As you can imagine, I was really upset.</u> But after that, I stayed another seven years in the rainforest, and had nine more encounters, all of which I captured on film.

P: Why is the jaguar so hard to find?

N: Because it's a threatened species, it lives only in the very remotest areas. You have to remember that the Amazon forest extends for

PHOTOCOPIABLE

thousands of kilometres and the <u>territory of a typical male jaguar</u> <u>extends to something like 170 kilometres</u> – in exceptional cases as much as 300 or more.

P: No wonder you don't see them much.

N: Exactly, that's why each sighting is such a thrill. Because what you have to remember is that jaguars are solitary, shy creatures, which have the ability <u>to get through the forest so incredibly quietly</u> that you can be only a few metres away and miss one completely.

P: So how did you eventually track them down, on those other occasions you mentioned?

N: I went thousands of kilometres inland into a less-populated area and made friends with the local forest people. It was while they were helping me look for the jaguar that <u>I had the chance to eat</u> <u>their local speciality – the world's biggest spider.</u> It's 26 centimetres, has eight eyes and tastes revolting. But it would have been very rude to refuse to eat what for them is a very special meal.

P: What do the forest people think about jaguars?

N: Well like me, they don't get to see them very often because jaguars tend to avoid places where humans make their homes. But they certainly wouldn't kill one unless it represented some kind of threat. They have a <u>great respect</u> for these animals actually, regarding them as fellow hunters rather than as potential prey.

P: Studying these animals can't be easy.

N: Oh it's not. One great problem is actually keeping count of how many of them are out there and where they go, because they're so rarely seen. In one project, researchers have been putting what are called '<u>radio collars</u>' on to any animals they catch, so that they can study their movements afterwards.

P: But you have to catch the animals first?

N: Yes, and they are very frightened of people. You see jaguars don't only live in the forest. In areas where there are <u>cattle and sheep,</u> <u>farmers</u> hunt and kill jaguars because they do attack farm animals, I'm afraid.

P: I see.

N: And when they get too close to civilisation, jaguars can face other problems too, erm, they can pick up illnesses from <u>domestic cats,</u> <u>even dogs</u>, which tend to have a different range of diseases from those found in the forest. But at least, they're not dependent on the one disappearing habitat like so many animals. And there's lots of research going on into jaguars at present, so I'm confident that the animal has a future.

P: Nick Gordon, thank you.

Speaking. Page 45. (Paper 5 Part 2). Exercises 3a and 3b.

E = Examiner; S = Student

E: Here are your two photographs. They show people working with animals. I'd like you to compare and contrast these photographs, and say what you think <u>is difficult about these jobs. Remember, you</u> <u>only have about a minute for this so don't worry if I interrupt you.</u> <u>All right?</u>

Speaking. Page 45. (Paper 5 Part 2). Exercise 3b.

S: They both show people who work with animals. In the one on the left the man – he's the farmer, probably – is in the country with the sheep, whereas in the other one there's a woman in a white coat – she's a, <u>a ... kind of doctor who looks after animals</u>. People bring in, er, <u>small animals who live in the home</u>, when they are ill or when they hurt themselves, like this dog.

<u>Personally, I</u> think both jobs must be very hard work. A doctor for sick animals has to study for a long time to learn about all the different animals, and she has to see a lot of, erm, 'patients' in a day. But <u>if I had to choose</u> I would say the farmer's job is more difficult because he has to get up very early in the morning and go out to the fields in summer and winter. He has to work a lot – it must be very tiring.

E: Thank you.

Unit 8

Listening. Page 58. (Paper 4 Part 3). Exercise 2a.

Speaker 1

My first parachute jump was the scariest thing I'd ever done. Nothing prepares you for falling out of a plane at 180 kilometres an hour. After all, you can't turn back if you change your mind, can you? When it came to actually jumping, I got very nervous. I had no choice but to do it though, because <u>the whole point was to get people to give</u> <u>donations to a medical research organisation</u>. If I hadn't jumped, I wouldn't have got any money for them. Once back on the ground, I realised I'd loved it and that was the beginning of my big hobby, *much to the amazement of my friends and family*.

Speaker 2

I grew up surrounded by water – you could see the Atlantic from my bedroom window, and yet I'd never learned to swim. See, I – I just never fancied it, even though my parents and brother swam like fish. I finally signed up for a five-week beginners' course at the age of 35, I mean not because I'd changed my mind about wanting to swim, but <u>just so that I could see the expressions of amazement on my kids'</u> <u>faces</u>. It was worth suffering those awful lessons just for that. But I must admit that, even now, I'd much rather relax at the poolside and watch <u>them</u> splashing about.

Speaker 3

I took up skiing while I was living abroad. I absolutely loved it from the word go – the scenery of course, the sense of speed and complete focus on the task. It's fantastic exercise, too. I hadn't expected to enjoy it though, *in fact I had to be talked* into doing it by my friends. They'd all skied since they were very small, and kept on at me until I agreed to give it a go. I'm much older now and obviously not as fit as I used to be, but if I could find the money I'd like to take the kids and see if I can still do it.

Speaker 4

I'm not really into risky sports, but I enjoyed snorkelling and quite fancied getting a closer look at exotic fish. My main motive for taking up scuba diving though, to be honest, is because my boyfriend, Tony, said I wouldn't be able to do it. I tend to panic you see, and in scuba diving you have to remain totally calm or things can get very dangerous. It took me ages to gain the confidence to do it, but <u>I was</u> <u>determined to show Tony that he was wrong</u>. So I persevered, and I've now passed all my exams and we're off on a diving holiday together soon.

Speaker 5:

When I was younger and much fitter, I was really into football in a big way. Not just playing it but, you know, going to every Liverpool home match, watching it on TV. And when I wasn't doing this, I was on the computer playing these games, like the one called FIFA and so on. I don't play football competitively any more but I do still enjoy a kick around with my mates or my kids. It's <u>the only way I can really</u> <u>unwind actually</u>, I have a really stressful job and football just helps me to switch off and think of something else.

Speaking. Page 59. (Paper 5 Part 3). Exercise 2a.

E = Examiner; S1 = Student 1; S2 = Student 2

E: Here are some pictures which show people doing different sports. First, <u>talk to each other about the advantages and disadvantages of</u> <u>doing each of these sports</u>. Then <u>decide which one would be best</u> <u>for someone who doesn't have much spare time</u>. You have only about three minutes for this, so don't worry if I stop you. Please speak so that we can hear you. All right?

Speaking. Page 59. (Paper 5 Part 3). Exercise 2b.

S1: OK, let's begin with swimming, shall we? I think it's a good sport to do because it keeps you fit and you can swim all year, if you have an indoor pool. Most cities and towns have a pool, I think.

S2: It's very boring, though. It's OK in the sea but I don't like public swimming pools. I prefer running because you can go in the open air and run round the parks and …

S1: Yes, and as well as that, you can go with a friend, and it doesn't cost anything. You can go when you want and you can – if you're not fit you can walk or jog. I don't know about golf, though – what would you say?

S2: Well, it's a good sport for meeting people and it's very relaxing.

S1: But it takes a lot of time. I think it's better when you finish work, how do you say – when you're older …

S2: Ah, when you retire. Yes, my father plays it – it's good for people with lots of time, but it's quite expensive if you have to join a club or something.

S1: So, maybe not so good if you have a busy job.

S2: That's true. Well, what about …

S1: Sorry to interrupt, but for me tennis is a good sport.

S2: Yes, tennis is good for meeting people but it's very expensive in my town. You have to join a club and wear, you know, special white clothes.

S1: It's good for fitness though; you have to run around a lot. But what about skiing?

S2: Oh, I don't know – I've never done it. Do you like it?

S1: I like skiing, but it's expensive. You have to travel to the mountains and pay for the lessons and the things you need – you know, you, you have to hire the skis, and the, er, …

S2: Yes, the equipment and clothes. I agree with you. And as well as that it's dangerous. You need to learn. Or you'll spend a lot of time in hospital! With football you can play in the street, with your friends or with …

S1: But you still need to practise and learn the rules, if you …

S2: Well, you can just kick a ball around. It's very popular in my country. What about riding a bike?

S1: I think it depends. If you live in a busy city it's not very good for your health and it's a bit dangerous, I would say.

S2: Anyway, we have to decide which one doesn't take much time. What do you think?

S1: Well, I suppose swimming might be the most suitable, or …

S2: I'm not sure I agree about that. You still have to go to the pool, change your clothes, and then afterwards have a shower, get dry and get …

S1: Or cycling, maybe cycling is better. You can just get on your bike and go.

S2: Well, only if you have a bike. And you should wear a … you know … a hat for safety. Running is even easier and quicker.

S1: So let's decide which one. Running?

S2: Yes, I think so.

Exam practice 2: Teacher's Book

Listening. Page 180. (Paper 4 Part 3).

Speaker 1

Because I'm a designer, people immediately assume I'm interested in the fashion pages in the newspaper, but actually we have specialised magazines for keeping up-to-date with developments in the industry – all you get in the newspapers is gossip, and there's enough of that in fashion anyway. No, the only newspaper I get is the local one. It tells me what's on at the cinema, and has really good coverage of my local football team. I'm a real fan, but it's only a local team, so they're hardly mentioned in the national press. The rest of the paper's mostly adverts – I wouldn't buy it just for those, but they're useful sometimes.

Speaker 2

I don't get much time for reading a newspaper, so I buy one of the smaller ones. It's useful for seeing what's on television and I like to know what people are saying about the latest films and plays, even if I rarely get time to go and see any myself. Admittedly, there's more advertisements than news in this paper, and most of the photos are of celebrities at parties, so I skip all that. Even the sports coverage tends to be full of gossip, it seems to be the fashion nowadays. Personally, I'm more interested in the game itself, so I get the results and match reports from the radio.

Speaker 3

My favourite daily newspaper is actually the one that's read by the smallest number of people – perhaps that says something about me! I like it because it only employs top-class journalists and photographers, and they seem to get just the right visual image to go with each story. Even the sports reports are intelligent and well written. I'm not a great one for the arts or fashion, but I find myself reading reviews of plays and concerts which I'd never go and see. And best of all, there's hardly anything about who's dating who and all that rubbish that seems to dominate much of the press these days.

Speaker 4

I work in the advertising industry and so I have a professional interest in newspapers. I'd like to pretend that by choice I'd go for one of the more up-market dailies and read the more serious reviews, but I'm afraid for me the important thing is who's getting coverage, whose photo is appearing on the cover. In my business, you have to know who's saying what about which fashion model or sports personality, otherwise you could easily find yourself using the wrong person to promote a brand. I tend to read one particular paper because the main columnist really does know everybody who's anybody, so you can believe what she says!

Speaker 5

To be honest, we generally manage without a newspaper. I'll look through someone's if I'm not busy at work, but it's usually only glancing at the headlines and pictures. The only time I buy one is when we're booking our holidays – because the Sunday papers are still the best place for those kind of adverts. But I get most of my news from the television these days and if I want up-to-date sports reports, or if I'm looking for a film to go and see, then I can find a much better range of reviews on the Internet. To my mind, newspapers are old-fashioned, they've been overtaken by modern technology.

Unit 10

Listening. Page 74. (Paper 4 Part 4). Exercise 2a.

N = Neil; T = Tanya

N: Today we're talking about inventors and Tanya's been doing some research about a modern-day inventor, haven't you, Tanya?

T: Yes, that's right. I've been finding out about Trevor Baylis, who's invented more than 200 useful gadgets.

N: So what did you find out? What made him become an inventor?

T: Well, it's not the sort of career where there's, like, a course in inventing you can go and do. But Trevor's father was an artist and his mother an actress, so they were creative people, although in a different way, and they must have recognised his talents. Because, as a child, apparently he was fascinated by machines; you know, taking things apart, seeing how they worked, all that, and they encouraged him in that.

N: So what did Trevor study?

T: He actually left school with no qualifications whatsoever. Apparently he had a choice: he could either go and work in a factory for £8.00 per week, or do what's called an apprenticeship – you know, where you work four days a week and the company pays you to go to college on the fifth. And although the pay was only half that of the factory, that was the one Trevor went for, and so he was trained as a mechanical engineer.

N: But how did that lead to inventing?

T: Well, I think he learned the basic skills you need to be able to make your ideas a reality. From what I've read about him, most of

Trevor's inventions start as a problem. For example, he saw a television programme about people living in a poor part of Africa where there's no electricity supply. You can get batteries, but they're expensive, so they didn't even have things like radios, which are really useful for, like, getting information to people about health issues and that sort of thing.

N: So he came up with a solution?

T: Well, according to the story, he went to bed thinking about this programme and then had a dream. In the dream, he could see an old wind-up record player. Apparently, he woke up with a start and suddenly thought 'Of course, people had machines long before there was electricity.' And that got him thinking about how you could power a radio by mechanical means, and the result was the wind-up radio, which works on the same basic principle as the wind-up clock. You turn a handle for 25 seconds and you get an hour's listening. That's his most famous invention and it's really changed the lives of lots of people.

N: Brilliant. And a lot of the best ideas are really basic, aren't they?

T: Yes, a lot of imaginative young inventors waste their time trying to come up with the latest complicated electronic gadget, like computer games or household appliances, because they see things like mobile phones, walkmans and think that's how they're going to make their fortune. But, to be honest, it's the research departments of big companies that tend to come up with that sort of thing, not individual inventors working at home.

N: But how does someone like Trevor take an invention, you know, from being just a good idea to something we can buy in the shops?

T: Well, you make what's called a prototype – a working example, which you then demonstrate to lots of companies until you find one that's interested in developing it further. That's the really hard part, apparently, especially if you're unknown. Because it's easy to believe people when they say your idea's no good, when actually you need to have faith in it if you're going to convince anyone. Then, when a company does show interest, the inventor has to get legal advice before signing anything, to be sure of keeping a fair share of the profits.

N: And what about Trevor Baylis. Has he made his fortune?

T: Well, I think he's made some money out of his inventions, but he's not really a big businessman. In fact, a lot of his best ideas were for things to help disabled people, like for example machines that can be operated by people in wheelchairs, that sort of thing. And often that means working with charities, so there's not much money to be made out of these inventions, but they're the ones that Trevor says he's proudest of.

N: He sounds a nice man, Trevor Baylis. Thank you, Tanya. Next on the programme …

Speaking. Page 75. (Paper 5 Parts 3 and 4). Exercise 2a.

E = Examiner; T = Tina; N = Nils

E: Here are some pictures which show useful inventions. First, talk to each other about the advantages and disadvantages of each invention. Then decide which two are the most important. You have only about three minutes for this, so don't worry if I stop you. Please speak so we can hear you. All right?

T: So we have to discuss all the photos and then choose the two most important?

E: That's right.

Speaking. Page 75. (Paper 5 Parts 3 and 4). Exercise 2b.

T: OK. Well, straightaway I can see the phone ...

N: Absolutely!

T: This is the most wonderful invention – without it I don't think I could live.

N: I completely agree with you – it's amazing that you can speak to each other in different countries as if you are in the same room. They're incredible! But the computer is also useful because it's – you can do in one hour what you used to do in one day.

T: Well, I don't agree because I've always had problems with computers – they always go wrong when I'm using them!

N: Perhaps that's because you're the same as me – you don't know how to use it very well.

T: Yes, perhaps – but with the phone you just …

N: But once you have learned, it will be a useful invention, much more than a CD player or …

T: Yes, but CD players are a good thing when you're travelling.

N: I agree, but it's just for your pleasure.

T: That's true. They aren't necessary. And this yellow paper here – what's it called? You can stick it everywhere; it's quite a good invention. I wouldn't have thought it but it's very useful.

N: It's quite unusual to see notes like this these days because with the phone and text messages you don't need …

T: I agree, but it's nice sometimes.

N: Yes, and of course you couldn't write messages like this without a pen and paper. It's my favourite way, but it's slow.

T: Yes, in my country letters take ages to arrive, but if you have a note or a letter you can keep it forever. It's really nice.

N: Email is faster! What about the TV? Is this a TV?

T: The TV – it can keep you up-to-date but there are more disadvantages, like the owner of the TV channel can brainwash you – you never know if the news is real or just what they want to make you believe. And there are too many advertisements.

N: But you can learn a lot if you watch some things. It depends what TV is like in your country.

T: I agree with you. And videos are fantastic. I love watching films … . We haven't talked about this pen.

N: A highlighter pen. I sometimes use it for studying.

T: Me too. Yes, yes, it's useful, but it's not the most important.

N: So we'd better make up our minds which two …

T: For me, there's no choice. I prefer the phone!

N: Yes, I think we agree that the phone is the most important! And the second one?

T: You think the computer, I know.

N: I do, definitely. Do you agree?

T: I suppose so. So, we think the computer and the phone are the most important inventions.

E: Thank you.

Speaking. Page 75. (Paper 5 Parts 3 and 4). Exercise 2c.

N: Yes, I think we agree that the phone is the most important! And the second one?

T: You think the computer, I know.

N: I do, definitely. Do you agree?

T: I suppose so. So, we think the computer and the phone are the most important inventions.

E: Thank you.

Speaking. Page 75. (Paper 5 Parts 3 and 4). Exercise 3b.

E: Do you like watching television?

N: I sometimes watch it at the end of the day to relax. But the problem is it's easy to sit there and be lazy and watch programmes even if they aren't interesting.

T: Yes, there's so much rubbish on television. I prefer to buy a video and watch films that I like.

N: But there are some good programmes if you decide what you are going to watch and then switch off afterwards so you don't waste your time.

T: Yes, I watch the news on TV and I like documentaries, where you can learn something new. And some comedy programmes.

E: And in what ways are computers good or bad for children?

T: I don't know. I've never had a computer, but when I go to my friends …

N: It's time you had one!

T: Yes, but I think for children it's very dangerous because there are so many computer games that are quite violent …

N: Well, it depends on the way you use computers, because nowadays if you want to get a job you need to use them.

T: Exactly, but as a child, …

N: You can teach them how to use computers.

T: But you have to control what they do because there's a lot of rubbish.

N: Nowadays you have rubbish everywhere so it's up to you to …

T: Yes, you have to teach them what's good and what isn't.

E: Do you think you could invent something?

T: Personally?

E: Yes.

T: No, I don't think so. Well, I'm quite creative, I have to say, but not in technical things – I like to work with paper, but not computers.

N: It would be my dream to invent something so simple, but so basic for the world that I could live for the rest of my life without working.

T: I couldn't agree more. But how could you do this? You can learn it if you work in a company, I suppose.

N: I always think about the man who invented Trivial Pursuit, you know the board game. If you think about it, it was such a simple idea but he thought of it, and now he must be so rich. He'll never have to work again.

T: That would be fantastic, but it would never happen to me, I'm afraid.

N: Me neither. But I'll try!

E: Thank you. That is the end of the test.

Unit 12

Speaking. Page 88. (Paper 5 Part 2). Exercise 2a.

E= Examiner; A = Alice; R = Robert

E: Here are your two photographs. They show different types of art. I'd like you to compare and contrast these photographs, and say which type of art you think is more interesting. Remember, you only have about a minute for this, so don't worry if I interrupt you. All right?

Speaking. Page 88. (Paper 5 Part 2). Exercise 2b.

A: Both pictures show art – it's completely different art. In one picture we can see classical art, and the other picture is definitely about modern art. In the first one there are a lot of people looking at the pictures that are on the wall, while in the second picture the people are walking down the street and I get the impression that no one is interested in this, this thing – they are just there. The statue could be a bird or a man – I really don't know what it is.

Well, I like some modern art but if you ask me to choose, I think I would choose classical art because I understand it. In the first photo you know what the painters wanted to say. If you want you can learn something about why they were painted. But in the second, if you don't understand it you …

E: Thank you. Robert, are you interested in art?

R: I'm not really very keen on art. I prefer listening to music.

Speaking. Page 88. (Paper 5 Part 2). Exercise 3a.

A: In the first photo you know what the painters wanted to say. If you want you can learn something about why they were painted. But in the second, if you don't understand it you …

E: Thank you. Robert, are you interested in art?

R: I'm not really very keen on art. I prefer listening to music.

Listening. Page 89. (Paper 4 Part 1). Exercise 2a.

One

Hi. Rachel. Thanks for phoning back. Listen, you're going to see the New York City Ballet, aren't you? … Have you still got the brochure there? … . Great. So do they give the exact dates? Oh, really? I didn't realise it was so soon. Thank goodness I phoned you because I'd hate to miss it. I'd better give them a ring. You're going next Friday, you say? Shall I see if they've got any for then because that would be nice, wouldn't it?

Two

To start with, I must admit that I had my doubts. I didn't think Alex Casey would be able to leave the film-script style behind. But even though the characters are a bit predictable, they are so colourful that you can't help but engage with them. And they're portrayed with a good deal of sensitivity, so you really care what happens to them. Then there's the very unusual plot, which keeps you gripped until the very last page. In fact, it would probably transfer very well to either stage or screen and because it's Casey, you immediately think of that. But, actually, it works well enough as it is.

Three

M = Man; W = Woman

M: Can I help?

W: Yes, I'd like to move to the back, so I'm not disturbed so much by the noise of the traffic.

M: Well, it is the holiday period, madam, so we're fully booked and …

W: I appreciate that. But if I'd known how much noise there'd be, I would've gone elsewhere. I might as well put my bed on the motorway.

M: I'll see what can be done. Would you like to take a seat in the bar over there while I have a word with the manager?

W: I'm just on my way to the dining room, actually.

M: Very well, Madam.

Four

S1 = Student 1; S2 = Student 2

S1: So what did you think of it?

S2: It was all right, but you know, it didn't really live up to the hype, did it?

S1: Oh. I thought visually it was really good.

S2: Well, the special effects were OK, I suppose, but I hadn't really expected all that in this sort of film. If you ask me, though, they'd have done a lot better to stick to the plot of the original a bit more closely. Much as I liked Julia Roberts, it just didn't hold my attention, I'm afraid.

S1: Well, I haven't read the book, so I don't know, but I think she was just brilliant.

Five

M = Man; W = Woman

W: I lent him that CD ages ago. I keep dropping hints whenever I see him in the canteen, but either he's forgotten or just doesn't want to give it back to me.

M: Some people are very thoughtless, aren't they?

W: Well, I wouldn't mind, except it was a birthday present and I haven't really listened to it myself yet. My son bought it for me. If I knew him better, I'd ask for it straight out, but I don't want to fall out with someone new like that.

M: It's difficult to know what to do, isn't it?

Six

Don't get me wrong. It's mostly worthwhile stuff they've got there. It's just the way it's been put together that I don't like. I mean, it would be much better if all the works were grouped in some kind of logical way – you know, according to period, theme or whatever. You can't argue with the amount of background information available, which is very thorough, but if all you want to do is see a particularly brilliant painting or watercolour or whatever, you've got to go past all this other stuff to get to it. Some people will be exhausted by the time they're half way round, if you ask me.

Exam practice 3: Teacher's Book

Listening. Page 184. (Paper 4 Part 2).

P = Presenter; F = Fiona

P: My guest today, Fiona Mulligan, runs her own business. Fiona, welcome.

F: Hello.

P: Now your company helps people in a very particular way, doesn't it Fiona? Tell us a little about it.

F: Well, it's all about public speaking. For some of us, standing up and speaking in front of a group of people comes very naturally, but for others it's a rather frightening experience, especially if it's part of their job. That's why I started my company which is called Presentation Skills. It aims to help people get over their fear and speak more confidently in public.

P: So you had experience of public speaking yourself?

F: Yes, because although I was working as an accountant at the time I started the company, I'd trained as an actress and worked in television for many years. But I'd reached the age of 40, it was getting harder to get work in my profession and I was tired of doing temporary work. I decided that I wanted to run my own business, but I wasn't sure exactly what I could do.

P: So where did the idea come from?

F: Well, a friend, a doctor actually, had to give a talk whilst attending a conference. He knew his subject, but was very nervous about actually giving the talk and asked for advice. That's when I realised that many people must suffer in the same way.

P: So how did you get started?

F: Well, the first problem was money – I had none! I applied to the bank for a loan, but they weren't interested. I talked to lots of friends and colleagues, but nobody could really help. In the end I had a lucky break. A rich uncle, who I'd lost touch with years before, heard about my idea through some cousins I'd written to. He was so impressed that he decided to lend me the £10,000 I needed to get started.

P: That was lucky.

F: Yes. Then I needed to find some customers. I telephoned lots of big companies and offered to run a free training session for their staff. I tried supermarkets, financial companies, travel agents, but nobody was interested. In the end, it was the managing director of a department store who asked me to help him with a speech he had to give. He was so impressed that he decided to arrange sessions for all his senior staff. Since then I haven't looked back.

P: So what do your clients get for their money?

F: The basic course involves two days of individual lessons on how to speak in public and costs from £2,500 to £3,500 depending on exactly what's included. For most people the problem is just one of confidence, although some people have to learn things like how to speak loudly enough or how to avoid going too fast – things like that. But some people have special needs, like they have to speak while showing statistics on a screen, which often means using computer equipment, so we train them to use that properly.

P: So you tell people what they're doing wrong?

F: We use a video studio, so that people can see for themselves and, at the end of the course, we take them to a real theatre where they practise giving their talks on stage.

P: And what's the commonest problem people have?

F: They just make the talk boring. They're so worried about how they feel that they forget about how the audience feels. You know, they don't look at the audience, they repeat themselves or, worst of all, just read from notes. That can be really dull.

P: And can you teach people to be more interesting?

F: Well, the important thing actually is for them to be themselves – that's how they'll be most comfortable, and that's how they get over feeling shy on stage. People who are nervous and tense sometimes seem to be angry for example. But when they see themselves on stage, they realise what they look like and that helps them to understand what they need to do.

P: How interesting. Fiona, thank you for … .

Unit 14

Listening. Page 104. (Paper 4 Part 3). Exercise 2a.

Speaker 1

I tend to wear fairly elegant clothes in the week at work – you know, fitted jackets, high-heeled shoes, straight skirts or trouser suits, that sort of thing. The first impression my clients get of me is really important so I spend ages looking for clothes that are businesslike but not too expensive. It's got to the point when I don't feel right in casual clothes, so even at the weekends and in the evenings I'll still wear the same kind of thing, but perhaps change the jacket and high heels for a sweater and flat shoes.

Speaker 2

I always wear the same things when I'm not at school – tracksuit bottoms, a fleece or a T-shirt and designer trainers. Nearly all my friends do. I've also got three different football kits – Man United, England and Barcelona. In the summer, I sometimes wear shorts instead of tracksuit bottoms but it's always sports stuff. There's no point in dressing up in smart clothes, anyway – they just get dirty. What matters is feeling relaxed and not having to worry about what you look like.

Speaker 3

Well, I've always had a clear idea of how I want to look – I want to be a designer when I leave school, and I'm always looking in magazines to get ideas. At the moment, the trend is to wear very short or very long skirts with trainers or high heels – nothing in between. Strong patterns and crop tops in bright colours like lime green are popular this season too. I wouldn't dream of wearing anything old-fashioned. I even try to adapt my school uniform a bit to make it more personal. I wear patterned or striped tights and so on with it.

Speaker 4

I don't think about clothes very much. I suppose I wear what I've always worn – a shirt and tie with trousers and maybe a sweater. I don't spend much money on clothes so most of them are a few years old. I sometimes go into charity shops and my son gives me things he's fed up with. I'll wear anything, as long as it's warm and not too scruffy. I'm certainly not trying to impress anyone!

Speaker 5

I like clothes, but I'm not a fashion victim and I don't dress up. Now I've got kids, my clothes have to be practical, so no high heels and tight skirts these days. Having said that, I don't want to end up living in tracksuits or jeans and baggy jumpers all the time like some mums. I go for casual but well-cut clothes in natural fabrics like silk or cotton. I do tend to spend quite a lot on my clothes but then I can wear them over and over again and they don't drop to pieces. It's an investment.

Speaking. Page 105. (Paper 5 Part 4). Exercise 4a.

E = Examiner; J = Julia; P = Paul

E: Do you think we can decide what a person is like by the clothes they wear?

J: No, I don't think you can judge someone's character from their clothes …

P: To be honest, I haven't thought much about it but I think, er, you can have an idea, for example if they are very casual or very formal. You know if they are similar people to you depending on the clothes they wear. Of course it's wrong to think like that – just because they aren't wearing jeans and T-shirt like me, it doesn't mean they aren't a nice person. Everybody should be allowed to wear what they want, and anyway it depends on what they're doing. If they're going to work they probably can't wear jeans or trainers so you can't really know…

J: Of course. And apart from that it would be very boring if everyone wore the same clothes. It's dangerous if you decide you don't like someone just because they have different clothes.

Unit 16

Listening. Page 118. (Paper 4 Part 2). Exercise 2a.

P = Presenter, R = Robin

P: Reading weekly magazines, you'd think that celebrities like film stars, top models, etc. spend their whole non-working lives at parties. But, according to a new book by psychologist Robin Clark, who's studied free-time activities, this is often far from the truth. Robin, welcome. Tell us more.

R: Hi. Well, things have changed over the years. Take the rock star Mick Jagger, lead singer of the rock group *The Rolling Stones*. When he was accused of being a <u>bad influence</u> on young people because of his wild social life, he replied 'That's great. It's what rock 'n' roll is about. I'd be more worried if they accused me of <u>stamp collecting</u>.' And what he meant was that we don't expect rock stars to enjoy doing things like collecting stamps, which people generally regard as a boring hobby.

P: It'd disappoint the fans.

R: Exactly. Being a celebrity is all about <u>image</u>, and their fans have certain expectations of these people. So even if a rock star is keen on that sort of hobby, <u>he or she will be keen to present another side of themselves to the public.</u>

P: But is this still the case today?

R: Well, less so. At one time, the only free-time interest that a self-respecting rock star would admit to was football, although it's not really a hobby. But recently, I discovered that Jarvis Cocker – the lead singer with the rock band *Pulp* – actually spends a lot of his time bird-watching. <u>I came across this information when I saw a video of the band</u> filmed in a wildlife park. 'Why there?' I asked, and discovered that, apparently, he spends a lot of time there. Not exactly the party-going stereotype, is it?

P: Not really!

R: And he's not so unusual because, believe it or not, quite a few rock stars collect things too; and not the CDs or musical instruments that you might expect either, but things like <u>old coins and matchboxes</u>. Though an awful lot of them seem to enjoy flying model aeroplanes and kites – probably because it gets them out into the fresh air, it's an escape from being surrounded by people, by so much noise, in their working lives.

P: Right. But what about film stars?

R: Well, of course, on a film set people spend a lot of time hanging about, waiting for things to happen. So actors bring along things to pass the time. During my research, I saw some very glamorous film stars doing crosswords or jigsaw puzzles, but the thing I saw most often were <u>board games</u>. They're obviously quite trendy at the moment amongst the stars.

P: So does it follow that non-celebrities, ordinary people in routine office jobs, do things to make their lives more exciting?

R: Adventure sports are certainly popular, bungee jumping was all the rage for a time, but the sport of the moment for young adults is one known as '<u>indoor climbing</u>'. Rather than go up mountains, people crawl up and across walls. These activities are seen as a more interesting way of keeping fit than jogging or just going to the gym.

P: And older people? I can't imagine my bank manager climbing walls, somehow.

R: You'd be surprised. One of my colleagues, he works in the library at the university, spends his free time playing the drums in a band. But if we look at all age groups, <u>dancing</u> seems to be the fastest-growing free-time activity in this country – classes are springing up in anything and everything, disco, jazz, salsa. Take your pick.

P: Sure. And what about you Robin, do you have a hobby? Come on, be honest.

R: Well, after a long day at work I do listen to music, I even collect antique books in a small way, but the thing that really helps me to wind down is <u>gardening</u>. And what about radio presenters, do you have a hobby? Let me guess, erm, I'd say true to the stereotype … buying designer shoes?

P: How did you know that! I think we'd better leave it there, Robin thanks very much …

Speaking. Page 119. (Paper 5 Part 1). Exercise 2a.

E = Examiner, G = Giorgio; A = Anna

E: My name is Katie, and this is my colleague Mark. He is just going to listen to us. So you are … Anna … and … Giorgio. Thank you. First of all we'd like to know something about you, so I'm going to ask you some questions about yourselves. Giorgio, where are you from?

G: I'm from Padova, in Italy.

E: What do you like about living there?

G: It's a very nice town, not too big, not too small. The people are very friendly, and they will help you, it doesn't matter if you are a neighbour, or a visitor to the town. The only thing is it can be a little bit boring sometimes – there aren't so many things for young people to do!

E: Anna, where are you from?

A: I'm from Zurich, in Switzerland.

E: Do you like living there?

A: Yes, I do, very much. Although we live in the city we have quite a big house with a lot of space and I love the garden. We always have barbecues, and it's on a hill so we have views over all the city and the mountains.

E: And what do you do in Zurich, do you work or study?

A: I work for an international bank, as a financial adviser.

E: What do you enjoy most about your job?

A: I have a lot of contact with clients and I really enjoy meeting them. And my, er, <u>the other people who work with me</u>, we like each other very much and get on well together.

E: Giorgio, could you tell us something about your family, please?

G: Yes, there are five of us: my mother, my father, and two brothers. One of them is younger than me and one is older. They say in Italy the one in the middle is the best one, but it's just a saying! My brother is a teacher, my father is a teacher and my mother is a teacher, but my other brother hasn't decided yet. I graduated last year and I don't know what I'm going to do. I studied law but I don't want to be a lawyer.

E: Anna, what do you like doing in your free time?

A: It depends on the season. In the winter I like skiing. In Switzerland we have a lot of mountains and it's very pleasant to go there for the weekends. In summer I go walking in the mountains with my husband. After work I like reading books – I like thrillers best.

E: Giorgio, what sort of music do you like?

G: I like rock music most, but I'm really quite, er, <u>how do you say it, I like many different kinds of music</u>. But when I'm quite tired and want to relax it's pop rock because I play the guitar and the best style to play is rock.

E: Thank you. Now, I'd like each of you to talk on your own for about a minute …

Exam practice 4: Teacher's Book

Listening. Page 188. (Paper 4 Part 4).

P = Presenter; J = Janice

P: Now it's time for that part of the programme where we talk to people just back from unusual holidays. Today's guest is Janice Dawley, who's been on a singing holiday to Spain. Janice, welcome.

J: Hi.

P: Now, how did you find out about a holiday like this?

J: Well, I've been to Spain a number of times and even had a Spanish boyfriend at one time who was a travel agent, so I know the country quite well. But <u>I found this deal on the Internet</u> where flights and accommodation are included as well as singing classes. I was actually looking for language courses in Spain, because I wanted to brush up my Spanish, and came across this by chance.

P: And you went on your own as well?

J: Yes, although that wasn't my original intention. I was meant to be going with a friend, but she had a fall and broke her ankle, so had to pull out at the last minute. I think if it'd been a simple beach holiday, she'd have come in any case. <u>But in the circumstances, I couldn't blame her.</u> I thought of cancelling myself, because I'd never been away on my own before, and then I thought. 'Well, why not?'

P: And was it lonely?

J: In fact, as it turned out, most people <u>were</u> alone, but we all shared a love of Spain and music, so got on really well. And, you know, at the end we all swapped addresses and promised to keep in touch. So I'm hoping I've made some friends to go away with in future. <u>Although I might consider going away alone again, I think, on balance, it's nicer to have someone to share things with.</u> But I must say it's opened my eyes to what's possible on your own.

P: So how was the trip organised?

J: We stayed in a lonely farmhouse deep in the countryside and, every morning, we'd do four hours of classes. They put us into two groups, with the best singers – some of them had lovely voices – in the higher class and those at elementary level, like me, in another. <u>Although I wasn't that good, I'd once been in a choir, so I already knew the basics of singing which was useful,</u> because the absolute beginners on the course found it very difficult.

P: But you made progress?

J: The classes were tough, but my singing definitely improved. That's because our tutors were professional singers. And they didn't speak any English, so that was fun, and a great way to practise two skills at once. Although we'd been warned about the language problem in advance, some people really didn't have enough Spanish to cope, and that did hold us up at times. It would be my only reservation about the holiday, actually.

P: And when the classes were over?

J: After the lessons, the rest of the day was free. <u>I was happy reading my novel in the sun actually,</u> although trips to different places were available if you wanted. The only one I went on was to Granada – a lovely city which I didn't know. We had a guide – an American student who'd been studying at Granada University for a few years – and she offered to show us around, but I don't think she really knew much about the city, so I didn't bother with that. In the evenings, after dinner, we'd all get together to sing songs and that was wonderfully sociable.

P: So would you recommend this experience?

J: Singing every day really makes you feel good and I felt a long way away from my daily life at home – which is what I wanted. <u>The holiday wasn't cheap, but I thought it was worth every penny.</u> I'd definitely go on another trip like this, but maybe not to the same place next time. There's a two-week tango holiday in Buenos Aires coming up – which I'm sure would be really challenging – but I'm quite tempted.

P: Janice, thanks. And if you'd like …

Unit 18

Listening. Page 135. (Paper 4 Part 1). Exercise 2.

One

How's your general knowledge? Reckon you can outwit the competitors on the TV quiz shows? Well, *Quiztime* gives you the chance to show what you can do. Beat the clock to answer questions on a variety of topics, ranging from football to soap operas, natural history to music, fashion to computers. <u>Throw the dice and race round the board, collecting points as you go. Based on the hit TV programme</u> of the same name, *Quiztime* comes in both adult and junior versions and is guaranteed to keep the whole family entertained for hours.

Two

W = Woman; M = Man

W: All I can do is either give you a jacket in another size or issue a credit note. <u>I can't give you a cash refund unless the product is faulty in some way,</u> I'm afraid, because you paid by credit card.

M: But supposing there isn't a blue one in the longer fitting?

W: Well, I expect there will be if you look, or we can order one in for you. A credit note would be valid for up to six months.

M: But that's no good to me, it's a 100-mile round trip from where I live.

W: I apologise, sir, but those are the rules.

Three

The thing is, last month I had a service done and the work alone cost me well over £100. And that's without the parts. What worries me is whether you can trust them or not. I mean, I don't know a thing about what goes on under the bonnet – how do I know they're not just ripping me off and saying they've put new bits in when they haven't? I suppose you'll say I should go to an evening class or something to find out how the engine works, but quite honestly I haven't got either time or interest. <u>I just wondered if you had any ideas on what I could do.</u>

Four

T = Tom; M = Miriam

T: Right. Here we are … I'm not so sure that this is a good idea, Miriam. They did say on the phone that there wasn't one. *Why don't we go to a shop* and buy a map of the area and then <u>get someone to mark the bus routes on it for us?</u>

M: Oh honestly Tom, why should we spend money needlessly? These places always have maps, it stands to reason. I'm going to go up to <u>that uniformed man over there and ask him to lend me one, then we'll take it next door to the library and photocopy it.</u>

T: OK, but don't say I didn't warn you.

Five

Look, I'm sorry. I accept it was a genuine mistake – these things happen, but surely I'm entitled to some kind of compensation. <u>Had I known there was a midday flight, I'd certainly have chosen it. But when I spoke to your employee on the phone, she said there was only one flight a day</u> and, as you know, with these cheap flights once you've booked, you can't change them. So we ended up having to get up really early in the morning in time to catch the flight she'd booked us on, then had to wait ages at the other end because we were too early – the rooms were still being cleaned.

Six

We're on the train and we'll be arriving around six o'clock, but what I want to know is whether we've got time for a round of golf before dinner, or whether we're down to eat at a specific time. Yes, I know that you didn't make the booking yourself, but I think I read something about the rest of the conference delegates arriving tomorrow morning, so I'm not sure what arrangements have been made for tonight. I seem to have mislaid all the paperwork somewhere, <u>it's probably on my desk somewhere – can you have a look? Or perhaps you could check with the organisers</u> and then get back to me, please? I'm on the mobile number. Thanks.

Seven

It's the latest idea to hit London. A company called Q4U has launched a new service that takes the tedium out of waiting around – be it for prescriptions at the chemist's, picking up dry cleaning or queuing for theatre tickets. Anything that people waste their time standing in a queue for. Customers pay the company £20 an hour and one of their professional queuers does the boring bit on their behalf. <u>The idea has caught on fastest when there's something to be picked up, especially holiday documents.</u> The company says that, given mobile-phone technology, the idea can actually be applied to any time-wasting task. Who knows? Maybe even the dentist's waiting room?

Eight

For both customers and e-commerce businesses, not to mention the mail-order industry in general, the question of delivery has long been an issue. The problem is simply this: that the people most likely to spend serious money having a purchase delivered are the least likely to be in when it arrives. After all they are the ones most liable to possess a job and a busy life. It makes you think that if e-commerce had been around first, then the invention of the walk-in shop would have been welcomed as a brilliant new idea. But, <u>fortunately it looks like a solution is at hand.</u> Tanya Wilde went to investigate …

Unit 20

Listening. Page 148. (Paper 4 Part 4). Exercise 2a.

V = Vicky; A = Alex

V: I think you hold fairly strong views about the way our town's changing, don't you?

A: I suppose so. What's really annoying me at the moment is the endless house-building that's going on. Every time a factory or other small local business closes down, more new houses spring up on the site instead. But there's not the work in the town to support the present population, let alone an increasing one … unemployment is actually rising amongst young people.

V: But people must want to live here, or there wouldn't be the demand for the houses.

A: Yes, but it's not local people who are buying them, it's people who move here and then catch the train into the city for work each day. Our town's fast becoming a commuter suburb. And that's where the problem of facilities begins, because although the city's close enough for work, it's not so handy when it comes to using its leisure facilities. The journey takes too long and costs a fortune because of the train fares.

V: Well, what worries me is that most of the new houses they're building are intended for families, you know, three- and four-bedroomed places, when there's already very little for teenagers to do here.

A: Well, that's not entirely true, is it? We have, after all, got a lovely new leisure centre, which lots of towns don't have.

V: Oh yes, and it's great. But the centre caters more for people of our age. You know, there's a gym, sauna, health treatments and so on. Well then, yes, there are activities available for little kids. But for older teenagers, you know, fifteen upwards, there's not much for them really.

A: Well, there is a bowling alley in the next town, they can go to that.

V: But how do they get there? Parents aren't always on hand to provide lifts, you know, and the bus services to other towns round here aren't exactly the most frequent or reliable, are they?

A: Well, perhaps we should be thinking about improving the existing transport options rather than building leisure facilities for an expanding population?

V: I know you're worried that the town's getting too big, and you're right to be, but on the other hand, what is there for teenagers to do in the evenings? In my day, we used to have a disco here as well as two cinemas. That kept us off the streets.

A: But it wouldn't make economic sense to build another cinema complex, surely, when there's a huge one only ten kilometres away. You can see all the films you want there.

V: Evenings are a worry, though. The kids just hang around the streets because there's nothing else to do.

A: Well, there's always the pizza place. Enough of them seem to go there.

V: Yes, but how often can they afford that? As far as I can see, teenage social life just consists of chatting on their mobiles on street corners. I think the solution is to build a new shopping complex on the outskirts of town with a cinema, a bowling alley, a skate park as well as more shopping. A nightclub would be ideal. Everyone would love it.

A: I'm sure they would, everyone except the shopkeepers in the town centre, that is. Surely, the one thing that is adequate in this town is the shopping centre. Anyway, when large numbers of kids get together like this, you're just inviting trouble – you know, fighting, under-age drinking, all that.

V: Actually, that sort of behaviour is much more likely if they're just hanging around getting bored.

A: But a shopping complex of this kind would change the nature of the town completely. I mean people like living here precisely because it is a small town. They come here to avoid the social problems associated with the big cities.

V: On the other hand, we do have to move with the times, unless we want it to become a retirement community for the elderly. It's just a question of how things are done.

A: Yes, but …

Exam practice 5: Teacher's Book

Listening. Page 192. (Paper 4 Part 3).

Speaker 1

Everyone had warned me that, though it was a wonderful experience, there was always a downside to any trip to Antarctica – long days at sea, rough weather, bitter cold, so I was well-prepared. But when the airline lost my luggage and I found myself standing on the harbour in an open-necked shirt, and lightweight jacket, it nearly put me off going any further. Fortunately, the ship had an impressive on-board shop where I was able to stock up on clothes and equipment. I spent a lot though, and I kept the receipts to send to the airline afterwards – it was their fault, and I wasn't going to let them get away with it.

Speaker 2

I'd come to Winter Park, in Colorado, as a novice skier looking to improve my technique away from the crowds, and it was well worth the extra I'd paid. My previous experience of skiing had been at cheaper resorts in Europe. And though I'd enjoyed it tremendously, I'd also become accustomed to fellow skiers using their poles like elbows to get ahead of you in the queues for the lifts. Here, two queues fed each lift, but there was no pushing, merely a polite 'after you' gesture from the person at the head of the other queue. In Europe, I'd been hopeless at skiing, but I'd become expert at holding my own in a queue!

Speaker 3

Diving is a sport I took up reluctantly 12 years ago whilst holidaying in the Caribbean. My friend decided that the beach was boring and, instead, dragged me out of bed every morning at 7:30 for theory classes, after which I was thrown into the ocean with lots of heavy equipment. It didn't cost much, but the instructors were real bullies and couldn't hide their amusement at how uncomfortable I felt. At the time I said: 'Never again', and meant it. Since then, I have actually tried diving again, and although I don't find it a particularly satisfying activity, it's very much easier than I thought then.

Speaker 4

I'd chosen to go on what's called an 'activity break', and the second day's activity involved climbing with ropes up a large rock, and then abseiling down it. I'd expected the other people to be fitness fanatics who'd make me feel inadequate, but I was pleasantly surprised to find a mixed bunch. Some wanted to overcome a fear of heights – others, like me, had heard it was good for your self-confidence, and didn't cost much. I managed the climb with no trouble, it was easy really and I could have handled something more challenging. Then I stood at the bottom giving shouts of encouragement to those who'd got stuck halfway.

Speaker 5

It's every schoolboy's dream – driving a Formula One racing car round the track. Well, in return for about a month's salary, I made that dream come true, and it was worth every penny. As I was lowered into the car, I was surprised to find no steering wheel. Apparently, they only fix that on once you're strapped into your seat. An instructor leant over and helped me find first gear, and I raced off down the track. But as I entered the first bend, suddenly the world started going round and round … . Moments later, the rescue team arrived, all laughing as they pulled me out. It was such a relief when one said: 'It's OK, the car's not damaged.'

Unit 22

Listening. Page 164. (Paper 4 Part 2). Exercise 2a.

P = Presenter; J = Jamie

P: In this special end-of-year edition of *Health Today*, we look back at some of the things the experts said were good for us over the last 12 months. Jamie, you've been keeping a record, haven't you? Let's start with food and drink. Any surprises here?

J: Well, we're always being encouraged to eat more fruit and vegetables, and I do try to do that, so I was quite interested to find out that our lungs increase their capacity to breathe if we eat around seven apples a week. I've no idea whether the same applies to pears, which I'm also fond of, or plums for that matter, but apples are highly recommended.

P: Right. And I was particularly pleased with the new research about chocolate.

J: I thought you might be! Yes, it seems that eating chocolate is not all that bad after all. We've always known it helps cheer people up, but apparently it also contains a chemical that actually helps in the prevention of heart disease. Although you've still got to watch your weight, obviously.

P: OK, I know. And I read somewhere that green tea was supposed to be really good for you.

J: I'm afraid that research was discredited earlier this year. But apparently, there is something in tea which does help to prevent holes forming in teeth. Milky tea is no good, though. It has to be black.

P: Really? I must say that I'm a coffee drinker myself. I bet that's not good for you.

J: Well, actually, believe it or not, some scientists say that coffee is a better and faster painkiller than a lot of stuff you buy at the chemist's to get rid of headaches. But, I'm afraid it does keep you awake, so it's not the thing to have if you have trouble sleeping.

P: But is sleep itself good for you?

J: Well, yes and no. Less than four hours a night is not good for your health. But research in the USA has now revealed that too many early nights and lie-ins may be just as bad. There's no need to sleep longer than six hours from the point of view of health, and in fact people who sleep over eight hours a night don't appear to live as long, although scientists can't explain why.

P: Presumably exercise is still good for you, though?

J: Yes, good health is still being associated with regular exercise, but what people are saying now is that this is better for you if it takes place outdoors, as opposed to the fitness training, you know, lifting weights and all that, that goes on in gyms. So jogging or walking, for example, anything like that.

P: Cheaper too!

J: That's right. So is laughing.

P: Laughing?

J: Yes. I read a report which said on average children laugh 400 times a day while adults only laugh 15 times in the same period. Laughter isn't just the best medicine, it's also an excellent way to give the body a really good workout, because apparently we use as many as 80 muscles when we have a really good laugh.

P: And if I want to live to be 100?

J: Actually, walking a dog has been highly recommended. Apparently, it's a good way to make friends – everybody stops to speak to you – and a good social life is said to be a key factor in long life.

P: It can't be that simple, though, can it?

J: Well, it seems that people who take up a hobby are also at an advantage here, because after they retire, or their children leave home or whatever, they tend to devote more time to that hobby and this keeps their brain active.

P: Right.

J: And, finally, remember that you're much less likely to live a long and healthy life if you live alone, so the message from all the research is that getting married is one way of increasing the likelihood of a long life.

P: Mmm. I'll have to think about that one. I don't know if I'm ready for that just yet. I'll stick with the coffee and laughter. Jamie thanks. Now if you …

Unit 24

Listening. Page 178. (Paper 4 Part 4). Exercise 2.

P = Presenter, M = Mike

P: My guest today, Mike Morgan has been a leading journalist on a national newspaper for more than 40 years. Mike, what made you decide to take it up in the first place?

M: I kind of drifted into it. I was always good at English and liked writing stories and so on at school, but I was initially quite keen on a career in business and, in fact, I'd accepted a place to study that at college. It was my father who talked me into doing journalism. He just thought I'd be better at it than I would at going into business.

P: What training did you get?

M: In those days, you were taken on by the newspaper straight from school as a kind of message boy. Rather than doing a diploma in journalism as you would now, you had to pick up the skills you needed actually on the job. You had to follow a senior reporter around and if he went to court, you'd go too and then write up the same story. He would look at it afterwards and give you feedback. It was some time before anything of mine actually appeared in the newspaper.

P: What was your first real reporting job?

M: I was a crime reporter, which meant I had to spend a lot of time with the police. In those days, you just hung around them to find out what was going on. They were terribly suspicious of us at first, I remember, but we were given an enormous expense account to buy them drinks, which helped! And after a bit, they felt sure enough of me to let me go out on jobs with them. Unfortunately, I wasn't always allowed to report the things I heard and saw!

P: Are there rules about what you can and can't report, then?

M: There are legal issues, obviously, with privacy and national security and so on. But there are also unwritten rules. I remember when Prince Charles was at university he had four bodyguards looking after him, but he sometimes used to try and lose them so he could meet a girlfriend. So he might go to the toilet in a pub or restaurant and then get out through the window. We always knew what he was up to, but we never printed it – all the journalists sympathised with his situation and didn't want to spoil things for him. It was an unspoken agreement amongst us.

P: So, what makes a good journalist?

M: Well, obviously you need to be confident and articulate and able to get on with all kinds of people. Being able to write well also helps. However good you are though, this is not as important as having bags of energy and commitment. When a big story breaks, you have to drop everything you're doing and work all hours if need be, often under tremendous pressure.

P: And do you still enjoy it?

M: I do, although I won't be sorry to retire. In my day, it was all going out and meeting people to get stories. Now it's much more office based. We have to be computer literate and we do a lot of stuff that printers used to do. In the satellite age, everything has to be instantaneous. It's still just as exciting, but quite honestly it's not what I set out to do.

P: Would you encourage young people to go in for it?

M: Let's face it. Even working on a best-selling tabloid paper you're never going to make your fortune, but you can earn a decent living. No two days are the same and it's great to be one of the first to know what's going on. In some ways it's competitive, like all jobs, but actually that's not such a problem as people might think, because there's also a great team spirit when you're working on a story. So, as long as your family commitments aren't going to be a problem, given the long and unpredictable hours – which is something that has to be borne in mind – then, yes, I'd say, go for it!

P: Mike, thanks for joining us today.

M: My pleasure.

Exam practice 6: Teacher's Book

Listening. Page 196. (Paper 4 Part 2).

P = Presenter; S = Sally

P: With me today is Sally Carson who takes part in round-the-world sailing races, but not, I should explain, as part of a crew, because Sally usually races alone in single-handed yacht races. Sally, welcome.

S: Hi.

P: Now, Sally you've just bought a new boat, haven't you?

S: Yes, it's called *Seabird* and it's much faster than the old one, which was called *Golden Globe*. I'd had it for a few years, and loved it, but it didn't have all the latest equipment, so I decided to change.

P: Yes, because I imagine that if you're out there, in the middle of the ocean, all alone, the technology is pretty important.

S: Absolutely. I usually make the comparison with motor racing, you know, if you put a really good driver into an inferior car, that person's not going to win. But in the same way, a poor driver won't win, even driving the best car in the race.

P: Right. But personal qualities must be important too.

S: Sure. Instinct and skill and technical knowledge are, of course, essential. But the design of the boat can make the difference between winning and finishing further down the field. And in long-distance races, reliability is equally important – if you can't repair your boat, you're not going to finish the race at all.

P: Which one gadget would you never be without in a race?

S: All boats are full of computers for navigation, steering and so forth, but the most important one is the one called the autopilot. If that goes wrong, you simply cannot carry on. That's because if your calculations are wrong by just one degree, and you don't notice, you can end up hundreds of miles off course.

P: Wow. Of the other gadgets, which do you value most personally?

S: Without doubt it's the onboard Internet connection. It means I can keep in touch with the family at home at a time when I'm very much alone, and find out what's happening in the news. But most significantly, it provides weather information, which is vital. If you're going to be sailing into a hurricane, it's best to know beforehand.

P: And what do you do about sleep?

S: When you're alone, tiredness is always the biggest danger because there's nobody else to take over if you've had enough. And there are things like icebergs to avoid, sails to change depending on the wind and so on. I average around five hours sleep over a 24-hour period when I'm racing, and the longest race I've ever done went on for 93 days. I find I sleep best in the afternoons, in bursts of between ten minutes and about an hour.

P: But don't you struggle to keep awake after weeks at sea without a break?

S: No, because you're so excited about the race, the course, the boat and everything that it's difficult to switch off. The problem is more being able to relax sufficiently to get off to sleep, and so sleeplessness can be a problem.

P: And what physical training do you do to prepare for such huge races?

S: Well, sailing is a very physical sport, so you have to be fit and strong with lots of stamina. It's nothing like training for athletics or team sports, though. The best way to train the muscles you need for sailing, is by going sailing. I also go to the gym and go jogging, but there's never enough time to prepare my body as well as I'd like to.

P: And you've written about your experiences too.

S: That's right. My book comes out next week – it's called *Across the Ocean*, and as you can see there's a picture of my old boat, *Golden Globe*, on the cover. Writing that was actually much tougher than sailing, I can tell you, but I was determined to do it all myself.

P: Determination – is that what motivates you to keep sailing and racing?

S: I love the sea. It's as simple as that. I love the sea and I love to race.

P: Sally, best of luck with the new boat and thanks for joining us today.

S: Thank you.